The PQ Factor

Stop Resisting and Start Persisting

by
Bernice L. Ross, Ph.D

Published in the United States of America by
RossdalePress.com, a division of Teleclass4U.com, LLC
12400 Hwy 71 W, Suite 350 Box 343
Austin, TX 78738

Cover Design: Klinginsmith & Company

First edition published May 2017

The Library of Congress Cataloging-in-Publication Data Applied For

Ross, Bernice L.
The PQ Factor: Stop Resisting and Start Persisting

ISBN: 978-0-9985573-0-4

Copyright © 2017 by Bernice L. Ross

All rights reserved in all media.

Printed in the United States of America

For information about special discounts available for bulk purchases, please contact our distribution center via email (shane@rossdalepress.com) or by calling 352-535-0685.

No part of this book may be reproduced, stored in a retrieval system, or transmitted by any means, electronic, mechanical, photocopying, recording, or otherwise, without written permission from the author.

The information in this book is designed to be helpful and informative. The author and publisher cannot warrant or guarantee that using the information in this book will work for you. References are provided for informational purposes only and do not constitute an endorsement of any websites, books, or other sources. Neither the publisher nor the author shall be liable for any physical, psychological, emotional, financial, or commercial damages, including, but not limited to, special, incidental, consequential, or other damages. If you need financial, medical, psychological, or any other type of professional assistance, please seek help from a qualified practitioner in your area.

To Byron Van Arsdale:

Husband, best friend, great cook, and the one who always makes me laugh—thank you for being in my life and for your many contributions to this book

Contents

Introduction 7

Prepare to PERSIST
Chapter 1: Triple Your Brain Power... 13
Chapter 2: Program Your Brain for Peak Performance............ 19

Perspire
Chapter 3: Leverage Attraction to Perspire Less and
               Achieve More.. 33
Chapter 4: Resist Falling Prey to Illusion 45

Embrace Your Strengths
Chapter 5: Embrace Strengths, Work Around Weaknesses..... 59
Chapter 6: Escape the Quicksand of Procrastination............... 75

Increase Your Resilience
Chapter 7: Optimism—The Key to Happiness
               and Resilience... 89
Chapter 8: Facing Adversity: What Story Will You Weave? .. 101
Chapter 9: Confronting a Life-Threatening Event............... 113
Chapter 10: When Death Comes Calling................................. 121

Be Self-ish, not Selfish
Chapter 11: To Nourish Others, Nourish Yourself First 141
Chapter 12: Sources that Block Self-ishness 153
Chapter 13: Moving from Source to Solution........................... 167

Become More Internally Anchored
Chapter 14: Take Control of Your Life.. 191

Serve
Chapter 15: Give the Gift that Gives Back 217

Time It Right

Chapter 16: Timing Is Everything 237
Chapter 17: What PERSIST Choices Will You Make? 249

About the Author 253
Acknowledgements 255
Appendix 259
Bibliography 261
Index 267

Introduction

It's the morning of September 11, 2001. The nation stares aghast as the unthinkable is happening. The Twin Towers are ablaze, people are leaping to their deaths, and we feel helpless to do anything about the horror unfolding in front of us. Our world has been shattered and we along with it.

Have you ever wondered what choice you would have made if you had been trapped in one of the Twin Towers with no way through the blaze and your only option was leaping out a window? Would you have chosen to fight the hijackers as the people did on United Airlines Flight 93? Would you have run into the fiery inferno, putting your life at risk as did so many of the first responders, police, and firefighters?

While these choices seem extreme, millions of ordinary people face equally difficult decisions daily. Our police, firefighters, and our military constantly put their lives on the line. Parents may sacrifice themselves to save their child's life. Bystanders often will risk their lives to rescue another person at the scene of an accident. Each of these individuals makes a choice to serve others, even when it means putting aside their own safety.

Take charge of your choice
Persistence, the ability to continue to pursue a course of action even in the face of numerous obstacles, requires taking control of your choices. People who feel that they control their choices are happier, more emotionally resilient, and live longer. In contrast, lack of control can result in depression and powerlessness. To illustrate how deadly this situation can be, when elderly people are forced to leave their homes against their will, 50 percent die within 12 months.

Former United States Senator Robert F. Bennett observed how critical the power of choice is:

> *Your life is the sum result of all the choices you make, both consciously and unconsciously. If you can control the process of choosing, you can take control of all aspects of your life. You can find the freedom that comes from being in charge of yourself.*

Make the Choice to Stop Resisting and Start Persisting

Few of us will experience what the people in the Twin Towers faced on 9-11. Increasing your *Persistence Quotient (PQ)* doesn't require a heroic effort, however. Instead, it starts with simple choices you make each day. This notion is summed up by the tag line for *The PQ Factor,* "stop resisting and start persisting."

A few weeks before I began writing this book I opened a fortune cookie that said, "It is easier to resist at the beginning than at the end."

Resistance and persistence work hand-in-hand. To illustrate how this concept works, what is the one food that you have the most trouble resisting?

In my case, it's avocado oil kettle-cooked potato chips. The only way I can avoid wolfing down a whole bag is to resist walking down the potato chip aisle at the market. Avoiding an aisle at the market is a much easier choice than resisting the clarion call of the chips in my pantry. By choosing to resist the potato chip aisle early in the process, it's easier for me to persist in pursuing my long-term goal of eating better and being healthier.

Ultimately, this is what *The PQ Factor* is about—raising your PQ by unlocking the secrets that will allow you to resist making the easy choices at the beginning so you can persist in making better choices in the long run.

How to Use *The PQ Factor* to Improve Your Life

You, and only you, are in charge of the actions you choose to take. In other words, you are in charge of helping you. There is no persistence, no solution to your challenges, or fulfillment of your dreams until you take the action to make it so.

The PQ Factor provides you with a buffet of ideas, proven strategies, and the underlying scientific research to support you on this journey. If you like what you take from the buffet, take more. If not, try something else. This is at the heart of persistence—when something doesn't work, try a different approach, preferably one that is best suited to your life and to your specific situation.

The PQ Factor begins by outlining the primary factors correlated with happiness and success. You will also learn simple ways to maximize your brain and body's performance, how to tune up your brain's messaging system, plus how to tap into your "happy brain."

Introduction

The balance of the book is devoted to the seven dimensions of persistence that compose the PERSIST model for increasing your PQ:

P: *Perspire*
E: *Embrace* Your Strengths
R: Increase Your *Resilience*
S: Be *Self-ish*, not Selfish
I: Become More *Internally Anchored*
S: *Serve*
T: *Time* It Right

There's no such thing as one size fits all
Because each individual has a unique combination of characteristics, strengths, and traits, there is no such thing as a "one-size-fits-all" approach to being more persistent. If you have ever tried to emulate someone else's road to success or happiness, you probably became frustrated and you may have even given up. On the other hand, when you feel inspired to take action, you are much more likely to experience satisfaction and success.

Taking action is infinitely easier when you work with your strengths. Strengths are a combination of your heredity, life experience, values, skills, and daily habits. They are as unique to you as your fingerprint. Identifying your unique profile of strengths lays the foundation for increasing your persistence.

The PQ Factor illustrates how to use your unique characteristics to create better outcomes in every area of your life. This knowledge will also make it easier for you to apply the PERSIST principles both at home and at work.

There are numerous self-inventories throughout the book, many of which look at past choices you have made. Identifying your past choices coupled with the results you experienced gives you a quick way to spot the strategies best suited to your individual needs. In addition to these self-inventories, there are scientifically validated assessments that you can take online for free or at a minimal cost. The list is at http://www.ThePQFactor.com/assessments.

There is one extremely important caveat to keep in mind about any scientific assessment. Scientific research relies on selecting a sample of subjects and then generalizes from that sample to the overall population. Consequently, while research can often tell us how most individuals will behave or respond, it may not be predictive of how you will behave or respond.

Overcome the Myths and Misconceptions that Block Your Happiness and Success

As you read *The PQ Factor* and dive more deeply into the seven factors in the PERSIST model, you may be surprised to discover that many of the obstacles blocking your happiness and success are based upon a myth. A major goal of this book is to dispel these myths and to empower you to make better long-term persistence choices that will result in the best possible outcomes in your life.

Choose the right tools for you

To take full advantage of *The PQ Factor*, think of it as a toolbox. There are some tools you will use all the time because they fit your unique profile and align with a specific situation you are experiencing. Other tools may have virtually no value to you because they don't apply to how you work or live your life.

While *The PQ Factor* provides you with a range of proven tools to assist you on your journey, you will definitely have your favorites. Choose wisely and your life will flow almost effortlessly. Choose poorly and you'll continue to encounter pain and struggle. Ultimately the fulfillment of your hopes and dreams rests firmly in your hands and the choices you make.

If you're ready to "stop resisting and start persisting" in having the life you want, take the next step and turn to Chapter 1.

Prepare to PERSIST

In the confrontation between the stream and the rock, the stream always wins. Not through strength, but through persistence.
H. Jackson Brown

Chapter 1:
Triple Your Brain Power

I believe in intuitions and inspirations…
I sometimes FEEL that I am right.
I do not KNOW that I am.
         Albert Einstein

It was 10:00 p.m. and I had just wrapped up my Monday night Psychology 1 class. I had a miserable cold, was totally exhausted from a 14-hour day, and was eager to get home. As I was putting away my class materials there was a knock on my office door.

An attractive, nicely dressed young man wanted to know more about the classes I taught. I explained that I had a nasty cold and was probably still contagious. If he wanted to discuss anything, I would be happy to see him during my regular office hours. I remember putting my left hand out in front of me, motioning him away because I was sick.

He continued to ask questions. I explained again that I was ill and now wasn't the time to talk. When a male colleague showed up, I quickly excused myself and followed my colleague into his office to ask a quick question.

The next morning, I told my husband Byron about the student from the night before. Byron insisted that I report the incident to the campus police. I explained it was no big deal—just that it was late and the guy didn't take the hint about leaving. Byron was adamant.

After wrapping up my classes for the day, I reluctantly went over to chat with the campus police about the interaction. I apologized for bothering the officer with this seemingly unimportant event and explained my husband's insistence that I contact them.

The officer asked for the student's description, his name, and exactly what had happened. Imagine my shock when the officer grew stern and said, "I've met this character. Your husband was right to have you contact us. He has harassed a number of women at another campus. I was a LAPD detective for 30 years and this guy is extremely dangerous. He has been charged with harassment, assault, and rape, none of which have stuck in court. He's smart, careful, and only targets attractive women when they are alone."

The former detective then gave me a chilling warning: "You are not to leave your office or class alone. An officer will escort you to your car after your classes. When this perp explodes, it will make headlines. Again, don't go anywhere on campus alone."

How did I misread this situation when Byron immediately identified that there was a cause for concern? The answer is that my left brain failed to note the very clear warning signals from my right brain. Byron picked up something in how I relayed the story that troubled him and hence, his insistence on reporting the incident to the campus police.

Does Intuition Trump Thinking?

Do you know who said that intuition is the only valuable thing? It was Albert Einstein, the greatest thinker of the 20th century. Why would one of the most important thinkers in history make such an extraordinary assertion?

The answer to that question explains what happened with the student. It also has a direct bearing on how you can make better conscious decisions by tapping into the power of your so-called gut, intuition, or unconscious, and integrating that with your conscious decision making process.

Brain Play

Maximizing your brain's performance is much simpler than you may realize. Improved mental performance will not only improve your PQ, it will also make the journey to achieving your personal goals and dreams easier. This approach goes beyond working harder or smarter. Instead, it's about understanding how your physiology works best and then using your brain in the most effective way possible. To achieve the best results from this process, it's important to understand the various roles different parts of your brain play.

Left brain vs. right brain

Your brain is divided into two hemispheres, each with discreet functions. The left brain controls the right side of your body and the right brain controls the left side of your body. Damage to left side of the brain shows up as loss of function on the right side of the body and vice versa. The corpus callosum joins the two hemispheres, allowing them to communicate and work together.

The dominant hemisphere (normally the left hemisphere for about 90 percent of the population) processes language and also controls the motor functions associated with speech. It relies on logic, does mathematical calculations, and accesses facts from memory. The non-dominant hemisphere handles facial recognition, spatial relationships, and processing music. It also helps you to comprehend visual imagery by making sense of what you see.

(For convenience, "left brain" as used in this book will reference the dominant hemisphere and "right brain" will reference the non-dominant hemisphere, even though for about 10 percent of the population, these functions occur on opposite sides.)

The left brain has words, but lacks feeling and emotion. A good analogy is a computer reading back a text message. In contrast, the right brain adds feeling and emotion to your speech, controls your body language, and interprets non-verbal communication signals, but understands very few words.

The Three-Brain Theory
Neuroscientist Paul D. MacLean (1990) was the first to propose the triune or three-brain theory. This theory claims that human beings have three brain levels: the reptilian, the limbic, and the cortex. The reptilian brain dominates your basic instinctual needs that are sometimes referenced as the "Four F's"—feeding, fighting, fleeing, and reproduction.

The limbic brain controls emotions. It helps you to develop social ties that allow you to experience love and belonging while also triggering anger or jealousy when you feel threatened.

The cortex governs logic and reasoning, abstract thinking, and complex processes such as long-term planning. Your cortex also controls your ability to resist the easy choice early on (e.g., the potato chip aisle) that leads to increased persistence in achieving the long-term better choice (e.g., the goal of being healthier by eating better).

Again, as with the left and right brain, using the reptilian, the limbic, and the cortical areas of your brain in concert with each other yields the best results.

The heart transplant research—transferring heart and gut memories
The late Paul Pearsall's (1999) research with heart transplant patients provides strong evidence that not only do the neurons in your brain

store memories, so do the neurons in your heart and gut. In one of his seminars called "The Healing Power of Aloha," Pearsall cited an extraordinary case that illustrates this point.

A little boy received a heart from another young boy who had drowned. A daytime talk show invited the boy, his parents, and the donor's parents to appear on the show. The two families had never met.

The donor's father was called in to do a last-minute emergency surgery and let the show know that he would be unable to make it. When the procedure took less time than anticipated, the doctor arrived in time to catch part of the interview. As the doctor walked in to take a seat in the audience, the little boy spotted him and said, "Hi dad—how's Toy?"

Toy was the donor's dog.

Pearsall's research documents numerous cases where recipients of a transplanted heart acquired memories from the donor, even when the recipient knew nothing about the donor's history. This research supports Pearsall's contention that the neurons in your heart and your gut store memories in the same manner as the neurons in your brain.

Together with your right brain, the limbic system, and the brain stem, these neurons are critical components in a powerful network that underlies our so-called intuitive or gut feelings. The challenge is that the left brain often fails to take note of the messages that this network constantly generates. You may feel that something isn't right but because you can't articulate what it is, you may ignore it.

Get the most from your brain and your gut

Going back now to the incident with the student. The moment he approached me, my unconscious or intuitive information system read the situation correctly—this person needed to be stopped. During the entire conversation with the student, I held my left hand out in a stop position. My left brain rationalized that I was merely trying to avoid exposing the student to my cold. My right brain (which controls the left side of the body, including my unconsciously extended left hand) recognized the threat, leading me to flee to the safety of a colleague's office.

A primary goal of *The PQ Factor*'s PERSIST model is to help you to integrate your logical thinking function with the often unconscious gut or intuitive information that your body constantly generates.

Chapter 2 walks you through the specific steps needed to program your brain for peak performance.

Chapter 1: Key Points

1. Resist the easy decisions in the beginning to persist in achieving your longer-term PERSIST goals.

2. Your brain has three primary areas—the cortex that governs higher-level thinking, the limbic system that governs emotion, and the brain stem (the reptilian brain) that governs instinctual needs.

3. You will make the best decisions when you integrate input from all three areas.

Chapter 2:
Program Your Brain for Peak Performance

When your brain works right, you work right. When your brain is trouble, you have trouble in your life.
Daniel Amen, *Making a Good Brain Great*

Once upon a time there was a woodcutter who asked a timber merchant for a job. The pay was excellent. When the woodcutter was hired, he was determined to do his absolute best.

The first day his boss issued him axe and showed him where to work. At the end of the day, he had cut down 15 trees. His boss congratulated him and encouraged him to keep up the good work.

Feeling motivated by what his boss had said, the woodcutter was determined to cut down even more trees the next day. Instead, each day that week he cut down fewer trees than the day before, even though he was trying harder and harder.

At the end of the week, the woodcutter went to his boss and apologized—he had no idea about why his production kept getting lower each day.

The boss asked, "When did you last sharpen your axe?"

Sharpen Your Axe

When you purchased *The PQ Factor*, you probably expected that becoming more persistent would entail a lot of "you-should-work-harder-advice." Granted, sometimes being persistent does mean working harder as many wise people have noted:

Genius is one percent inspiration and ninety-nine percent perspiration.
Thomas Edison

Energy and persistence conquer all things.
Benjamin Franklin

Patience, persistence, and perspiration make an unbeatable combination.
Napoleon Hill

A little persistence, a little more effort, and what seemed hopeless failure may turn to glorious success.
L. Ron Hubbard

As the story of the woodcutter illustrates, perspiration alone can be a poor strategy. To be successful, you must also sharpen your axe. The best place to begin is with the structure that controls the entire process: your brain.

Tune Up Your Brain's Messaging System

Have you ever wondered why some people have sunny dispositions while others fight anxiety and depression? Differences in neurotransmitter levels, the chemical messengers that control your brain and nervous system, are often the cause. Neurotransmitter imbalances can result in mood swings, memory problems, addictive behavior, low energy, and sleep issues.

You constantly alter your neurotransmitter levels by what you eat, the activities in which you engage, and any prescription and recreational drugs that you ingest, including commonly consumed substances such as alcohol, caffeine, and nicotine. For example, your morning cup of coffee raises your adrenaline and dopamine levels. A long run or eating chocolate increases beta-endorphin levels. Chocolate provides the double benefit of also raising dopamine levels in the nucleus accumbens, the brain's primary pleasure center.

Increasing your PQ is much easier when your brain is functioning at optimal levels. This chapter addresses specific steps to take to put your brain into peak performance mode.

How to Optimize Your Neurotransmitters Levels

Below you will find a list of six of the most important neurotransmitters, what they control, and simple steps for maintaining them at optimal levels. Please note that serious imbalances normally require medical intervention—not self-help suggestions.

Acetylcholine: the building block for memory and learning

Have you ever forgotten the name of someone you have known for years? As people age, these occasions become more common due to a decline in acetylcholine, the neurotransmitter that governs memory. This loss is most pronounced in Alzheimer's patients where acetylcholine levels may drop up to 90 percent. Although there is no cure at present, drugs that inhibit the breakdown of acetylcholine do reduce the rate of cognitive decline.

You can slow down the decline in your acetylcholine levels by switching from drinking coffee to drinking green tea. Foods that increase your acetylcholine levels include egg yolks, fish, meat, and poultry. (Egg yolks and whole eggs are by far the most effective.) On the other hand, antibiotics, antihistamines, and antidepressants typically reduce your body's acetylcholine levels and can make you feel drowsy or groggy. Given the benefits that many "anti" drugs provide, the drowsiness is often a much better choice than having an allergic reaction, depression, or a relapse of an infection.

Adrenaline (Epinephrine)

The fight or flight response is tied to adrenaline (epinephrine). Your body releases adrenaline when you are in a threatening situation, under stress, or even when you're caught in traffic. Adrenaline increases your heart rate and blood pressure. It also redirects your blood circulation from the internal organs to the muscles, dilates your pupils, and releases both glycogen and glucose. Each of these responses is designed to help you to flee the situation or to survive a fight.

Many people today turn to adrenaline as a source of quick energy, especially when they are dealing with a stressful situation. The result is that much of the population lives in a state of adrenaline overload, which can lead to ulcers, cancer, and heart disease.

If you would like to reduce stress and be more effective, adrenaline is one of your worst enemies. Adrenaline can numb your senses to the point where it blocks feelings of sadness, inadequacy, or not being loved. In fact, adrenaline responses are so strong that some athletes have played with broken bones and not experienced any pain until after the game.

To reduce the potentially damaging effects of adrenaline, begin by reducing your caffeine intake. Caffeine stresses the adrenal glands, your heart, and circulatory system. If you skip your coffee in the morning and get a headache, you're addicted to caffeine.

> **Prepare Tip #1: Kick the caffeine**
> To kick the caffeinated coffee habit, begin by mixing 3/4 of a cup of regular coffee with 1/4 decaf. After several days, shift to 1/2 and 1/2. The next step is to mix 1/4 regular with 3/4 decaf. The final step is to move to 100 percent decaffeinated coffee. You can also substitute herbal tea or decaffeinated cola. (Please note that decaffeinated coffee still contains some caffeine.)

Beta-Endorphin

Beta-endorphin, the best known of the neuropeptides, governs pleasure and alleviates pain. Neuropeptides regulate sleep, wakefulness, alertness, mood, memory, pain, hunger, pleasure, and sexual behavior. Low endorphin levels have been tied to being overly sensitive to emotional and physical pain, difficulty recuperating from grief, and numbing behaviors such as eating sweets, drinking alcohol, using marijuana, tobacco, or OxyContin.

> **Prepare Tip #2: Raise your beta-endorphins naturally**
> Safe ways to raise your beta-endorphin levels naturally include exercising (the so-called runner's high), acupuncture, and the most important one of all—laughter. Paul Pearsall's (1999) research showed that laughter is one of the best ways to avoid heart disease and cancer.

Dopamine: the pleasure neurotransmitter

Most physical pleasure originates from increased dopamine levels in a brain structure called the nucleus accumbens. Dopamine regulates the body's pleasure-reward system, coordinates smooth movement, and is also involved in sensitivity, information processing, relaying information, cognition, motivation, attention, and focus.

When dopamine levels are too low, Parkinson's disease results. Low dopamine levels are also associated with apathy, addictions, and self-destructive behaviors. When dopamine levels are too high, concentration becomes more difficult and may even result in schizophrenia. Autism has also been tied to dysfunction in the production and/or the uptake of dopamine.

Humans regularly self-medicate with substances that increase dopamine levels. Common examples include caffeine, alcohol, sugar, nicotine, and recreational drugs. Behaviors correlated with low dopamine levels can include drug and sex addictions as well as compulsive gambling and shopping.

> **Prepare Tip #3: Healthy ways to raise low dopamine levels**
> Healthy ways to increase your dopamine levels include exercising, meditation, and achieving the goals you set. Foods that raise dopamine levels include avocados, green leafy vegetables, apples, beets, chocolate, oatmeal, nuts, and seeds. (Please note that abnormally high dopamine levels usually require medical intervention.)

GABA (Gamma-aminobutyric acid): the relaxation neurotransmitter

If you're easily stressed out, suffer from anxiety attacks, experience heart palpitations, shortness of breath, or if your brain races all night and you cannot sleep, your GABA levels may be low. GABA is often referred to as "nature's Valium" due to its relaxing properties. When GABA levels are low, your brain stays in "on" position most of the time.

> **Prepare Tip #4: Naturally raise your GABA levels**
> Exercise, especially yoga, increases GABA levels as do probiotics that contain lactobacillus rhamnosus. Fermented foods such as yogurt, kefir, sauerkraut, kimchi, and miso also increase GABA levels. Other foods that increase GABA include bananas, broccoli, brown rice, citrus fruits, fish, lentils, nuts, oats, organ meats, spinach, and whole grains.

Serotonin: the happiness neurotransmitter

Serotonin plays a pivotal role in the moods that people experience. When serotonin levels are high, you will generally feel positive and happy. Low serotonin levels are associated with anxiety, depression, eating disorders, insomnia, obsessive-compulsive disorder, and seasonal affective disorder. Other symptoms associated with low serotonin levels include carb cravings, binge eating, excessive alcohol consumption, impulsivity, insomnia, mood swings, negativity, and low self-esteem. Most antidepressants are believed to work by raising serotonin levels.

> **Prepare Tip #5: Serve up more serotonin**
> Tryptophan increases serotonin levels. Foods that are rich in tryptophan include dairy, chicken, and turkey as well as B-complex vitamins, magnesium, and omega-3 fatty acids. You can also increase your serotonin levels by exercising daily, getting enough sleep, and having adequate exposure to sunshine.

Multitasking—The Great Myth of the 21st Century

If you were to ask a group of people whether they engage in multitasking, most people would say that they do. The truth is that multitasking is a myth. No one is able to multitask due to how the brain is wired, specifically in "Brodmann's Area 10," the primary regulator of concentration and attention. Neuroscientists have nicknamed Brodmann's Area 10 "Mother."

Mother can only conduct one conscious process at a time. The same is true of computers. They do multiple tasks, but a single processor still completes only one function at a time. In Mother's case, she takes 0.7 seconds to shift gears from one task to another. Again, it is impossible to multitask because Mother can only do one thing at a time.

According to molecular biologist John Medina (2014) in his book *Brain Rules*, people who claim to be multitasking are actually task shifting. Medina's research illustrates how costly task shifting can be. If you interrupt an activity to answer a phone call, respond to a text message, or look at a Facebook notification for 30 seconds, it takes you a full five minutes to regain full concentration. Medina further claims that multitasking confuses Mother and can even lead to ADHD (attention deficit hyperactivity disorder). Additional studies have shown that people who engage in multitasking (i.e., task shifting) take 100 percent more time to complete tasks and they make 50 percent more errors.

Researchers (*Nass, Ophir, et al, 2009*) lend additional support to Medina's claims. Ophir's group conducted three different trials where they split their subjects into those who were heavy multitaskers and those who did little multitasking. In each of their three experiments, the low multitaskers had no problem with the three different tasks while the high multitaskers performed poorly.

The researchers concluded that the high multitaskers couldn't help thinking about the task they were not doing. "The high multitaskers were always drawing from all the information in front of them. They can't keep things separate in their minds." Furthermore, when multitaskers are "in situations with multiple sources of information coming from the external world or emerging out of memory, they are unable to filter out what's not relevant to their current goal. That failure to filter means they're slowed down by the irrelevant information."

Rule-Shifting: How to Make Even More Mistakes

Rubinstein, Meyer, and Evans (2006) showed that when people shift tasks, they take more time to complete the tasks than if they had completed each task separately. Their research also suggests that the switching process has two parts—goal (task) shifting ("I want to do this task now instead of that task") and rule activation ("I'm turning off the rules for that task and turning on the rules for this task.") Mother controls the task shifting process, but when the task shift also requires a rule shift, Mother requires twice the time to complete both shifts.

A good example is text messaging and driving. The rules governing how fast you drive, when to slow down due to a change in the speed limit, or where to turn off, are quite different from the rules that turn on your phone and that govern how language is entered into your mobile device. As Meyer points out about drivers using their cell phones, "A mere half second of time lost to task switching can mean the difference between life and death because during that time the car is not totally under control and can travel far enough to crash into obstacles the driver might have otherwise avoided."

To really drive this point home, all 50 states have now set .08 percent blood alcohol concentration (BAC) as the legal limit for driving under the influence (DUI) or driving while impaired (DWI). According to Medina, driving and texting is the equivalent of having a BAC of .12 percent—that's 50 percent higher than the level for DUI.

> **Prepare Tip #6: Save time and make 50 percent fewer errors**
> To cut your "perspire" time in half and to make 50 percent fewer errors, avoid interruptions and focus on completing one task at a time. The text messages and the Facebook notifications can wait 20-30 minutes until you take a break or complete the task at hand.

Tap Into Your Happy Brain

Everyone has those days when nothing seems to go right. You're mentally foggy, your body feels sluggish, and you can't wait to get home and crawl back under the covers. Then there are those wonderful days when you feel great and everything seems to go right. So what can you do to turn those foggy, sluggish days around?

Each hemisphere of your brain generates separate brain waves. When these waves are in synchrony, optimal performance occurs. When you're feeling cranky and out of sorts, chances are your brain waves are not in synchrony. To synchronize your brain waves quickly, listen to any type of music that makes you want to snap your fingers to the beat. If you're using a music app that plays songs based upon what you have liked and disliked in the past, the app will generally select songs that have the same distinct beat. While the beats that cause brain synchronization vary from person to person, you can recognize which beats are optimal for you when you want to snap your fingers and dance to the music.

> **Prepare Tip #7: Triple your brain's benefits**
> In order to increase the benefits you receive from brain synchronization, move to the music and snap your fingers to bring your whole body into alignment. You will get the triple benefit of brain synchronization, exercise, plus increasing your preparedness for whatever is ahead.

Anchor Happiness

Another way to immediately shift your mood comes from Neurolinguistic Programming (NLP). NLP practitioners believe that emotions can become physically anchored in your body. For example, if you lost a loved one and several people patted you on the back during the funeral, you may feel like bursting into tears when a friend pats you on the back five years later. Your grief was physically anchored at the funeral.

For years I did the following exercise in my psychology classes to illustrate a powerful positive anchor that most people carry. This anchor is so powerful that it allows people to quickly shift their mood, even when they're having one of those days when nothing seems to be going right.

Here's what to do: stand up, look straight up at the ceiling, and then wave your hands in the air above your head as if you were on your feet cheering for your favorite team. Be sure to keep looking up at the ceiling as you wave your hands.

Unless your mother was "Mommy Dearest," this particular body position is a strong anchor for feeling cared for and happy. The reason is that when you were a baby and you cried, you would reach up to your mother and she would pick you up to care for your needs. By the same token, every time you raise your arms to cheer for your favorite team or dance with your arms above your head, you are reinforcing this powerful anchor from your infancy.

When Byron read this chapter, he decided to try this approach with one of his one-on-one coaching clients. His client is a very direct, get-it-done type of person who has been told that she has a perpetual scowl on her face. Byron explained what he wanted her to do. She put down the phone and a few seconds later he heard her laughing out loud in the background.

Prepare Tip #8: Anchor happiness

If you would like to anchor happiness or laughter, the process is simple. Every time that you laugh for the next week tap your shoulder three times. Then, the next time you have an unhappy or down moment, tap your shoulder three times. Don't be surprised when you feel an overwhelming urge to laugh.

"How a Few Minutes Changed My Life"

One of our readers shared this powerful story about what happened when he decided to resist the urge to do "just one more thing" before he left for an appointment.

> *Ever since I was a teenager, I had the habit of trying to squeeze in just one more thing before I left the house to go to work or to keep an appointment. I was always running a few minutes late. If there was an accident or a delay due to roadwork, I would go ballistic, cursing and swearing at the lights and traffic. I knew every short cut in town, but I was always running late. My stomach was bothering me, I wasn't sleeping, and my neck and back muscles ached constantly. As an experiment, my coach asked me to try leaving ten minutes early for all work and commitments. The difference was amazing—my stomach settled down, I was more effective at work, and the tension in my neck virtually disappeared. I definitely feel calmer and more balanced—it's amazing how much difference those few extra minutes have made.*

Prepare Tip #9: The 10-minutes early experiment

If you are typically late for appointments, note your current stress level and how you feel. Next, experiment for one week by leaving ten minutes early for work or for any other appointments. At the end of the week, were there any improvements in your stress level or how you felt? If so, continue to persist in your new habit of leaving early.

What Action Steps Will You Take?

The PQ Factor is packed with tips to help you raise your PQ and have a better life. A key point that we have learned from our business and personal coaching practices is that people who try to do too much at once become overwhelmed. The result is that they often end up doing nothing. A better approach is to choose one tip and then implement it. If that works, keep on working with it and then add something new.

For example, if you are experimenting with synchronizing your brain waves by moving to your favorite music, note whether you feel more or less energized after you listen to the music. If you notice that you're feeling particularly good or happy, you could then do the tap-three-times-on-the-shoulder exercise to anchor that good feeling. Please remember, it's the process of being in action that results in significant long-term change.

Chapter 2: Key Points

1. Tune up your brain's performance by getting enough sleep, limiting your caffeine and sugar intake, and making simple improvements to your diet.

2. Multitasking is a myth—Brodmann's Area 10 (Mother) can only process one piece of information at a time.

3. Task shifting not only doubles your error rate, it will take you 50 percent longer to complete your tasks.

4. Texting and driving is equivalent to driving with a blood alcohol level 50 percent above the level for a DUI violation.

5. Exercise not only increases your feel-good neurotransmitters, it also synchronizes your two cerebral hemispheres to help you achieve peak performance.

6. Tap into your happy brain by listening to music that makes you want to snap your fingers and dance.

Perspire

*The key of persistence opens all doors
closed by resistance.*
John Di Lemme

Chapter 3:
Leverage Attraction
To Perspire Less and Achieve More

*Success is not to be pursued;
it is attracted by the person you become.*
Jim Rohn

Attraction is constantly at work in your life whether you realize it or not. While the previous chapter focused on physical changes to improve your brain's performance, this chapter focuses on how to reset your attraction mindset. As the story below illustrates, your thoughts and words are often much more powerful than you may realize.

Be Careful What You Ask For

It was March 2007. I had just secured a training contract, which required me to be in Los Angeles every Thursday for six weeks. At the time, we were handling the hundreds of decisions required in building a custom home while simultaneously staging our current residence for sale. Contractors were in and out almost every day, ripping out flooring, painting, and changing fixtures. I was also only a few weeks away from hosting my first conference for women in real estate leadership (Awesome Females in Real Estate). With all the hotel arrangements, meal planning, audio visual, and finding speakers to fill a three-day program, the conference had turned out to be the equivalent of throwing a three-day wedding in another city.

I was feeling completely overwhelmed by all the stress and disruption. I found myself repeatedly saying, "I don't want to deal with this move." "I wish this contract could start a week later so I would have another week to be better prepared." "I really wish I could get some downtime for a break."

Well, I attracted exactly what I asked for—I got my downtime for a break, I didn't have to deal with the move, and the training was delayed a week. The reason? I fell and broke my arm.

As the story above illustrates, your thoughts and words shape what you attract in your life. Mastering how to use attraction will raise your PQ dramatically. While there are many different versions of attraction, we have worked with the simple five-step model below for over 20 years. This model works in all types of situations. In order to obtain the best results, address each of the five areas outlined below.

Attraction Step #1: You Attract Who You Are

Have you ever noticed that the people who share similar interests always seem to end up together at social gatherings? The law of attraction explains this phenomenon: we are attracted to those who are like us and who share our interests and values. If you are happy and well adjusted, you are likely to have happy and well-adjusted people in your life. If your personal life is in chaos, you will attract others whose personal lives are in chaos. What you attract reveals both the positive and the negative consequences of your thoughts and actions.

Toddlers are a great case in point. You may have told them, "Don't use that word!" but in most cases, they're simply repeating something you said. Children imitate what their parents do rather than doing what they say to do. Thus, the child who is physically punished at home may end up fighting at school. The child whose parents read to him learns to love books. Parents who exercise extreme control over their daughter may find that she develops anorexia and/or bulimia; her controlling behavior with food mirrors how they attempt to control her behavior.

While it may be painful, take a realistic look at what and whom you have attracted in your life. Are the people in your life caring and trustworthy or do you constantly experience betrayal? Do things in your life run smoothly or do you seem to constantly experience one disastrous situation after another? Do you attract truthful people or people who misrepresent the truth? Take the Personal Standards Inventory to identify opportunities where raising your standards can improve what you are attracting in your life.

Perspire Tip #1: Personal Standards Inventory
Answer each item as "true" or "false."

____ 1. The last time a clerk or restaurant forgot to charge me for an item, I brought it to the person's attention.
____ 2. I fudged on my tax return last year—the government already gets enough of my money.
____ 3. I have remained friends with someone who gossips and says hurtful things about me and other people.
____ 4. The last time someone told me a lie, I let it go by without saying anything.
____ 5. The last three times I promised to be somewhere or to help someone else, I was on time and did what I promised.
____ 6. I paid one or more of my bills late last month.
____ 7. The last time I made a mistake at work or elsewhere, I owned up to making the mistake and took responsibility for it.
____ 8. It has been at least three years since I received a traffic ticket.
____ 9. The last time someone told me a secret or asked me to keep a confidence, I shared the information with someone else.
____10. The last time I went to a restaurant, I thanked the person who seated me, the waitperson, and the person who brought the water or bussed the dishes.

Scoring:
Give yourself one point if you answered "True" on questions 1, 5, 7, 8, and 10.

Give yourself one point if you answered "False" on questions 2, 3, 4, 6, and 9.

The areas where you earned points represent core strengths. The areas where you did not score a point represent opportunities to raise your standards and to increase the quality of what you attract in your life.

For example, your friends, family, and co-workers may not know that you pay your bills late, but the credit bureaus track this data in detail. More importantly, the pattern of paying bills late may show up elsewhere as in being late for appointments or missing deadlines at work. Raising your standard to always being on time, whether it's with bills, deadlines, or people, will reduce the stress and the hassle in your life significantly.

By the same token, if you are attracting disloyal people, where have you failed to keep your word or do what you promised to do? If people always seem to be taking advantage of you, where are your actions causing harm to someone else?

> **Perspire Tip #2: Seek the source**
> To better understand how the mirroring element of attraction works, list at least five positive things in your life. Next, list five areas that you currently find challenging or that make you unhappy. Areas to consider include your health, family, friends, work, finances, etc.
>
> For each area that is working well in your life, did you model your behavior from a parent, teacher, colleague, friend, or mentor? Where did the thoughts, beliefs, and feelings that support these areas originate? How did your environment support your growth in each area? Leveraging your strengths is the best way to cope with the areas where you experience challenges.
>
> Now consider the areas where you are facing challenges. Where did these challenges and sources of unhappiness originate? Whose behavior did you model? What beliefs, emotions, or thoughts are contributing to the challenges that you are currently facing? What aspects of your environment are making your life more difficult? Again, identify the sources. The next step is to replace these ineffective approaches with the strategies that you identified that work well for you.

Chapter 3: Leverage Attraction To Perspire Less and Achieve More

The PERSIST model is based upon leveraging your current strengths to tackle the areas that you would like to improve.

Good people sometimes attract toxic individuals and situations
Here's an important point to note: even if you are functioning at high levels of attraction, you can still attract a toxic person or situation. The key is being able to recognize when someone's behavior is out of alignment with your behavior and to remove yourself from the situation as quickly as possible.

For example, if a friend says hurtful things about someone else behind their back, chances are the same friend is also saying similar things about you. While it may be difficult, you can either ask the person to stop saying hurtful things or you can stop spending time with him or her. By choosing to persist in maintaining your standards and resisting the temptation to ignore the behavior, you increase your level of attraction.

Once you can distinguish between behaviors that support your growth as opposed to the behaviors that increase the pain and struggle in your life, it becomes easier to persist in choosing the behaviors that will nourish you in the future. As the lyrics to an old Michael Jackson song say:

> *I'm starting with the man in the mirror,*
> *I'm asking him to change his way*
> *And no message could have been any clearer,*
> *If you wanna make the world a better place*
> *Take a look at yourself and then make a change.*

Attraction Step #2: Create Space

An old Chinese proverb says, "You cannot fill a cup that is already full." Before something new and better can come into your life, you must rid yourself of the old stuff that is blocking it. To illustrate this point, there's no room for a shiny new car when there's an old, beat-up junker in the garage. Getting rid of the junker creates the space for a new car to appear.

In the real estate industry, when an agent plans a vacation, their business often picks up dramatically a few days just before they are scheduled to leave. In scientific terms, nature abhors a vacuum. The act of creating space makes room for something new to come into their business or personal life.

Consequently, if you want to attract more business, more love, or just about anything else in your life, an important question you must answer is whether you have room for it. Many people are looking for Mr. or Ms. Right, even though they have no room in their life for a full-time relationship. Instead, they believe they can make room once they meet that person. Unfortunately, it seldom works that way—you must create the space first.

> **Perspire Tip #3: Create more space**
> Over the last 20 years I have given the following exercise to thousands of real estate agents. Those who implement it usually see a substantial increase in their business. By the way, this approach will also work in your personal life. To make more room for new business, a shiny new car, or the relationship you want, clean your closet, clean your desk, clean your garage, file those stacks of papers, and stop hanging out with people who drain your energy or waste your time. It makes no difference where you start. The goal is to eliminate whatever is taking up unnecessary space and is the easiest to do. In other words, get a trashcan and use it often.

Perspiration required

Attraction requires perspiration but it's not necessarily about working harder on the task at hand. The critical shift is in your mindset. As strange as it may seem, creating space in your schedule and in your physical environment, can result in significant benefits in other parts of your life. Remember, nature abhors a vacuum.

Attraction Step #3:
Have Clarity about How and What You Want to Attract

A number of years ago I was leading a coach training class on attraction. One of the coaches on the call asked, "What does it mean to have clarity about what you want to attract?" Here's how a new coach who had generated over $200,000 in fees during his first six months in the business answered the question:

> *The first thing I did was to sit down and write a list of characteristics of my ideal client. It was 15 pages long, right down to the type of belt and tie he wore.*

When I asked if his ideal client had shown up yet, his response was:

> *No, but a lot of his brothers and sisters sure have.*

Be definite with the infinite

Having clarity about what you want to attract and how you would like it to appear is another way of saying, "Be definite with the infinite." The coach in the example above illustrates the power of this approach. In contrast, one of my friends desperately needed money and prayed for it to appear. It did when she had a major car accident and was seriously injured.

One way to increase the clarity about what you want to attract is to visualize yourself in your new situation. For example, if you want a new car, go to the dealership and drive the car. Be sure to take a picture of yourself at the wheel and then post it as a screensaver on your computer or mobile device. Another approach is to make a storyboard of what you want to achieve. Writing down your goals and sharing them with another person also helps. To get the best results, combine your written goals and your storyboard or photo and share them with at least one other person.

> **Perspire Tip #4: How to create recreational time with your loved ones**
> If you would like to have more recreational time with your loved ones, write down the specific details of what you would do. Would you spend more time playing with your children? Would you be at home, at a park, or the beach? Would you make a picnic lunch or explore a new fun place to eat? Next, schedule a specific time to enjoy this activity as soon as possible. Once you've made room for this activity the first time, it's much easier to schedule time in the future.

Have clarity about what you will not accept

While it's important to have clarity about what you want to attract, it's equally important to have clarity about what you are unwilling to accept. One of my personal coaching clients created a 25-point list for what her ideal man would be like. As we worked together, the quality of the men she attracted continued to improve. After a number of months, she attracted a man who had virtually everything that she had on her list. The problem was he was emotionally available (he had been separated for five years), but was still legally married. She had forgotten to put that being emotionally available also meant that he was single. She added being single to her list and is now in a long-term, committed relationship.

> **Perspire Tip #5: How to attract your ideal**
> As noted above, whether it's a romantic partner or the ideal client, a certain amount of perspiration is necessary to make attraction work. Begin by making your ideal partner or client list. Identify not only what you want, but also be clear about what you are unwilling to accept.
>   Once you have finished that list, go back through it and identify how many of the characteristics that you listed actually apply to you. Now note which of those characteristics you lack. Keeping in mind that you attract who you are —if you want to attract someone who

appreciates you, make sure you regularly tell others how much you appreciate them. If you want to be treated well, treat others well.

Attraction Step #4: Give Back

There's an old adage that says,

When you give to a giver what do they do? They give back!

No matter how scarce things may seem, everyone has things they do not need or use. Whether it is old clothing, household items, or anything else you are not using, the question to ask is, "Does someone else need this more than I do?" If so, give it away.

If you truly have nothing to give away, read to a sick child, give someone who cannot drive a ride, or visit a shut-in. In general, the adage, "You get what you give" is true. What you give to others is almost always returned with interest.

Attraction Step #5: The Attitude Is Gratitude

This final component of attraction can be summed up in a simple question:

How can I ask for more when I don't appreciate what I already have?

In the mid 1990s, I was living in my custom-built house in a Beverly Hills guard-gated community, owned a shiny new Jag, designer clothes, and had most of the trappings of success. The problem was I was working 12-14 hours per day juggling my full-time college teaching position and running the real estate training program for 4,000 agents.

How could I have all this success and yet still feel unfulfilled? Fancy cars, expensive clothes, and a seemingly glamorous life selling Westside real estate should have made me happy, but didn't. If pursuit of physical possessions wasn't the answer, what was?

The answer was simple: gratitude. I was focused on what I lacked rather than on all the abundance I did have. Making the shift to regularly expressing gratitude wherever possible has profoundly influenced my level of happiness. The same approach can help you too.

How to create an abundance mindset

The sense of abundance is independent of how much money you have. Robert Frank (2007) in his book *Richistan* catalogs the characteristics of the ultra-wealthy ("Richistanis"). Many Richistanis report that having only $20 or $30 million is not enough to even get by. As you may have already concluded, the Richistanis are chasing physical possessions, a losing game where someone always has something bigger, better, and more beautiful than what you have.

In contrast, one of my friends lives on her husband's modest military pension and the small gifts she receives for helping others. She repeatedly acknowledges how she has more than she needs. She has an abundance mindset while many Richistanis do not.

When people lack abundance, they may try to bring you to their level (like attracts like) or they may envy what you have and become angry. Sometimes your best option will be to walk away. While this is not always possible, do your best to limit your exposure to them because their toxicity can negatively impact your well-being.

Practice gratitude daily

At Thanksgiving, most people pause to express gratitude for the abundance in their lives. Expressing gratitude daily by acknowledging others, not only makes them feel good, it makes you feel good as well. What's fascinating is that the more gratitude you express, the greater your sense of abundance will be. This in turn increases your attractiveness, making it easier to attract even more abundance.

Expressing gratitude has an extremely positive influence on your brain. When you actively search for ways to express gratitude, your brain releases beta-endorphins. This in turn improves your mood and increases your immunity. The more gratitude you express, the better you feel and the easier it becomes to find more things for which to be grateful.

Expressing gratitude in times of adversity

While it is relatively easy to express gratitude when things are going well, what about expressing gratitude when you are feeling angry or hurt? Often our most valuable lessons result from facing adversity. This is the time people are least likely to express gratitude, yet if you can find something positive in the situation, it can help you weather the storm until things improve.

To illustrate this point, the Great Recession left us swimming in a sea of debt. As we were struggling to hang on and work through the process, I remember coming across a quote about how to be grateful about your debt: "Be thankful to your creditors—they had an abundance of faith that you would pay them back."

Not long after that, one of my friends shared how she had worked through a spate of similar financial challenges. Although it took several years, what she experienced helped us to persist until we were able to pay everything off. We had to make some serious changes in our lifestyle, but those changes have actually resulted in much greater happiness while also improving our quality of life.

> **Perspire Tip #6: Keep a gratitude journal**
> Showing gratitude for what you have is an excellent way to become more attractive. A simple way to express gratitude is to look for opportunities to acknowledge others. Along the same lines, take a few moments each day to record at least five things in your life for which you are grateful, whether it's something as simple as your health, a roof over your head, the electricity that powers your lights, clean water, or food. You can keep track in a journal, in your appointment book, or in your contact manager. A great way to start your day is to do this before you begin work. Remember, if you want more of anything in your life, express gratitude for what you already have.

If you are still skeptical after reading this, I challenge you to an experiment: use these principles for one month and see if your life improves. Chances are you will be pleasantly surprised by the results.

Chapter 3: Key Points

1. You attract who you are. To improve the quality of the people you are attracting, raise your personal standards.

2. If you are attracting toxic people, they either reflect something negative that you are doing or you are not enforcing a boundary regarding the behaviors you are willing to tolerate.

3. To attract a higher quality of life, create space and be clear about what you want to attract—be definite with the infinite.

4. Give back and express gratitude as often as possible. A great way to do this is with a gratitude journal.

Chapter 4:
Resist Falling Prey to Illusion

Your problem is how you are going to spend this one odd and precious life you have been issued. Whether you're going to spend it trying to look good and creating the illusion that you have power over people and circumstances, or whether you are going to taste it, enjoy it, and find out the truth about who you are.
Anne Lamott

A critical step in embracing who you are is minimizing the negative impact that illusions have on your life. Illusions hurt you in a wide variety of ways. They set up unrealistic expectations, they fail to allow for the shortcomings that every person has, and they can rob you of the happiness and joy that you do have. In other words, resisting illusions makes achieving your goals and dreams easier.

The dictionary definition of illusion is, "something that deceives by producing a false or misleading impression of reality. It is also the state or condition of being deceived."

> **Perspire Tip #7: What do you like about you?**
> Here's a quick exercise. List ten things that you like about yourself. Next, list ten things you dislike about yourself. If you're like most people, it was easier to name what you dislike about yourself than what you like. The next step is to add another ten things to the list of what you like about you.

Now you may be wondering why people are so clear about their faults while they struggle to state what they like about themselves. The reason is that the advertising industry, the self-improvement gurus, and many so-called experts use every possible online and offline marketing medium to persuade you that you're not good enough unless you buy their product or service. Furthermore, advertisers continuously bombard us with Photoshopped images of perfect people who appear to be living perfect lives.

These are illusions; no one has a perfect life. Everyone has their disappointments, hurts, and struggles, no matter how wonderful their lives may appear on the outside. As noted in the last chapter, having gratitude for what you do have, rather than disappointment, envy, or anger about what you do not have, is a powerful way to create greater happiness and satisfaction in your life.

Recognizing Illusions

Being able to recognize illusions is the first step required to resist falling prey to them.

How many of these commonly held illusions have you experienced during in your life?

- My parents should understand me.
- If I go to college, I will definitely get a well-paying job.
- He/she will change once we get married.
- Having a child will save our marriage.
- If I try hard enough my spouse will stop drinking/taking drugs.
- My baby will always love me unconditionally.
- I will never treat my children like my parents treated me.
- My life would be great if I could just make enough money to pay off all my debts.
- My way is the right way.
- I'm in control—I can stop doing _____ whenever I want to.
- _____ could never happen to me.

A reliable way to spot an illusion is by its all-or-nothing nature. If X happens, then only Y can be the result. This is what makes illusions so insidious. When you start with a false premise that there is only one acceptable outcome, you shut down the possibility that other beneficial outcomes are possible. In addition, the more heavily you are invested in a single outcome, the harder it will be to shatter the illusion that blocks your progress.

Illusions Start with "Should"

Have you ever noticed how often people use the word "should"? Almost all illusions have a "should" attached to them, whether it is stated directly or implied. When you use, "I should," it generally represents something you have internalized from an external source such as a parent or authority figure.

When someone else tells you what you "should" do, that person is usually trying to manipulate you by using fear or guilt. For example, "You should stop eating so much junk food. If you don't, you'll end up having a heart attack." While this is a legitimate request, adding the word "should" and then coupling it with a fear-provoking threat turns this request into an attempted manipulation.

Now note how omitting "should" changes the request. "The doctor recommended cutting back on the junk food to decrease your heart attack risk. Would you like to join me in having more heart-healthy meals?"

"You" and "should"

When it comes to personal relationships, the moment "you" creeps into the conversation coupled with "should," an argument may be only moments away. For example, "You should do your fair share of work around the house."

A better approach is to use "I." While this can be challenging, mastering this approach can improve your communication dramatically. It will also reduce the amount of conflict you experience.

Using the previous example to illustrate how this process works, begin by eliminating "should." Next, make a request and couple it with a benefit. "Would you pitch in with the house cleaning this weekend? If we tackle it together, we could go to that new movie you wanted to see."

Consequently, the next time you're being "should" upon, ask yourself if this person is using guilt as a way to manipulate you. Does agreeing to their request require you to compromise your standards or beliefs? Are you responding to someone else's values or expectations? Before you decide what to do, analyze the consequences and choose based upon what energizes and supports you, not on what you "should" do.

Choice is sustainable; "should" is not

For a substantial part of the population, exercise is a "should." How many times have you heard someone resolve to start going to the gym regularly and then drift back to being physically inactive? "Should" is not a sustainable strategy. A better choice is to resist using "should" and to use the PERSIST strategy of "choice."

My personal wake-up call about exercise came when a dear friend who has osteoporosis broke seven ribs and literally died (and was resuscitated) five times while being airlifted to have coronary bypass surgery. Years of physical inactivity almost killed her.

A bone scan alerted me that I was at risk for osteoporosis. Making matters worse, heart disease killed my father, his three siblings, and a number of my cousins. It became crystal clear that I had a choice: take care of my heart and bones or face a similar fate. Now, when I don't feel like exercising, I remind myself that my actions are a choice: good health and vitality or heart disease and disability.

The key for me is doing my exercise first thing in the morning. If I wait until later, it almost never gets done. As one anonymous author observed, "I have to exercise early in the morning before my brain figures out what I'm doing."

Perspire Tip #8: Reframe "exercise" to "moving your body"

Reframing is a powerful tool that helps you make better choices by couching the choice in different language. Here's how it works. First, substitute the words "moving my body" for the word "exercise." Second, think of some of the fun ways to move your body—shopping, dancing, golfing, tennis—whatever works for you. Third, take at least 30 minutes three times a week to engage in any of these activities you enjoy. For example, your exercise program may include shopping, country western dancing, or a round of golf. When moving your body means doing something that is fun and enjoyable, it is much easier to sustain. Couple that activity with your favorite music and you also reap the benefits of brain synchronization.

Chapter 4: Resist Falling Prey to Illusion

Five ways to eliminate "should"

If "shoulds" are so damaging to your PQ, what can you do to decrease them? Here are five strategies:

1. The first step in eliminating "should" is to increase your awareness. Listen for when you and others use "should" and note the context in which the word is used. In almost every case, you will observe that "should" is a strategy to alter behavior using guilt and manipulation.

2. Immediately stop using "should." When you catch yourself using it, see if you can identify the nature of the manipulation and reframe the statement without using "should."

3. Once you have eliminated "should," ask those closest to you to restate what they want without using the word "should." While this can be difficult, the improved communication that results is well worth the effort.

4. There are certain situations where you may be unable to ask another person to restate their request. When that occurs, restate the request in your head without the "should." For example, if your child's teacher says, "Every night you should make sure Jane has done her homework," rephrase the request as, "Jane's teacher just asked me help Jane by making sure she completes her homework every night." Notice the shift from "should" to "help." Being told what you "should do" can create resistance. Being asked to help someone you love creates an entirely different dynamic.

5. Let go of past "shoulds" that resulted in poor outcomes. You cannot change the past but you can stop using a past "should" as a way to punish yourself. For example, if you dropped out of college, that's in the past. The question is what choices do you have today about rectifying that situation? Is it really worth the time and effort required to go back to school? If so, start exploring the options. If not, it's time to identify the reason that you are holding on to this "should." Is it that you don't want to admit to failure, you didn't live up to your "should" of being a good role model for

your children, or something else? Once you identify the reasoning behind the "should," it's much easier to release it and move on.

Perspire Tip #9: "No" is a complete sentence
One of Byron's favorite sayings is, "No is a complete sentence." You do not have to explain your reasoning or justify your decision-making process to anyone but yourself. Consequently, when someone tries to "should" you into doing something you don't want to do, all you have to say is, "No." You can then change the topic or leave the situation. If the person demands to know your reason, simply reiterate your answer, "No."

Confirmatory Bias: When There's No Changing Your Mind

Do you have a close friend or family member whose political beliefs are diametrically opposed to your beliefs? If so, you may be completely mystified as to how they can have these beliefs when you have accumulated so much evidence that they are wrong.

Confirmatory bias is defined as the tendency to seek, interpret, favor, and recall information in way that reinforces one's preexisting beliefs, while giving disproportionately less consideration to alternative possibilities.

When the Republican presidential campaign kicked off in 2015, anyone who believed that Donald Trump would defeat nine governors and five senators to capture the Republican nomination and then go on the win the presidency was considered to be delusional. In fact, two days before the election, the *Los Angeles Times* predicted that Secretary Clinton would win with 352 Electoral College votes. How did they and so many other people get it so totally wrong? The answer is confirmatory bias.

In an article on confirmation bias, David McRaney (2010) argues that your opinions are based upon years of paying attention to information that confirms what you believe and ignoring information that challenges your preconceived notions. McRaney explains:

Punditry is a whole industry built on confirmation bias. Rush Limbaugh and Keith Olbermann, Glenn Beck and Ariana Huffington, Rachel Maddow and Ann Coulter—these people provide fuel for beliefs, they pre-filter the world to match existing world-views. If their filter is like your filter, you love them. If it isn't, you hate them. Whether or not pundits are telling the truth, or vetting their opinions, or thoroughly researching their topics is all beside the point. You watch them not for information, but for confirmation.

Recognizing when confirmatory bias is strengthening an illusion
Remember that illusions normally allow for only one outcome and frequently have a "should" component. Denial and blaming are two additional clues that confirmatory bias may be propping up an illusion.

For example, assume that your friends and your family keep nagging you about your drinking. Using confirmatory bias, you deny their arguments, saying that you just drink socially or that having a few drinks once or twice a week is no cause for concern. Oh, by the way, did they notice that Joe had way more to drink than you did last weekend? After all, you can stop whenever you want. Besides, when you drink during the week, it's justified—who doesn't need a drink when the boss is a jerk, a co-worker just cheated you out of a promotion, or the office busybody is spreading lies about you. You also point out that you have never had a DUI, you have a great job, and you're the person who makes every party fun.

If people you love and trust are saying that you have a problem, is it possible that they may right? This is especially true if you are blaming your drinking on other people's actions rather than taking responsibility for your choice. These are all signs that your belief you are in control of your drinking is an illusion.

How to limit the effects of confirmatory bias
Robin Dreeke (2011), the former head of the FBI's Behavioral Analysis Program and the author of *It's Not All About "Me:" The Top Ten Techniques for Building Quick Rapport with Anyone,* has an excellent strategy for avoiding confirmatory bias. When you meet new people, Dreeke

argues that the most important thing you can do is to listen and seek their thoughts and opinions.

When someone says something you disagree with or that you don't understand, avoid judging that person. Instead say, "Oh that's fascinating. I never heard it put quite that way. Help me understand. How did you come up with that?"

Part of the reason this approach is so powerful is that people derive more pleasure from talking about themselves than they do from food or money. The same is true about giving advice.

The reason Dreeke's approach works so well is that it prevents the other person's brain from shutting down. When people hear something that goes against their confirmatory biases or contradicts their beliefs, two things happen: first, the logical part of the brain shuts down and second, the brain prepares to fight.

A more effective way to build trust and rapport is to ask about their challenges. Everyone has them and, as noted above, people derive great pleasure from talking about themselves. By being open to what others say, you limit your risk of confirmatory bias and decrease the probability of falling prey to illusions.

Lose Your Illusions

Because illusions are self-created, they can be uncreated. People typically cling to illusions because there is some benefit to holding on to them.

> **Perspire Tip #10: Learn from past disillusionments**
> Recall a time when one of your illusions was shattered. Perhaps you had a broken heart, a trusted friend betrayed you, or some long held dream did not materialize. Next, list the benefits you achieved from holding on to the illusion such as avoiding painful events elsewhere in your life. One of the greatest benefits of shattering illusions is releasing the energy needed to hold the illusion in place. Once released, this energy then becomes available for taking action to raise the quality of your life.

Dream, goal, or illusion?
Illusions can sometimes be confused with achievable dreams and goals. For example, most students who attend college expect to be hired into a well-paying position once they graduate. Very few anticipate how hard it may be to get hired, even for entry-level jobs with much lower salaries than they anticipated.

Leah Goodman's (2015) article in *Newsweek*, "Millennial College Graduates: Young, Educated, Jobless," explains the difficulties today's college graduates are encountering. One Georgetown graduate reported that her friends averaged 60 applications before being hired. Another voiced her frustration about not even being considered for entry-level jobs.

> *"So far, I have applied for around 30 jobs and have heard back on two of them. I didn't get either job because I don't have enough experience. These are entry-level jobs but experienced people are taking them."*

Pray for sunshine, be prepared for rain
An old friend from my graduate school days used to say, "Pray for sunshine, be prepared for rain." This is a simple strategy for eliminating illusions while simultaneously allowing you to persist in achieving the best possible outcome.

Given the high unemployment rate among millennials (some experts place it as high as 40 percent), it's smart for students to have a backup plan. Many employers prefer to hire people with experience. Thus, students can be better prepared to enter the workplace by pursuing internships or volunteering in an area where they hope to be hired. They can also broaden their background by taking additional classes outside their major. In each case they gain valuable experience while making contacts that may help them in the future. The wise course of action is to pursue their dream, but to also be prepared with a backup plan.

Moving from disillusionment to happiness and satisfaction
Releasing illusions frees you to pursue new possibilities as this story from one of our company's coaching clients shows:

All through my twenties and thirties, I desperately wanted to get married and have children. When I went to parties and class reunions, I always felt like I was on the outside looking in. When I turned 40, I finally came to terms with the fact I wasn't going to have children and I probably wasn't going to get married. While my friends were raising their families, I was building a successful company. Now at age 50, I have a life most people dream of—travel, a great home, lots of golf, and a great life filled with wonderful friends. More importantly, I've started a program for young adults with Down syndrome where they can work to make their own money. My company provides transportation, they work a few hours a day, and we all have a ball. If I had raised my own family, I wouldn't have had the time or the money to devote to these wonderful young people.

Perspire Tip #11: Is there an illusion holding you back?
Here's a quick checklist to spot any illusions that may be holding you back.

1. You have a cherished belief or goal, but there always seems to be obstacle after obstacle in the way of achieving it.

2. When you consider this belief or goal, there's only one outcome that will be acceptable to you—it's an all-or-nothing proposition.

3. You find yourself using "should" when you talk to others about this belief or goal.

4. You become defensive or angry when anyone shares information that contradicts what you believe about this belief or goal.

5. Achieving this goal means that most of your problems will disappear.

Chapter 4: Resist Falling Prey to Illusion

You have amped up your brain and your attraction level, but what are the best ways to persist when you feel the urge to procrastinate, are feeling stuck, or when you have done your best and it's not good enough? The best place to start is by embracing your strengths, which is the second step in the PERSIST model.

Chapter 4: Key Points

1. Identify illusions by recognizing their all-or-nothing nature coupled with the word "should."

2. Replace "should" with "choice." "Should" is almost always attached to an attempt to manipulate others or yourself using guilt.

3. "No" is a complete sentence.

4. Escape confirmatory bias by being willing to listen to viewpoints that differ from yours.

5. Avoid having the other person's brain shut down when you disagree with him or her. Instead say, "Oh that's fascinating. I never heard it put quite that way. Help me understand. How did you come up with that?"

Embrace Your Strengths

Embrace your differences and the qualities about you that you think are weird. Eventually, they're going to be the only things separating you from everyone else.
Sebastian Stan

Chapter 5:
Embrace Strengths, Work Around Weaknesses

*Life is too short to perfect
your weaknesses.*
Joeann Fossland

A critical component of increasing your PQ is to shift from focusing on your weaknesses to focusing on your strengths. As mentioned before, the advertising industry spends billions of dollars trying to exploit your fears and insecurities in order to sell you their products or services. Rather than buying into their hype, embracing your strengths is the foundation for achieving happiness and success while simultaneously increasing your ability to persist in achieving your long-term goals.

Identify Your Strengths

While most people can easily identify their weaknesses, identifying their strengths usually proves to be more challenging. The dictionary definitions for strength include "the inherent capacity to manifest energy, to endure, and to resist" and "the quality that allows someone to deal with problems in a determined and effective way." In terms of the PERSIST model, your strengths are your assets—they provide the energy required to persist in taking effective action and to resist choices that fail to support your long-term goals.

Embrace Tip #1: How to identify your strengths
Identifying strengths is not as easy as it may seem because your strengths are easy for you. Consequently, you may not recognize them as strengths. They seem ordinary, something others must be able to do as easily as you do.

Identifying your strengths is a two-step process. Begin by writing down at least 5-10 strengths that you have. Examples include exercising, serving your community, being a hard worker, or making others laugh. It's about what energizes you and what you do well. Strengths can also include patience, your ability to endure adversity, and your choice to resist activities such as smoking, drug use, overeating, or other temptations that do not support your long-term health and well-being.

The second step is to ask 10-20 people from your personal and work life about what they perceive your strengths to be. Take note of the top five things that people repeat the most often. When people repeatedly cite something you do and you feel like saying, "Well that's not a big deal," you have identified a strength. As you address your illusions, weaknesses, or any other challenging situation, remember that relying on your strengths will be the most effective way to resolve whatever you must face.

Address Your Weaknesses

Like illusions, weaknesses can be barriers to success. Rather than allowing the barrier to stop you, the issue is how to get around it. Here are some of the most common ways that people deal with their weaknesses.

Avoidance

People often go to great lengths to avoid exposing a weakness. Children who have test anxiety are an excellent example; their emotions can cause them to vomit and to even run a fever.

When it comes to weaknesses, avoidance can be a two-edged sword. For example, assume that you are a college student who is prone to panic attacks when you are in a large group. A required class is available online or live in an auditorium that seats 600. In this case, avoiding the large class is a positive choice. On the other hand, if you were to stop attending required live classes, that negative choice could ultimately force you to drop out of school.

Delegate

Delegation is a powerful strategy for proactively dealing with weaknesses. If you are a get-it-done type of person who can't be bothered with details, hire a detailed-oriented assistant. Your combined strengths and weaknesses complement each other. The downside of delegation occurs when you fail to monitor results. As the saying goes, "Inspect what you expect."

Denial
Denial is a poor approach for addressing weaknesses. To illustrate this point, the woman who notices a lump in her breast and denies that anything is wrong may put her life at risk. Denial also robs individuals of their sense of control and can even lead to feelings of victimization.

Compensation and overcompensation
Sigmund Freud observed two other strategies that people use to cope with their weaknesses: compensation and overcompensation. When someone compensates for a weakness, they do so by becoming strong in another area. For example, the guy who is not very athletic may compensate by developing a great sense of humor.

In overcompensation, the person actually develops strength in an area where there is a major weakness. An excellent example is someone who has had a leg amputated due to cancer and who takes up running marathons to raise money for a cure.

Workaround
Prior to the last presidential election, a close friend whose politics are the polar opposite of mine seemed unconcerned about who was going to win. I was stunned by her attitude. She went on to explain:

"It makes no difference which candidate is elected. Ultimately, America is the great workaround society—we'll figure it out no matter who wins."

She was right—when something doesn't work, the American mindset is to figure out a workaround. When you are unable to avoid being in a situation that forces you to rely on a weakness, figuring out a workaround can be an excellent strategy. A workaround typically uses one of your strengths to combat a weakness. Here's an example of how this process works.

She Can't Keep Her Numbers Straight
You have just enrolled in Statistics 1. After the professor passes out the syllabus she asks:

> *Is there anyone here who does not know how to push the add, subtract, multiply, divide, and the square root keys on their calculator?*

A few students laugh nervously, but no one raises their hand. She continues,

> *Good. If you know how to push those five keys, that's all you will need to do to solve the problems in this class. By the way, there's something else that you need to know. I have a type of learning disability called an auditory sequencing problem. What it means is that when I'm solving a problem on the board, I may transpose some of the numbers. So I need your help—if you spot a mistake, please call it to my attention.*
>
> *Also, if you are having a problem understanding something we're discussing in class, please ask me to repeat what we have just gone over or to explain it in more detail. If you're not following what I'm saying, chances are other students may not be either.*

The little speech above was my standard opening for my Statistics 1 class; it accomplished four things. First, because so many students were terrified about taking the course, it reduced some of their fear about the difficulty of the math. Second, if someone with a learning disability could learn statistics, then maybe they could too. This provided hope that they could indeed pass the class. Third, anyone who brought an error to my attention was helping me, not criticizing me for making a mistake. Fourth, if the student had a question, it was safe to ask, especially in light of the fact that their question could help other students in the class.

Embrace Who You Are

I remember when my department chair first told me that I was being assigned to teach two sections of statistics the following semester. My first thought was, "Are you serious? My degrees are in English and Educational Psychology. Yes, I took three graduate classes in statistics but given my auditory sequencing problem, there is no way I should

Chapter 5: Embrace Strengths, Work Around Weaknesses

(notice the "should") be teaching a math class where numerical accuracy is critical."

This response illustrates the resistance part of the decision-making process. Notice that there was only one acceptable option—not teaching the class. Making that choice, however, would require taking a partial leave and would also result in a 40 percent cut in pay. This is an extremely important point to note. You always have choices; you just may not like any of them.

People often justify their resist behaviors by providing legitimate reasons for their weaknesses. In my case, I was using my auditory sequencing problem as an excuse to avoid spending an extra 100 hours to prep for this course. Besides, the students already had enough issues with this class—they didn't need me confusing them further with the mistakes I was bound to make. This example highlights how confirmatory bias plays into the resistance aspect of the decision-making process.

Once I realized that Statistics 1 was going to be part of my reality for the foreseeable future, the best option was to let go of my resistance and to persist in tackling the course. It was time to shift from making excuses to implementing a solution. This is another key point: when you make excuses, there is a high probability that you are in resistance mode, whether it's an illusion or a perceived weakness.

Marshall your resources

The PERSIST model emphasizes shifting your focus from your weaknesses to your strengths. I began my process by identifying a workaround. Because my department chair had been teaching statistics for many years, I asked for his help. He graciously agreed to share his notes, tests, and other resources.

I also knew from teaching remedial reading that if I worked at it, I could present the material in a way that would be relatively simple for the students to understand. I was going to make mistakes, but helping more students to pass the course and to obtain their degrees would be worth the effort. The moment you shift from focusing on yourself to focusing on others you are at the pivot point in moving from resistance to persistence.

Once I made this pivot and I had obtained the supporting materials from the department chair, the next step was to take what had worked well in my other classes and to adapt it to statistics.

My "Advance Organizers" were quite popular with my students. This concept comes from learning theory. The notion is that if you want someone to learn something, provide them with the key points they need to learn, give them practice problems, and list the key vocabulary terms that they need to master. The beauty of the Advance Organizers was that they helped to reduce the student's anxiety about the exams.

I also needed a workaround strategy to handle the auditory sequencing errors I was prone to make. My students always appreciated the detailed set of lecture notes that I provided for each of my classes. I decided to do the same thing for statistics and to include sample calculations. This freed students to concentrate on the concepts rather than frantically copying my calculations from the board. It also reduced the number of errors that I would make in front of the class.

Ultimately I discovered that I enjoyed teaching statistics. What was really rewarding, however, was repeatedly hearing from former students about how well they did in their required upper division statistics classes, especially when most of their classmates were struggling.

The bottom line was that by resisting the urge to wiggle out of teaching statistics and by persisting in finding a workaround, I helped hundreds of students. So what if I transposed a few numbers?

> **Embrace Tip #2: Hang it out on the front porch**
> The next time you feel like hiding a weakness, take a tip from my long-time friend Marilyn Naylor: "If you try to hide your dirty laundry everyone wants to find out about it. When you hang it out on the front porch nobody gives a damn."

Let Go of Being a *Homo Perfectus*

Perfection is an illusion. As noted in the previous chapter, it has the elements of "should" and there is only room for one possible outcome (perfection). Moreover, trying to achieve perfection in everything you do (being a *Homo Perfectus*) creates struggle that slows your progress to achieving what matters most. Besides, even if you could be perfect, would you really want to spend time around a person who actually was?

Embrace Tip #3: There's no such thing as a 100 percent house…or spouse!

Jon Douglas, the CEO and founder of the real estate company where I worked for 18 years, used to say, "There's no such thing as a 100 percent house." I used to joke with my psychology students that the corollary to that saying is, "There's no such thing as a 100 percent house or a 100 percent spouse. You have to choose which set of warts you're willing to live with, whether it's a person or a house."

There's never time to do it right, but there's always time to do it over

The flip side of being a perfectionist is that there's never time to do it right, but there's always time to do it over. Have you ever noticed how often you have to redo a task that you thought was complete? Is this a frequent or a rare event in your life? On the occasions where you had to redo a task, how much extra time would it have taken to do it right the first time vs. the amount of time wasted on handling the redo?

Vince Lombardi once said, "Perfection is not attainable, but if we chase perfection we can catch excellence." When it comes to how much effort to apply to a task, how do you navigate between being a *Homo Perfectus* and having to do the task over?

An important part of *Homo Perfectus* behavior is that the people with this behavioral style usually apply a very high standard to everything they do. Those who have to redo projects suffer from the flip side of this—their standard for completion is consistently lower than what is required across the board. In other words, for both sets of people, their resist strategy is a one-size-fits-all approach as opposed to the more effective PERSIST strategy of varying the amount of effort required based upon the importance of each task.

In both cases, these individuals spend too much effort on unimportant activities and too little effort on the crucial activities that yield optimal results. It's important to realize that applying excess energy to a task that only requires a 70 percent effort to be sufficiently complete has the same consequences as putting only 90 percent toward an essential task that really needed 110 percent.

For example, when you do your taxes, it's wise to give a 110 percent effort—check and double check your figures before submitting them to the IRS. On the other hand, when you are setting the table for a dinner party, a 70 or 80 percent effort is probably acceptable. You can put each item in the appropriate place, but there is no need to spend additional time making sure that each plate, napkin, glass, and piece of silverware is perfectly placed.

Most people yearn for more time in their lives. By applying the PERSIST strategy of varying the amount of effort required to do tasks to the appropriate point of completion, you can avoid wasting time by working too hard on some tasks and having to redo others.

The Pareto Principle (the 80-20 Rule)

Chapter 2 discussed the importance of narrowing your focus by eliminating multitasking behavior and focusing on completing one task at a time. The Pareto principle is a powerful tool that can help you to achieve this goal.

The Pareto principle (the 80-20 rule) states that 80 percent of the benefits or results come from 20 percent of the causes or input. Italian economist Vilfredo Pareto based his principle upon his observation that 80 percent of Italy's land was owned by 20 percent of the population. As he conducted research in other countries, he found the same principle applied as well. For example, 20 percent of the salespeople in most businesses generate 80 percent of the sales. What was really surprising was what Pareto found in his garden: 20 percent of his pea plants had 80 percent of the total pea pods!

Perry Marshall (2014) in his book *80/20 Sales and Marketing* expands the original Pareto principle (80-20 rule) showing that the top four percent of salespeople represent 64 percent of sales. In other words, the top four percent of your activities/causes are responsible for 64 percent of your results.

What is number one on your to-do list?
In *The One Thing*, *New York Times* best-selling authors Gary Keller and Jay Papasan (2013) explain that life is too complex to have it all. Each of us has the same 1,440 minutes per day. The secret to success is shifting from what you "could do" to focusing on what is at the top of your to-do list. To illustrate this point, when Keller asks anyone about their to-do list, he always asks the same question: "Of all the things on

your to-do list, what is number one? It's important to know what #1 is before going on to #2."

Using Marshall's model, follow these three steps to identify your top four percent for each important area in your life:

1. Identify your to-dos.
2. Prioritize them.
3. Implement them one at a time starting with the most important.

Embrace Tip #4: Where are you spending your time and effort?
Take a moment to identify the three most important personal activities in your life as well as the three most important activities outside your personal life. For the next week, track how much time is devoted to these essential activities vs. everything else. Next, examine your totals. Was the time spent on non-essential items greater than the time spent on your highest priority items? To illustrate this point, did you devote more time to growing your job skills, eliminating debt, or spending quality time with your loved ones or did you waste hours of time playing video games and engaging in non-essential chatter online? Because the first step in changing your behavior is awareness, discovering this information can be life changing.

Start pruning

If 20 percent of your activities produces 80 percent of your results, spending time working on the bottom 20 percent is almost always a wasted effort. Eliminating the bottom 20 percent of your activities not only lets you place more focus on what does work, it also frees up the equivalent of one full work day each week.

Gardeners prune plants and trees to eliminate what is dead and to improve growth. In terms of raising your PQ, pruning means eliminating what is unnecessary, undesirable, as well as what is contrary to your values, integrity and ethics.

In addition to pruning off the bottom 20 percent of your activities, here are some other places to consider pruning:

- Anything you feel that you should do, yet no longer serves your present goals and purpose.
- Habits, patterns, or decisions that rob you of your energy, confidence, or emotional well-being.
- Any tasks that are a weakness for you that can be delegated and completed more quickly and successfully by another person.
- If your life has taken a turn that no longer supports you, it's much like a large branch growing over the neighbor's fence. The sooner you deal with it, the less likely it is to cause you problems.
- When you buy a new piece of clothing or a new pair of shoes, prune at least one item from your wardrobe either by throwing it away or giving it to charity.

Conquer Your To-Do List

A powerful strategy for conquering your to-do list is to identify the three most important tasks that you must complete each day at work and at home. It typically takes less than two minutes to complete the list and is well worth the effort.

Next, as Brian Tracy (2007) recommends in his book, *Eat That Frog!*, do the biggest, ugliest task (the "frog") on your list first.

Where many people get into trouble is that they fail to prioritize their list. Even if they have established priorities, they seldom complete the top items first. The result is they often fail to complete what was really essential. In other words, the resist strategy is to do what is most convenient in contrast to the PERSIST strategy of identifying your top three to-do's and completing them first.

When you "eat that frog" first, the rest of your day is much more enjoyable because the frog is no longer hanging over you. There is also an energy boost as you rid yourself of the frog, which makes your other tasks seem easier. Furthermore, when you complete your top three items, you're much less likely to feel guilty about not getting to the bottom items on your to-do list.

Remember, the bottom 50 percent of your to-do list is responsible for less than ten percent of your outcomes. Moreover, two decades of coaching salespeople has shown us that when a person takes the energy they used working on their bottom 50 percent of activities and they apply it to the top 50 percent of their activities, their sales increase exponentially.

> **Embrace Tip #5: Persist at what you love**
> "Choose a job you love and you will never have to work a day in your life." Confucius

Identifying the Amount of Effort Required for Your Best Outcome

Are there specific parts of your life or business where you always give your best no matter what the circumstances? And where in your life or business do you routinely give less than your best?

One of our past coaching clients made the following observation about not giving her best:

> *What immediately comes to mind are the many times I didn't bother giving my best when I could have. A friend calls this "being a 90 percenter." He likes to give 105 percent just to make sure he does the job right. Even though I seldom encounter situations where my best is not good enough, shifting to concentrating on completing what I start has made a huge difference in my overall effectiveness.*

> **Embrace Tip #6: What amount is the right amount?**
> Most performance experts agree: you cannot give 100 percent of your effort 100 percent of the time. The secret lies in knowing when you need to give a 105 percent effort and when 80 percent (or less) is enough. To see how this process works, identify a project you are working on and then answer the following four questions:
>
> 1. What level of effort am I currently giving?
>
> 2. What would be the impact (cost and benefit) of giving 105 percent effort to complete this project?

> 3. What would be the impact of giving 80 percent (or less) effort to complete this project?
>
> 4. To what extent will this project impact future projects?
>
> Any project that has a long-term impact on your life or business is a project worthy of a greater level of effort.

Train Yourself to Give Your Best

It's easy to give your best when things are going well. When you are confronted with a challenging circumstance, it can be much more difficult. The suggestions below can help you be better prepared to provide your best no matter what happens.

1. Are you giving your best
Learn to recognize when you're giving your best and when you're not. Keep in mind the detrimental effects of multitasking as well as the performance benefits of having both your left and right brain working in synchrony.

2. Be patient with the growth process
Ignore the resist strategy that claims that you are already doing your best and that you cannot do any more. Instead, use the PERSIST approach that says no matter how good you are, there's always room for improvement. Also, small improvements over time add up to big changes in overall effectiveness.

3. Create a support system
Whether it's a family member, a trusted friend, a coach, or mentor. Seek someone who encourages you to be at your best, even when it's painful.

4. Have a learning mindset
Read books, listen to podcasts, attend training, or engage in any activity that helps you to improve and grow. Making learning a

consistent habit will help you to be better prepared to give your best.

5. **Exercise your persistence muscle**
   Learning to handle difficult situations is like learning any other skill. It begins with awareness and a decision about what actual steps to take, followed by action, repeated practice, and incorporating feedback on how to improve. It is wise to start this process now so that you will be able to access this skill when you need it.

6. **Give your inner critic a holiday**
   Always ask, "Did I do the best I could do?" If you did and something didn't work out, determine what you could have done differently and then move forward.

7. **How have you overcome past challenges?**
   Make a list of five challenges that you faced in the past and include the strategies that you used to overcome them. Then, the next time that you face a challenge, review the strategies that worked before. Often the list will contain a solution that you can apply to the challenge you are facing now.

8. **Take baby steps**
   When you are in a situation that requires you to work with a weakness, take small steps to minimize the threat of failure. Remember, small steps over time yield major results.

9. **Express gratitude**
   Express gratitude to those who help you and acknowledge that it also takes guts to push yourself beyond your current limits.

10. **Stay present**
    A challenge that seems overwhelming right now may resolve itself effortlessly two days from now. Work with what you have available today and avoid worrying about yesterday or what may happen tomorrow.

11. Failures can be your best teachers
When you push yourself, there will be failures. Nevertheless, your worst moments may become your most valuable teachers and even occasionally, your most precious memories.

Mistakes and failures: blessings in disguise?
No one enjoys making mistakes or struggling to achieve a goal and not succeeding. Nevertheless, your mistakes and failures can be blessings in disguise. For example, the man I was engaged to in college could never seem to get around to agreeing to a date for the wedding. After five years, I was heartbroken and walked away. I compensated by going back to school to pursue my doctorate. We stayed in touch with a phone call or holiday card every year, but that was it. In 2014, I learned how very different my life would have been had we been married. He was suffering from Alzheimer's disease and had also become a compulsive hoarder.

Find Your Path

Your combination of strengths and weaknesses is unique to you. When you work with your strengths, it's fun and sustainable; trying to overcome weaknesses usually results in pain and struggle. If you hate where you work or some aspect of your personal life, take steps to identify the illusions that may be holding you back, the strengths you bring to the table, as well as the various options you could implement to improve the situation. At that point, you can determine whether you want to pursue the present course, change direction, or leave the situation. As Arnold Schwarzenegger once observed:

> *Strength does not come from winning. Your struggles develop your strengths. When you go through hardships and decide not to surrender, that is strength.*

Finally, always keep in mind that a decision to do nothing is almost always a decision to resist rather than to persist.

Chapter 5: Key Points

1. Identify your strengths by writing down what you do well and then asking at least 10 people at home or work about what they perceive your strengths to be. The items mentioned most often are your key strengths.

2. The six ways to address your weaknesses are avoidance, delegation, denial, compensation, overcompensation, and searching for a workaround.

3. The Pareto principle (the 80-20 rule) states that 80 percent of the benefits or results come from 20 percent of the causes.

4. Focus on your top four percent and prune off the bottom 20 percent of your activities that provide little, if any benefit.

5. Embrace who you are and if you're a perfectionist, experiment with completing tasks at the 90 percent level rather than the 110 percent level.

6. Give your best by exercising your persistence muscle, having a strong support network, focusing on your strengths, and delegating your weaknesses.

7. A decision to do nothing is almost always a decision to resist rather than to persist.

Chapter 6:
Escape the Quicksand
of Procrastination

*Procrastination is like a credit card:
it's a lot of fun until you get the bill.*
Christopher Parker

During the past week what did you postpone until tomorrow that would have been better handled today? Filing your income taxes? Saving for a rainy day? Going to the dentist? Paying your bills? Calling a loved one?

The dictionary defines procrastination as "intentionally putting something off until a later time because you do not want to do it."

Napoleon Hill described procrastination as, "The bad habit of putting off until the day after tomorrow what should have been done the day before yesterday."

When you procrastinate, you make a conscious choice to delay or to avoid taking action. That choice typically harms you in two ways. First, it results in increased stress and struggle, because you spent time and have nothing to show for it. Second, the longer you procrastinate, the more difficult it becomes to take the necessary action required to complete the task. In other words, procrastination makes easy tasks harder and harder tasks even more difficult.

Knowing What to Do Is Not Enough

Are you currently struggling with an issue where you know you need to take action but you are stuck in the muck of procrastination and resistance? If you're like most people, you probably know what to do. The issue is finding the motivation to take action and complete the task. A good analogy is being caught in quicksand. Once you get stuck in the quicksand of procrastination, it can be difficult to escape.

For example, if you have stopped exercising regularly, the longer you procrastinate about starting to exercise again, the harder it becomes to get back into the habit. The converse is also true; the more you exercise, the easier it is to continue exercising. Whether it's being stuck in the quicksand of procrastination or engaging in a PERSIST behavior that supports your well-being, the more energy you put into resisting or persisting, the more likely you are to continue doing that same behavior.

What Causes Procrastination?

You know what needs to be done, but when you procrastinate, you make a conscious choice to resist taking action. Procrastination often results when you do not make completing the task a priority. The reasons for your decision may be perfectly valid—the timing isn't right, you're not adequately prepared, or some other event occurred that required your attention.

When you become aware that you are procrastinating, look for the cause underlying your resistance to taking action. Are you focused on achieving a perfect outcome? Are you afraid of failing? Will the task take too much effort? Are you having trouble staying focused? Are you feeling overwhelmed because you have too much else to do? Was it some other reason? Each time you procrastinate, evaluate what is stopping you and determine if any of the following causes are responsible.

Being a *Homo Perfectus*

If you are a *Homo Perfectus*, you spend more energy completing all types of tasks as compared to those who spend more energy on high priority tasks and less energy on low priority tasks. This can be particularly daunting when you are required to master something new and are more likely to make mistakes. Unwillingness to make mistakes is a major reason people resist change. Their resistance often shows up as procrastination and/or avoidance. If you were focused on achieving a perfect outcome, would a 90 percent effort be satisfactory to anyone else? If so, try stopping when the task is 90-95 percent complete and see what happens.

Fear of failure

If you're afraid of failing, remember that failure and success go hand-in-hand. Failure is not the issue; it's the decision not to persist (i.e., to try again). If your fear of failure is getting the best of you, recall a time when you were afraid that you would fail and you succeeded instead. Another approach is to recall when you first learned to ride a bicycle, drive a car, or tried another new skill. You probably made mistakes, but you kept persisting until you succeeded.

Fear of failure can sometimes cause a strange type of lose-lose avoidance. As strange as it may seem, the individual attempts to cut their losses by limiting the impact of any failure. A common example is the student who skips studying for an exam. If the student passes the exam, it's a winning scenario—the student passed without studying. If the student fails the exam, it was because the student chose not to study. In contrast, had the student studied for the exam and failed, the impact of failing would have been much more damaging.

Low energy levels
Low energy has multiple causes including lack of sleep, poor diet, stress, illness, or an underlying medical problem such as hypothyroidism. If your low energy is resulting from lifestyle decisions, Chapter 11 "Self-ish" addresses how to make simple changes to increase your energy. If you suspect you may have a medical issue, please see your health care professional for an evaluation.

Lack of focus
If you lack focus, make a list of what you need to complete and then prioritize it. Next, complete the toughest item on the list before going on to the next task. Remember to complete the tasks in priority order so that the most important tasks are always completed first.

Another excellent approach is to shift your focus from what is not done to what you can accomplish right now. This simple approach eliminates the "should" in "What-I-should-do." When you couple focusing on what you can accomplish right now with a focus on your highest priority activity, the temptation to procrastinate diminishes significantly.

Overwhelm
Overwhelm occurs when you attempt to do more than your internal or external systems can handle. The result is that you become so drained by trying to manage it all that you find it virtually impossible to accomplish anything. When you are overwhelmed, what stops you is not a lack of ability; it's merely a lack of space and/or time.

> **Embrace Tip #7: Apply the 80-20 rule to tackle overwhelm**
>
> A large number of unfinished projects is a clear sign that you are in overwhelm. If this is true for you, now is an excellent time to apply the 80-20 rule. Many times unfinished projects are something that you agreed to do out of obligation, guilt, or shame. Identify your top 20 percent and then focus on completing what is easiest first. Please note that tackling high priority tasks first is usually the best approach. *When you're feeling overwhelmed, however, the opposite is true. It's better to complete a single easy task than to do nothing at all.*
>
> If your case of overwhelm is severe, begin by taking a single action step on the easiest item. As Lao Tzu said, "A journey of 10,000 miles begins with a single step." In other words, rather than focusing on the magnitude of the entire task, break it into bite-sized chunks. Accomplishing multiple small tasks en route to completing a larger more complex task gives you a sense of achievement. With each step that you take, you gradually build momentum and the process becomes easier. Furthermore, the process of stringing these small action steps together is what yields the greatest results. Once you complete one or more of the easier tasks, you can tackle the more difficult ones. Remember to concentrate on completing your top 20 percent first before moving to items lower on your list.

Strategies for Escaping the Quicksand of Procrastination

What can you do to escape the quicksand of procrastination in your life? Here are nine strategies:

1. Stop adding things to your to-do list

As the old saying goes, when you find yourself in a rut the first thing to do is to stop digging. Stop making any new commitments and focus your attention on completing the commitments that you have already made.

2. Create a personal procrastination profile
To create your personal procrastination profile, begin by noting the types of activities that you complete vs. those where you consistently procrastinate. Next, compare how you feel when you procrastinate to how you feel when you choose to take action. If you're like most people, completing the task made you feel good. On the other hand, the incomplete task probably resulted in increased stress and frustration. Once you are aware of where you are most likely to procrastinate, you can leverage your positive feelings about completing tasks as an additional way to motivate yourself to take action when you're tempted to procrastinate.

3. Delegate it or dump it
If there's a consistent area where you procrastinate, it's time to delegate it or dump it. Many times people become trapped by their belief system, especially when it comes to what they "should" do. For example, you may believe that you "should" bake a cake for a special birthday when a cake from the market would be just as good and would require less effort.

4. Tackle the simple items first
If you try to stop procrastinating all at once or tackle the hardest items first, you'll only create more struggle and stress. Instead, start with what you can easily handle and then move to the more difficult items.

5. Put a time limit on what's not handled
Here's an example of how to put a time limit on what you're not handling. If you subscribe to a print magazine and you didn't read it this month, put the magazine in the next month's stack. If you haven't read the magazine after 90 days, discard it. Allowing the magazines to pile up is a constant reminder of your procrastination and only makes you feel worse as the pile continues to grow. You can also use the same approach when facing a more daunting task such as returning a call to a difficult client or making an

appointment to have your doctor look at that strange lump on your leg. Set a short deadline for completing the task. Your agreement with yourself can be that you complete the task any time before the deadline, but no later. If you want to put some teeth in your agreement, try what one of my friends did. When he missed a deadline, he had to make a $50.00 campaign contribution to the political figure he despised the most.

6. Most mistakes can be fixed
Failure is seldom fatal. Furthermore, most mistakes can be fixed. It's important to realize that failure to take action is actually worse than trying and being unsuccessful. When you never try in the first place, you have nothing to show at all.

7. Alter your environment
If you are using time blocking (allotting specific time periods for completing specific tasks), turn off your computer's internet connection or place your mobile device in airplane mode. Using an example from real estate, an agent might block 9:00 a.m. to 11:00 a.m. for prospecting, 11:00 a.m. to 12:00 p.m. for following up on leads and handling transaction problems, 12:00 p.m. to 1:00 p.m. for lunch, and 1:00 p.m. to 4:00 p.m. for showing buyers property, and 4:00 p.m. to 5:00 p.m. to handle any other important tasks. The agent would take quick breaks to check messages and notifications, at 10:00 a.m., 11:00 a.m., 12:30 p.m., 1:45 p.m., 3:00 p.m., and 4:00 p.m. Time blocking allows you to avoid unimportant social media notifications or other unwanted interruptions. Check your messages every 30-60 minutes and get up to walk around if you are sitting. Research shows that both activities enable you to achieve more in less time.

8. Partner up
Alcoholics Anonymous, Parents Without Partners, Weight Watchers, and a host of other organizations assist people facing major life challenges by providing a supportive relationship where positive action is acknowledged and reinforced. Many people find that it is easier to take action when they have the support of others who are facing the same challenges they face.

9. Use the "one-pushup" approach to move from resistance to persistence

In *The Art of Persistence*, Michal Stawicki (2015) discusses how he conquered his lack of discipline around exercise by committing to do at least one pushup each day. When he knew that he had to only do one pushup to meet his goal, there was little need to procrastinate. Of course, once he had done one pushup, more followed until it became a regular part of his routine. This is another example of how taking baby steps can banish resistance and help you move to persisting in healthier behaviors.

Embrace Tip #8: Have fun tackling the elephant
There's an old joke about how to eat an elephant—one bite at a time. If you're tackling the equivalent of an elephant-sized task, having fun with it will make the task easier to complete. This also decreases the probability you will procrastinate.

One of our private coaching clients described how she tackled dealing with hundreds of storage boxes. She had taken a three-year assignment in the United Kingdom and had placed all of her belongings in storage. When she returned, her new home was too small to hold everything she had in storage. She made the tedious task of downsizing more fun by treating it as a treasure hunt. In each box, she searched for one treasure she could take to her new home. Because she didn't have space, everything else in the box went to charity or was thrown away.

Feeling Stuck?
Use This Simple Approach to Get Unstuck

Have you been frozen with indecision from having too many options to choose from? For example, you need a new mobile phone but you can't decide which model is right for you. You want the iPhone but you don't like the wireless ear buds. On the other hand, Android would be great, but it won't work well with the new iPad you just purchased. The result is you are stuck because you can't make up your mind.

Being stuck differs from procrastination. Procrastination generally involves taking action at some point in time. When people are stuck they often end up doing nothing. Doing nothing is still a decision—it's a decision to remain in limbo. When someone is stuck they resist change because it requires too much effort to decide which choice is best. As long as they're stuck, they are in resistance mode.

Embrace Tip #9: How to get unstuck
If you find that you are feeling stuck, here is a simple three-step process to get unstuck.

1. **Write down all the potential solutions to the issue no matter how silly or illogical they may seem.** When someone is stuck they normally replay different solutions to the problem over and over. The secret to getting unstuck is to write down as many solutions or alternatives as possible. For example, if you are in sales and you are angry with one of your clients, it's all right to write down, "I'm going to fire him," even if you would never consider doing so. The idea is to create as many options as possible.

2. **Choose the best possible solution.** After you complete your list, pick the one option that has the greatest probability of success. If you're unhappy with your options, seek the help of a friend or other trusted resource such as a colleague, coach, or mentor to help you sort out the best decision.

3. **Get unstuck by taking action.** The final step is to break out of the quicksand of procrastination and being stuck—take an action step now.

When Procrastination Isn't Really Procrastination: Lag Time

Have you ever wondered why changing some behaviors is easy and changing others is so difficult? *Lag time,* the length of time it takes between taking action and experiencing the result of that action, may be the reason.

Psychological research has shown that the best time to reinforce a new behavior is right after the behavior occurs. What's challenging is that many of the changes we would like to implement in our lives take time to create. In fact, activities such as earning a college degree, raising a child, or fulfilling your life's purpose take years to accomplish.

Because the process of obtaining reinforcement often takes more time than many people are willing to spend, they often give up on the new behavior before the full effects have a chance to take hold. This is partially due to today's on-demand society that expects instant gratification. When life doesn't cooperate immediately, they give up. Here are three suggestions to help you avoid being trapped by lag time.

1. Let go of expecting change to happen instantaneously

In most cases, whatever distress you are experiencing in life took a fair amount of time to get that way. Obstetricians routinely tell women it will take nine months to totally lose the weight from their pregnancy. Furthermore, it takes a full three years for a mother's body to return to the state she was in prior to the pregnancy. In other words, determine how long it took you to reach your current state and realize that it can take an equal amount of time to totally resolve the situation.

2. Focus on the process, not the goal

A major obstacle in dealing with lag time is focusing on the goal rather than the process. Imagine that you are driving from Los Angeles to New York. If you only focus on how quickly you can get to New York, the time you spend on the road will be a source of inconvenience and frustration. In contrast, if you focus on the process of enjoying each part of your drive, the drive itself becomes as fulfilling as reaching your destination. In other words, make the most of each moment and enjoy the process rather than focusing exclusively on the goal or the destination.

3. Baby steps taken in the wrong direction can lead to disastrous results

Throughout this book we focus on taking the baby steps that lead to positive change. On the other hand, baby steps taken in the wrong direction can lead to disastrous results. For example, eating an extra sandwich a day doesn't seem like much. Yet, if you maintain this behavior for a year without changing your exercise or other eating habits, you will gain 52 pounds over the next year. Small, incremental changes over time, whether these changes are positive or negative, can produce extraordinary differences in your life.

Reducing procrastination requires a series of small steps over a long period of time. If you're ready to stop procrastinating, how about completing one item right now that you've been putting off?

Chapter 6: Key Points

1. The longer you are stuck in the quicksand of procrastination, the harder it will be to escape it.

2. Procrastination is a conscious choice to not take action.

3. Primary causes of procrastination include perfectionism, fear of failure, low energy levels, lack of focus, and overwhelm.

4. Strategies for escaping the quicksand of procrastination include taking small, action steps, clearing out your to-do list by avoiding taking on new projects, eliminating what is not being handled, and finding a support system.

5. Move from resistance to persistence with Michal Stawicki's "one pushup" approach.

6. Get unstuck by listing all available options and then choose the one that will work best for you and your situation.

7. Avoid being trapped by lag time by letting go of expectations, focusing on the process rather than the goal, and remembering that baby steps in a positive or in a negative direction can cause major changes over time.

Resilience

*Courage doesn't always roar.
Sometimes courage is the quiet voice
at the end of the day saying, "I will try
again tomorrow."*
Mary Anne Radmacher

Chapter 7:
Optimism—the Key to Happiness and Resilience

A pessimist sees the difficulty in every opportunity; an optimist sees the opportunity in every difficulty.
Winston Churchill

In his book *How Ronald Reagan Changed My Life*, Peter Robinson shared one of Ronald Reagan's favorite jokes.

Parents of two twin five-year old boys were concerned that their boys had developed extreme personalities and decided to take the boys to a psychiatrist for treatment. One boy was a total pessimist and the other was a total optimist.

The psychiatrist treated the pessimist first. Trying to brighten his outlook, the psychiatrist took him to a room piled to the ceiling with brand-new toys. But instead of yelping with delight, the little boy burst into tears.

"What's the matter?" the psychiatrist asked, baffled.

"Don't you want to play with any of the toys?"

"Yes," the little boy bawled, "but if I did I'd only break them."

The psychiatrist treated the optimist next. Trying to dampen his outlook, the psychiatrist took him to a room piled to the ceiling with horse manure. But instead of wrinkling his nose in disgust, the optimist emitted a yelp of delight that the psychiatrist had been hoping to hear from his brother, the pessimist. Then he clambered to the top of the pile, dropped to his knees, and began gleefully digging out scoop after scoop with his bare hands.

"What do you think you're doing?" the psychiatrist asked, just as baffled by the optimist as he had been by the pessimist.

"With all this manure," the beaming little boy replied, "there must be a pony in here somewhere!"

Are you more like the optimist or the pessimist in this story? Most people fall somewhere between these two extremes. Unless you're already as optimistic as the boy in the story, increasing your current level of optimism can provide lifelong benefits including better health, happiness, and longevity. It is also a critical component in increasing your PQ.

No one can escape life's ups and downs. Sadness, loss, and despair help you to appreciate happiness and joy. Nevertheless, most people would prefer to maximize their happy moments and to minimize their pain and adversity. The research clearly shows that the higher your level of optimism is, the happier you will be. Moreover, optimism is highly correlated with increased resilience and persistence.

Self-Fulfilling Prophecy

Robert Merton (1948) coined the term, "self-fulfilling prophecy" to describe when a person unknowingly causes a prediction to come true, due to the simple fact that he or she expects it to come true. For example, if a woman believes that her husband will cheat on her, she may act jealous when she is around other women or look for signs of cheating. Her actions strain her marriage, especially if she falsely accuses her husband of cheating on her. The result is that he may grow so frustrated with her behavior that he decides to leave.

One of the most stunning examples of self-fulfilling prophecy comes from quantum physics. Researchers created an experiment designed to settle the dispute about whether light was composed of waves or particles. The results surprised everyone. This objective experiment yielded waves for those who expected waves and particles for those who expected particles. In other words, what the researchers expected is what the experiment yielded.

> **Resilience Tip #1: Focus determines your experience**
> Here's a quick exercise that illustrates how focus works. First, look at a picture of a room and identify everything in the picture that is green. Now look away and recall everything that is red. The point here is that where you place your focus determines what you will experience.

Choosing Between Optimism and Pessimism

Pessimists believe that they are much more realistic than optimists. After all, the world is filled with horrific events—murder, disease, starvation, war, financial meltdowns, natural disasters—the list is endless. They argue that the optimists need to get their heads out of the sand and see things as they really are. Contrary to what most pessimists believe, however, pessimism can be detrimental to both their physical and emotional well-being. Decades of research support this conclusion.

Optimism is highly correlated with health and longevity

Your degree of optimism has a profound impact on not only the quality of your life, but also on your health and longevity. Up until age 40, your health is determined primarily by how healthy you are at age 25. Being a pessimist has no effect. From ages 40-65, however, being positive and optimistic leads to improved health and longevity. Pessimism results in increased illness and a shorter lifespan. Specifically, longevity is highly correlated with the type of happiness typified by tranquility and peace of mind (Seligman, 1995, 1998, 2004).

Optimism reduces risk of early death

Quitting smoking decreases your risk of death by 5-10 percent. In contrast, increasing your optimism creates a protective effect that is almost 100 percent higher than quitting smoking. This massive correlation highlights how truly dangerous pessimism can be as compared to the benefits from being optimistic (Maruta, 2000).

Optimism fights disease

Optimism also plays an important role for those facing life-threatening disease. Multiple studies have demonstrated that optimists experience less distress when faced with a life-threatening cancer diagnosis. They also have a better quality of life while undergoing treatment. Optimism may also protect against the development of chronic diseases. One study tested pessimistic and optimistic women with precursors for atherosclerosis and then repeated the test three years later. The women who reported higher levels of pessimism at the baseline assessment were significantly more likely to experience thickening arteries; optimistic women did not experience any increase in arterial thickness (Carver, 2010, et al.; Matthews, et al., 2004; Schou, et al., 2005).

Optimism increases antibodies and strengthens immune response
Studies on people suffering from HIV plus research on influenza in the elderly have shown that higher levels of optimism are correlated with increased antibody production and a stronger immune response. In HIV patients, people with the highest level of optimism had more T-helper cells and a lower mortality rate. Other studies have found that changes in levels of optimism are directly correlated with the immune system's response to infectious disease. Furthermore, optimism appears to provide some degree of protection for those who carry a family risk for alcoholism. (Haney, 2014; Milam, et al. 2007; Ohannessian, et al. 1993.)

These studies all illustrate how optimism can boost your immune system, prevent chronic disease, and help you to cope when you receive troubling news. The bottom line is that optimism may be one of the most important predictors of good physical health.

What the Brain Scans Show
Daniel Amen's research (2005) vividly demonstrates the effects of pessimistic thinking vs. optimistic thinking. When Amen asked normal people to focus on pessimistic or angry thoughts, their brain wave scans no longer appeared normal; instead, their scans resembled the scans of those suffering from schizophrenia. In other words, pessimism causes your healthy brain wave pattern to shift to a brain wave pattern associated with a serious mental disorder. (Please note that schizophrenia is NOT what many people call "split personality." Instead, it is a serious disorder characterized by excessive amounts of dopamine that can result in being "split" from reality, including having delusions, hearing voices, and experiencing hallucinations.)

How to Raise Your Level of Optimism

Given the benefits of being optimistic, what can you do to raise your level of optimism? The research indicates some people are born with sunny dispositions and others are not. Nevertheless, you can increase your personal level of optimism, even if you're basically pessimistic by nature. While you may not be able to eliminate exposure to negative events entirely, you can choose more optimistic ways of responding to the negative events that you do encounter. Here are four steps that can help.

Chapter 7: Optimism—the Key to Happiness and Resilience

1. **Describe the situation in detail**
   When you encounter a problem, describe it in detail. Include who is involved, what happened, and where it happened. Keep your description factual. For example, "My boss laid off everyone in our department today." Notice that that there is no explanation or interpretation about the cause of the layoffs—just a simple descriptive statement.

2. **Record what you were thinking and how you felt while the event was happening**
   Write down your thoughts exactly, even if they're not "G-rated." Next, note which of your thoughts were optimistic, neutral, or pessimistic. For example, "This company is struggling; leaving now is actually a good thing" is an optimistic statement. "The company decided to eliminate our entire department, not any single individual." This statement is neutral (factual).

   If the layoff was unexpected, it's common for self-doubt to pop up in the form of pessimism: "Why am I always at the wrong place at the wrong time?" "What's wrong with me—my luck is awful." "Maybe I should just give up." "I should have known this company was going down the tubes—why did I ever accept a job here?"

3. **List all the possible actions that you could take plus their probability for success**
   A simple way to apply this approach is to list all the available options for any challenge you are facing. Next, review the options to determine which will have the highest probability for success.

   Be aware that the thoughts and feelings that you listed in the step above can have a powerful influence on whether you will succeed. For example, pessimistic statements such as, "I have bad luck" or "I'm always in the wrong place at the wrong time" could hinder your ability to find a new job. If you go on several job interviews and you are not hired, your pessimistic mindset will reinforce the idea that you have bad luck and that you are always in the wrong place at the wrong time. Due to self-fulfilling prophecy, each rejection only serves to strengthen your pessimism, making it increasingly harder to persist in obtaining a positive result. Consequently, when you decide which option is the best for you, make sure that it is at least neutral, but preferably optimistic rather than pessimistic.

The result is that when you choose an optimistic solution and you receive a positive result (in this example, a new job), the positive result reinforces your optimism making it easier for you to be more optimistic the next time you face a challenge.

If you do not succeed right away, look for ways to view the situation from an optimistic viewpoint. Some examples include, "Every 'no' brings me closer to the next 'yes'" or "There is a high demand for people with my skillset—I just haven't found the right opportunity yet."

4. Follow the energy
As you confront a challenge and you experience a pessimistic thought and feeling, take a moment to note what happens to your energy. The next step is to quiet the negative self-talk and visualize yourself successfully overcoming the challenge. In the example above, picture yourself being hired, starting your new job, and getting a raise. Now notice which set of thoughts and feelings gave you the most energy. In virtually every case, optimism increases energy while pessimism zaps it.

Martin Seligman (1998) explains why optimism is so important when it comes to persistence. His research shows that pessimistic people tend to give up more easily. In contrast, optimists are continually forging ahead in spite of the most devastating occurrences. Furthermore, optimists experience less stress as compared to people who identify themselves as realists. This is because optimists easily overcome minor setbacks and bounce back from major negative events more quickly.

Handling Rejection

There's nothing like rejection to put you into a pessimistic tailspin. While a small percentage of people use rejection to motivate themselves to try even harder, what can you do to bounce back from rejection and stay as optimistic as possible?

Jia Jiang, in his book *Rejection Proof*, documents his personal 100-day journey on how he learned to handle rejection. In the process, he walked into a Krispy Kreme donut store and asked the woman at the counter to rearrange the donuts into the shape of the Olympic Rings, asked a police offer to drive his patrol car, and knocked on a stranger's front door and asked permission to play soccer in his backyard.

Failure vs. rejection
According to Jiang, "When you fail at something such as a business venture or a career, it feels unfortunate but understandable and often tolerable, because it could be due to a host of factors. In fact, entrepreneurs love to tell and hear stories about failure because those letdowns are often stepping-stones toward eventual success."

In contrast, "Rejection involves another person saying no to us, often in favor of someone else, and often face-to-face…When we experience rejection, we are left with two unhealthy choices. If we believe we deserved the rejection, we blame ourselves and get flooded with feelings of shame and ineptitude. If we believe the rejection is unjust or undeserved, we blame the other person and get consumed by feelings of anger and revenge."

This is part of the reason that when you experience rejection and someone tells you, "Don't take it personally," or "Be tough and move on," it does little to help you cope with rejection. In fact, Jiang maintains that it is actually easier to talk about failure than it is to talk about rejection.

Five ways to become rejection proof
What does it take to lessen the negative effects of rejection? Jiang's journey shows that it may be easier and more fun than you realize.

1. Laughter defuses the pain associated with rejection
In terms of your physical response to social rejection, it is identical to your response to physical trauma. The warfare against rejection is not just psychological; it's biological and rooted in your DNA.

One strategy that lessens physical pain also works to cope with rejection. Robin Dunbar's (2012) research shows that pain thresholds increase when people watch comedy. Paul Pearsall (1999) found that laughing 100 times a day was a powerful force for warding off cancer and heart disease. In each case, it's due to the release of endorphins. Endorphins relieve the physical part of the pain while simultaneously reducing anxiety. If you have ever defused a tense or unhappy situation with laughter, you know how powerful this approach can be.

2. Ask "why" before good-bye

When Jiang first began his journey, he scuttled off the moment someone told him, "No." He then decided to try a different strategy. When he asked a stranger if he could plant a peach rosebush in the man's yard, the man turned Jiang down. At that point, Jiang asked, "Why?" The man explained that he didn't like flowers in his yard. On the other hand, the woman across the street would probably be delighted to receive the rosebush. This was exactly the case. By politely asking "Why," Jiang received a referral that appreciated his gift. Consequently, the next time you encounter a "No," politely ask "Why?"

3. When you receive a "no," ask for something less

Jiang went to McDonald's and asked for a McGriddles sandwich in the afternoon. The woman serving him couldn't help him because the machine that cooked the eggs and sausage had already been cleaned. Jiang shifted gears and asked, "Can you make me something like a McGriddles?" She was able to serve him a griddlecake with cheese.

Jiang explained that the McGriddles moment taught a powerful third way to cope with rejection: retreating, reassessing, and trying a new approach. The secret here is that when you experience a rejection, try making a lesser request or asking for what you want from a different angle. For example, if you are buying a car and the dealership turns down your offer, ask if there is a different concession that the salesperson could make to move the negotiation forward.

Robert Cialdini's 1984 book *Influence* outlines what makes this approach so powerful: people don't want to feel like jerks and are much less likely to say no to a second request.

4. Collaborate, don't contend

Jiang says, "Arguments are a magnet for rejection" and "Arguing turns potential collaborators into enemies." To shift this pattern, rather than arguing with someone who disagrees with you, make it clear that he or she has the freedom to say, "No." Then look for a way to collaborate with the individual by identifying where you agree.

For example, if you are selling your house and you receive a ridiculously low offer, rather than walking away, look for the places where you do have agreement. Are there any terms of the offer that are acceptable? By looking for points of agreement you increase the probability that you will make the deal. In my own experience, when sellers decide to negotiate with a buyer who made a very low offer on their house, about 50 percent of the time they end up closing the deal.

5. Switch up, don't give up
Sometimes no matter what you do, the only response you will receive will be "No." Continued persistence would only make the situation worse. Jiang says, "Before deciding to quit or not to quit, step back and make the request to a different person, in a different environment, or under a different circumstance."

A classic example would be if the car dealership refuses your offer during the first week of the month. If you visit the dealership on the afternoon of the 31st and they haven't sold their quota of cars, they may be much more willing to accept your offer.

Consequently, the next time you encounter rejection, tap into your rejection toolbox. While you may not get exactly what you expected or wanted, what you do get will almost always be better than walking away and feeling rejected.

Increase Optimism by Avoiding Vicarious Trauma

Today's news cycle is a fountain of never-ending negativity that bombards you through your mobile device, print publications, radio, and television. It's virtually impossible to escape.

The danger here is twofold. First, negative news makes staying optimistic more challenging. The second, more serious risk is what psychologists call "vicarious trauma." You may see the images of a mass shooting, a devastating earthquake, or semi-trucks flying in the air due to a swarm of tornadoes. While your cortex knows that those events are not actually happening to you, your reptilian and emotional brains cannot tell the difference. The emotions you feel watching a movie or a televised event are just as real to the reptilian and emotional parts of your brain as if you were experiencing the event first hand. Vicarious trauma can increase your stress, disturb your concentration, and decrease your effectiveness almost to the same degree as experiencing the trauma first hand. The long-term effects can be so devastating that they can even lead to life-threatening stress-related illnesses such as cancer and heart disease.

How to Increase Your Optimism

What can you do to increase your level of optimism and to avoid vicarious trauma? Here are five additional tips.

1. Limit your exposure to vicarious trauma

First, there's little you can do to control external events such as terrorist attacks, natural disasters, loss of loved ones, etc. A great starting place, however, is to limit your exposure to the stress-inducing onslaught of the 24-hour news cycle.

2. Respond rather than reacting

Rather than reacting to events, step back and consider the various options available prior to responding. Taking time to consider options is a powerful, proactive approach that yields much better results. When you experience a personal loss or challenge, you will recover more quickly when you take the point of view, "When one door closes, another one opens." In other words, look back at both the good and the bad in the situation, identify what you have learned, and then formulate at least one action step you can take now to move beyond the situation.

3. Create a positive environment

Fowler's (2008) study tracking 4,800 individuals over a 20-year period demonstrated that happiness is contagious. The more happy friends you have, the happier you will be. Thus, a simple way to avoid being swallowed by the doom and gloom is to create an environment where you surround yourself with others who are also optimistic and positive.

4. Take control

You are in charge of your life. As coach Philip Humbert described it:

> *"My well-being and optimism, my values and work-ethic and daily success are not determined by politicians in Washington or revolts in the Middle East or horrific earthquakes (as important as those things may be). My daily success is determined by my alarm clock, my to-do list, my use of time, and hugs from my friends. My success is determined by whether I do the things that I know are useful or whether I am distracted by the news, by gossip, or by worry."*

Humbert recommends focusing on yourself, your work, and the "small tribe of about 100 people" with whom you interact on a regular basis.

5. Help someone else

Study after study has illustrated that helping others increases our well-being and makes us feel better about ourselves. Granted, you can't change the world but as Ronald Reagan observed:

> *"We can't help everyone, but everyone can help someone."*

Seize Control

Is being positive and optimistic worth the effort? As Daniel Reardon once said, "In the long run the pessimist may be proved right, but the optimist has a better time on the trip."

The bottom line is that being optimistic will help you to seize and maintain control of the choices you make. Optimism enhances your persistence while pessimism can undermine it completely. The PERSIST model argues that you are in control of the choices and the decisions that you make. The question is, will you choose anger, fear, pessimism, and schizophrenic brain waves? Or will you choose an attitude that searches for the opportunity in the challenges you face and is optimistic about better times ahead?

Chapter 7: Key Points

1. Self-fulfilling prophecy: what you expect to happen, will happen. (Energy flows where attention goes.)

2. Optimism has huge benefits, including better health, increased longevity, and strengthened immune response.

3. Choose optimistic responses to life's challenges by describing the event in detail, recording what you experienced during the event, listing possible actions that you could take, and then choosing the one action that best supports your long-term PERSIST goals.

4. Ease the sting of rejection with laughter, digging deeper to see what the reason is that you're being rejected, and if you receive a "No," make a second request for something less.

5. Increase your optimism by limiting your exposure to vicarious trauma, responding rather than reacting, creating a positive environment, taking charge of your life, and helping others.

Chapter 8:
Facing Adversity:
What Story Will You Weave?

*Always seek out the seed of
triumph in every adversity.*
Og Mandino

Whether it's a book, a news story, a movie, or something amusing about ourselves, stories help strengthen our bonds with each other. Your memories are also stories—stories that you and others have woven about what matters in your respective lives. The stories you communicate provide a wealth of information about who you are, what matters most in your life, what makes you effective, and what undermines your success.

By choosing optimism rather than pessimism, you can paint a story with brightness of the future—a key element associated with good health, resilience, and being able to overcome adversity. Brightness of the future refers to looking forward and seeing positive events ahead. To illustrate this point, when a couple buys their first house, they often dream about the happy times they will have with their kids, the fun they will have entertaining their friends in the backyard, and how wonderful it will be to no longer have a landlord.

As Og Mandino's quote above suggests, triumph comes from seeking the glimmer of brightness present in virtually every situation. Pessimism sees only the dark with no hope of triumph or positive outcome. In fact, being able to envision positive possibilities ahead is essential to becoming more resilient and to achieving the best possible outcome no matter what challenges you face. By simply paying more attention to the stories you create and being consciously aware of how you are creating them, you will not only raise your PQ, you can also improve every aspect of your life.

When you face adversity, the challenge is not the adversity itself but the story you choose to tell about that adversity. The way you frame the story will determine how resilient you will be in coping with that adversity. The right story will help you to achieve the best possible outcome; the wrong story can leave you stuck in pain and misery. Moreover, in those cases where the adversity is life threatening, the right story can greatly increase your chance of survival.

To illustrate this point, assume that you are engaged to be married and have set the wedding date a year from now. A few weeks later your fiancé gets cold feet and decides to break off not only your engagement, but the relationship as well. You now find yourself in the awkward position of telling everyone the story of why you're not getting married.

How would you write your story? Would you cast your fiancé as an ogre and yourself as the horribly wronged lover? Would you point out all the things that bugged you about your fiancé and explain how this was a mutual decision? Would you lie by saying that you initiated the breakup?

The key take-away here is that *you are 100 percent in charge of the story you will tell about this event.* Granted, you can't control another person's actions or what others will think or say. That doesn't change the fact that you control your story and how you choose to respond.

What Stories Attract Your Attention?

What types of stories have attracted your attention over the last few days? Were the stories about another person's tragedy, gossip about another person, or a funny event from someone else's life? Were the stories future-focused or were the stories about some event in the past? For example, reminiscing about the past can be a fun way to strengthen your connections to others but it can also be a way to exclude those who did not share the same experience. Also, when someone keeps repeating the same old story they not only bore their listeners, they also miss the joy of creating something new in the present.

Once upon a time

There's a reason that "Once upon a time" and "they lived happily ever after" stories have endured for centuries—they're stories about hope, resilience, overcoming adversity, and the ultimate triumph when the characters walk away to a happily-ever-after future.

We are also drawn to stories about human tragedy, whether it's the classic fall from grace where the hero or heroine commits a fatal error and loses everything, or a murder, bombing, or some other horrific event. The tragic story draws us but what intrigues us even more is how people respond in the wake of the tragedy. The stories of the phoenix rising from the ashes inspire us and give us hope that we can bounce back from the adversities in our own lives.

Pain creators
While stories can inspire and support, they can also create pain for both you and others. For example, when most people repeat a piece of gossip, they're using the story to connect with others but they are also using it to make themselves look better. These "compared to you" stories usually appear when someone is experiencing fear, feeling inadequate, or experiencing some sort of deficiency in their lives.

The next time you hear yourself saying something that resembles, "I can't believe he did that—I would never dream of doing such a thing," step back and dig for what is really underneath that statement. If it is a comparison that puts someone else in a negative light, chances are you're telling the story to make yourself feel better at the expense of the other person. A better approach is to address the underlying issue that is causing your pain.

Another type of story that can result in long-term pain is called *future projecting* (creating a story about how the future should be). Future projecting often produces expectations that close the door to other possibilities. For example, I may future project the characteristics that I want my soul mate to have—he would have to be good looking, make lots of money, and be taller than I am. While I'm waiting for Mr. Right to show up, I miss the opportunity to marry the guy who lives in the apartment next door, who makes me laugh, and who has all the qualities we would need to have a wonderful life together. I miss the opportunity because future projecting has closed off my ability to see other possibilities.

Stories People Tell

There are a number of ways that people use stories to gain attention and to block forward movement in their lives. Are any of the stories below blocking forward movement in your life?

The Martyr: "Look what I've sacrificed for you"
When someone plays the martyr, they want the listener to appreciate and acknowledge them for their self-sacrifice, even though the listener never wanted or asked for the martyr to engage in those actions. A classic example is the parent who constantly reminds their child of all the sacrifices he or she has made for the child. In this case, the parent is attempting to use guilt to make the child feel responsible for the

parent's choice. If you are playing the martyr, remember that you (and no one else) are 100 percent in charge of your story and your choice.

The Victim: "This horrible event happened to me and I deserve special treatment because of it"

Whether it's being the victim of a horrendous crime, a terrible illness, or a disfiguring accident, you can allow the event to control the rest of your life or you can move forward by looking at how you can make each day the best possible. Playing the victim years after the event occurred is an attempt to gain attention and affection through pity.

If you find yourself playing the victim, here's an important question to ask: "Do I want people to value me for the person I am today or do I want them to pity me because of an event in my past?"

Keep in mind that people love hearing the story about how you overcame that horrific event. The reason is your story provides hope that they can overcome the obstacles they face in much the same way that you did. On the other hand, when you wallow in the negative, they don't want to be around you. Remember, people gravitate to those who are optimistic.

The Child: "I can't do it! It's too hard for me! I'm not ready yet"

The adult who responds by saying, "I can't do it!" is allowing their "child" to hold them back. The "child" is fear—fear of failing, of not being good enough, or not performing up to personal expectations. To stop playing the child, shift from using the word *can't*, to using the word *choose*. *Can't* disempowers you; *choose* puts you in charge as you decide which choice you will make. For example, "I can't possibly ask the boss for a raise" as opposed to "I choose not to ask the boss for a raise."

Next, ask yourself what is really holding you back. In other words, "I choose not to engage in this activity because I'm afraid of…"

On the other hand, and this is an important point to remember, some fears are healthy: "I choose not to drink and drive, because I could seriously injure myself and others."

The Parent/Expert: "You should listen to me because I know what is best for you"

The trap here is twofold: first, the parent/expert experiences an increase in their self-esteem when someone else follows their advice. Second, what's in back of the "I'm right-you're wrong" story is a need to be in control, usually coupled with a need to avoid being wrong.

To stop playing the parent/expert game, two steps are necessary. First, let go of the "should." Replace it with, "What worked for me," or "When I was confronted with X, this is how I dealt with it." This allows your listener to formulate their own response and avoids making you wrong if they happen to choose an option different from the one you selected.

Second, each situation has different players and different circumstances. Just as a forward pass may work in one football game, it can be disastrous in another. Let go of the expectation that others are having an experience identical to yours and that what worked for you will work equally well for others.

> **Resilience Tip #2: Change your story for the better**
> The two stories below illustrate how two individuals freed themselves from an old story that was holding them back and moved forward by creating a new story that resulted in a more positive outcome.
>
> **Releasing old energy**
> *I made a lot of money in the real estate market and then lost everything except my BMW when the market crashed. I kept the car 14 years and drove it over 250,000 miles. The heating and air conditioning were broken, as were a variety of other things. I couldn't let go of the car because having a "Beamer" was who I thought I was. I was "stuck" thinking my only choice was to drive the old car and wait until I could afford a new BMW. My coach helped me to see that replacing the car was a way to release the old energy that was holding me back. I bought a new Nissan with all the bells and whistles. It was great having a car where everything worked. More importantly, getting rid of the story freed me up from focusing on what was wrong with my car to refocusing on building my business.*

> **You can choose again**
> *My husband began disparaging my friends not too long after we were married. Eventually, he wanted nothing to do with any of them. He also had no interest in my work and was unwilling to share very much about what he was doing. The story that trapped me was, "I made a lifelong commitment—I have to keep it." My coach helped me understand that "When you make the wrong choice, sometimes you need to choose again." Today I'm married to a wonderful man with whom I can share every aspect of my life—I'm so thankful I let go of the old story and made a different choice!*

Escape the Downward Spiral of the Win-Lose Game

Our society thinks in terms of winners and losers. It's certainly true that there can only be one winner in an election or in a sporting event, but that doesn't mean that you have to rely on that approach when you face adversity. In fact, the fear of losing is what stops many people from ever taking action to achieve their goals and dreams.

Several years ago I heard Boston Philharmonic conductor Benjamin Zander give an extraordinary keynote speech that addressed how the win-lose game traps people in an "up-down" spiral. To see if you're playing this costly game, take the brief quiz below.

> **Resilience Tip #3: How to escape the up-down spiral**
> Answer the following questions as either "yes" or "no."
>
> 1. When you play a game do you become upset when you or your team loses?
>
> 2. When you make a mistake do you blame someone else for it?
>
> 3. Do you constantly go over your shortcomings?

4. At work, do you believe that winning requires someone else to lose?

5. Do you define yourself in terms of what you do rather than who you are? (That is, when someone asks you about who you are, is your first answer, "I work for XYZ.")

6. Do you believe that there is no middle ground—you either succeed or you fail?

7. When you speak, do you often use the words "you should," "you must," and "you need to"?

If you answered, "yes" to two or more of these questions, chances are that you're caught in the up-down spiral.

Zander's answer to breaking the up-down spiral in order to escape the win-lose game is to step into the realm of possibility. All this requires is a shift in how you tell your story. The beauty of making this shift is that instead of being hemmed in by just two choices (win-lose) Zander's approach can create hundreds of possibilities. Here are three strategies that can help you step out of the "win-lose" game and into the realm of possibility.

1. It's all invented
According to Zander, the secret of life and business is that "It's all invented." What constitutes being a winner or loser is like baseball or football—it's a game someone made up. Consequently, there's no requirement that you play win-lose. Instead, you can make up your own game with its own stories where there are no winners or losers.

For example, if you are in a sales position, rather than focusing on how much money you earn or how many deals you close, focus on how many times you added value to your customers. When you play win-lose, there is only one way to win—you must make the sale. In contrast, when you shift from being "me-centric" to being focused on how you can provide value to your customers, there are thousands of ways to win. Better yet, this shift also results in increased sales and happier customers. Zander suggests that in order to master the practice of possibility, constantly focus on all the unique ways you can contribute to others.

2. How fascinating!

If you're like most people, you fear making a mistake or looking foolish. Zander says these fears result in a "downward spiral." In contrast, when Zander or one his students makes a mistake his approach is to shout, "How fascinating!"

Now you may not be ready to shout out "How fascinating!" the next time you make a major mistake, but rather than becoming angry or berating yourself for doing poorly, what would it be like if you approached the situation by asking yourself about other possibilities besides losing?

For example, if you are bypassed for a promotion at work, instead of being angry or resigned to the situation, you could ask, "What new possibilities are open to me now that this position is no longer an opportunity?" Or, "Is it time for a much needed vacation?" In either case, the questions open up an abundance of possibilities while simultaneously freeing you from the up-down spiral.

3. Don't take yourself so seriously!

Zander says the key to the kingdom of possibility is, "Don't take yourself so seriously." When you are committed to being right you're invested in "win-lose." When you catch yourself in this cycle, seek ways to change the story so that you focus on a wide variety of possibilities rather than the single outcome of winning by being right.

When it comes to how you live your life, Zander believes that you have three choices—resignation, anger, and possibility. You cannot live a full life under the shadow of resignation, bitterness, or anger. Instead, consider the realm of possibility. The path there is through the stories you choose to tell.

Resilience Tip #4: Did you really get the story right?
Sometimes the issue with a story is the story itself. While you may believe that the story is accurate, keep in mind that your cerebral cortex is quite capable of coming up with excuses and rationalizations for why an event happens. This is especially true when the right story means that the emotional and the reptilian brain will feel better. Here's a story one of our coaching clients shared that illustrates this point:

> *I thought my first professional job was going along quite well and was even thinking of asking my boss for a raise when I was terminated. I went into a complete tailspin while telling everyone that I was just fine. My parents knew better and said let's go over some options. I chose to go back to school and finish my degree. A few years later I ran into my old boss at the airport. The company had been sold not long after I was laid off and he said that I was actually lucky to have left when I did.*

Overcoming Obstacles Blocking Your Path

The best way to overcome obstacles in your path is to rely on your strengths and to identify the tools and resources you will need to bypass the obstacle. The next step is to determine the options available to you. The final step is to implement the best possible choice using the "I have/I choose" model.

Before discussing the model in more detail, recall two different situations; the first situation is one where you overcame an obstacle easily and you experienced a positive outcome. The second is a situation where you handled the challenge poorly and the outcome was negative.

For each situation, identify the actions that you took that led to the outcome. For example, did you rush into a solution without considering your options? Is there something you could have discovered that would have helped you if you had taken the time to search for it? What could you have done differently that could improve the outcome, even if the outcome was positive?

The next step is to take these two situations and implement the "I have/I choose" model:

1. "I have the following strengths"
The "I have" step asks you to identify strengths that could assist you in meeting your challenge. Take a few moments to jot down the strengths you could have used to overcome the obstacle you faced in the two situations above.

2. "I have the following people who will support me"
This step asks you to gather your external resources—people who could support you or who could serve as a mentor or role model.

3. "I have the following tools and resources"
In addition to your strengths and support network, identify any technology tools, systems, or other resources that could help you to overcome this obstacle.

4. "I have the following options"
In this step, lay out all the possible options available to you no matter how ridiculous you may believe them to be. This is the equivalent of laying out different endings for your story. Because you are 100 percent in charge of how you create the story, choosing the best possible ending is one of the best ways to guarantee the best possible result.

5. "I choose"
At this point you have evaluated your strengths, your resources, and the options available to you. Looking at all these factors together, make your final choice and then take action on it.

This approach maximizes the probability you will obtain a positive result while also allowing you to avoid the poor outcomes that come from making a knee-jerk reaction.

Is this really mine?
Sometimes you may find yourself focused on an obstacle that really isn't yours, such as trying to help a friend resolve a situation where they work. Consequently, it's always important to ask the question, "Is this mine?"

Carefully evaluate whether the emotions you are experiencing about this event are really yours or whether they belong to someone else. Did someone dump this on you or are you carrying it even though no one asked you to do so? Honor those emotions that are yours and let go of those that are not.

It is difficult enough to process and deal with your own emotions. It is even more difficult to deal with emotions that don't belong to you. Energy spent dealing with someone else's emotions is energy that could have been applied to meeting your challenges and maintaining your brightness of the future. As Byron likes to remind me, "Not my monkeys, not my circus."

Life presents a wide variety of obstacles but none more difficult than a life-threatening event. When you or someone you love is injured in an accident, receives a life-threatening medical diagnosis, or faces some other severe crisis, this is when every PERSIST skill that you have acquired will be put to the test. The next chapter provides a road map for surviving and perhaps even thriving as you navigate through these difficult times.

Chapter 8: Key Points

1. You are 100 percent in charge of the story you tell about the events in your life.

2. People seek out stories with happy endings, but gossip and negative stories are often repeated as a way to make the storyteller feel better about themselves or to feel more important.

3. Stories can support your long-term PERSIST goals. On the other hand, types of stories that hamper your ability to persist include the martyr, the victim, the child, and the parent/expert.

4. Escape the downward spiral of the win-lose game by realizing it's all invented, being fascinated by your mistakes, and not taking yourself so seriously.

5. Use the "I have/I choose" model to overcome obstacles that block your ability to persist.

Chapter 9:
Confronting a Life-Threatening Event

*The secret of health for both mind and body
is not to mourn the past, worry about the
future, or anticipate troubles, but to live in
the present moment wisely and earnestly.*
Buddha

Life-threatening events can quickly upend your optimism by depriving you of your hope for a bright and happy future. By choosing to weave your story about difficult times in the most optimistic and resilient way possible, you can ease the pain and difficulty you experience substantially. On the other hand, when someone loses their capacity to experience hope and to see brightness in the future it can literally cost them their lives.

Looking backward rather than looking forward
I recently learned that a long-time friend has lymphoma. She was widowed several years ago and bounced back remarkably well, creating a new shared life with her children while also pursuing a whole new interest in classical music.

The cancer diagnosis devastated her. Her entire conversation was about all the great years she had been married, the joys she had experienced as a mother and a grandmother, her work accomplishments, and what she had loved about her life. She expressed gratitude for all that she had experienced. These are all positive stories but there was no brightness of the future story about successfully surviving her cancer, even though the survival rate for her type of cancer is high.

I attempted to paint a brightness of the future scenario by sharing how laughter and acupuncture could strengthen her immune response. I also shared that two other close friends who had advanced lymphomas are now cancer free. My attempts seem to fall flat as she stayed completely rooted in the past and "the time I have left." After we hung up, I wondered to what extent her lack of brightness of the future would undermine her recovery.

"I can't control what happens"

When I can't sleep, one of my guilty pleasures is watching the vet shows on television. While you see the pain that comes when a beloved pet dies, all these shows essentially repeat the same story: the worried pet owner brings their pet in for treatment, the vets seek the correct diagnosis, they successfully treat the animal, and the story ends with the tail-wagging, happy reunification of the pet with its owner.

The night before I wrote this chapter I tuned into the latest episode of *Rocky Mountain Vet*. Dr. Jeff Young of Planned Pethood Plus is the star of the show. He is also an outspoken critic of the incompetence and greed in his industry. Young is a strong advocate for spaying and neutering and charges a fraction of what many other local veterinarians charge. He also finds ways to treat cases where the owner of the pet may be homeless or has no money for treatment. For example, his staff will often volunteer their own dogs to provide whole blood when the owner cannot afford a transfusion. The clinic currently has over 100,000 patients in their database.

This episode had the usual stories about animals being turned away elsewhere and being saved at Young's clinic. In this episode, however, there was an entirely new twist: Young had been diagnosed with lymphoma that included an eight-centimeter mass in back of his heart.

Despite the diagnosis, Young continued to work while he was undergoing chemo. When his hair began falling out, he decided to shave his head. The film crew captured the moment as Young's wife, Petra, shaved off his shoulder length, scraggly locks while his entire staff looked on. Young went on to elaborate how he was doing everything in his power to recuperate and repeatedly assured his staff and family that he would be all right.

However, he was also very frank about the feelings he experienced on those bad nights when he found himself confronting the real possibility of his death. Despite this very real threat, he continued building his new clinic where he could serve even more pet owners in the future.

Given Young's actions, I found it puzzling when toward the end of the show he said, "I can't control what happens." Unlike my friend who had seemed pessimistic and focused on her memories, it seemed as if Young was doing everything he could to create a brightness of a future scenario and to take control of what he could in his fight to recover.

Young's remark made me wonder about the role hope and resilience play in creating the miracles where people recover completely as well as their role in those battles that end in death.

Speaking the Language of Miracles

In her book *Speaking the Language of Miracles*, Deanna Scott (2015) shares the specific steps she took to help her son Brandon survive terminal cancer. Scott's primary premise is that adversity and other challenging life events are merely situations. In other words, "The situation is not who you are." Scott goes on to explain that when you "walk in the situation, you become powerless. The goal is to walk in solutions."

Scott strongly believes that whatever you say, you create. Again, this is at the heart of self-fulfilling prophecy—what you expect to happen, will happen.

Consequently, when Brandon asked his mother, "Am I going to die?" her response was, "The illness is not who you are—it is only a situation."

Scott argues that when people focus on the illness, it persists. Scott's beliefs are supported by Howard Friedman's research (1987, 1991) on "disease-prone" and "self-healing" personalities. Disease-prone personality occurs when a person receives special attention due to their illnesses. The extra attention reinforces the illness rather than wellness. According to Friedman,

> *The disease-prone personality is associated with a pervasive negative mood, depression, anxiety, and irritability. They tend to dwell on the negatives of life and are often dissatisfied. As a result, they are more prone to stress-related illnesses, including coronary artery disease.*
>
> *In contrast, self-healing personality is associated with being conscientious, emotionally secure, having enthusiasm for life, and strong social relationships. These characteristics lead to more healthful behaviors—avoiding smoking, better adherence to exercise programs, and maintaining a healthy diet. This leads to greater resistance to stress-related illnesses.*

Scott asked everyone who interacted with Brandon to treat him as they did before his illness. Her goal was to keep the interactions the same rather than changing how people talked or played with him. She also did her best to make the hospital room environment as close to his home environment as possible. This meant focusing on wellness by eliminating as much of the "sick" paraphernalia as possible.

Resilience Tip #5: Walk in the outcome that you want to achieve

To "walk in the outcome you want to achieve," Scott recommends that you begin by separating the person from the situation. Examples of "situations" include the media, bad news, drama, gossip, divorce, death, illness, jealousy, hate, he-said, she-said, and liar-liar. Scott describes people who create drama by sharing these types of stories as "joy stealers."

To walk in the solution you must control your environment. Hang out with people who are happy and optimistic instead of those who walk in pessimism and drama—both are contagious. As Scott says, "It's impossible to walk in solutions when you are walking in the situation."

Next, describe the situation in a few words on a piece of paper. Tape the paper to a wall, read what you wrote, and then ask, "What are you going to do about it?" and "What is the positive outcome that you want?"

At that point, you're ready to search for the solutions you will need to handle the situation.

Finally, detail the steps needed to accomplish the solution you want and then take the actions necessary to complete them.

On a subsequent episode Dr. Jeff Young got his miracle. His scans were clear and he was cancer free. He is still very aware of the risk of a reoccurrence, but he chooses to walk in his solution by continuing to help as many pets and their owners as possible. His work allows him to live in brightness of the future every single day.

Becoming a Miracle Worker

Dr. Paul Pearsall was the author of over 200 professional articles and eighteen international best-selling books. In his SoulfulLiving.com blog and his book *Miracle in Maui* (2001), he shared the nightmarish treatments he experienced as a dying patient who undergoes bone marrow transplant surgery in a last heroic attempt to save his life. Yet amidst the terrible pain, constant vomiting, repeated infections, the festering sores, and the knowledge that half the patients on the ward would die from their exposure to radiation or their cancers, a little girl named Patsy taught Pearsall about being a miracle worker.

Pearsall describes Patsy's delight as she watched the Detroit Thanksgiving Parade from her window:

> "I see the balloons!" little Patsy shouted. "I see the balloons! They're blowing them all up right there for the parade. But that little balloon won't stay up. It just can't hold air. It can't keep the air inside it. It must feel like me."
>
> Patsy loved to ride what she called her Christmas IV stand… She would often drag her dolls along in her own parade and demand that other patients join her. We had to keep in line because that was Patsy's way.

Pearsall observed that Patsy had grown unusually pensive over the days preceding the parade.

> We all noticed that Patsy's parade was not taking place as regularly as it once did. The day of the Thanksgiving parade, she became somber as she pressed her nose to the hospital window. We pretended we could not hear her murmur, "That's just the way."
>
> Suddenly, the little balloon inflated and floated away from its handler and up into the sky. "There it goes," yelled Patsy. "It's going to heaven, but the parade is still to go on, isn't it? There are lots of balloons and air is everywhere. That's the way it will be." With her words, the little balloon's journey seemed to be a meaningful coincidence for Patsy and for us all.

Pearsall reminds us that small miracles are everywhere around us and that we don't need to go to what he calls "spiritual athletes" to experience a miracle—we just need to look for people like Patsy.

Making miracles

I heard Pearsall speak at several live events on "The Healing Power of Aloha." In that presentation everyone laughed and cried as he shared his journey using his well-honed sense of humor and optimism.

When it comes to making miracles, however, Pearsall believed that something more was required:

> *Too often some people practice a pseudo-psychology of mind-over-matter healing that suggests that we be upbeat, courageous, and maintain a positive attitude at all times. While there is nothing wrong with cheerfulness, I have found reflection, yearning, and private searching for life's meaning also to be key steps in the making of miracles. Crying in awe of the endurance of the human spirit is as healing as laughing in hope...*
>
> *The suffering of cancer and its related treatments forced my attention away from "me" and toward a deep reflection on the nature of life and its meaning, a sense of my connection with everyone and everything, and direct, personal experience of the "Way" things are...*
>
> *While they (my medical staff) battled my disease on a "particle level," my little "medicine girl" Patsy, my family, and the other courageous patients on my transplant unit kept me connected with the life-saving "waves" of love...*
>
> *Miracles are not reserved for heroic "survivors." Miracles are made when people live life with meaning and satisfaction, even when negative circumstances surround them.*

Pearsall's six characteristics for being miracle prone

Based upon his experience as a patient and his clinical studies on meaningful coincidences, Pearsall identified the profile of those who are "miracle prone." These characteristics are:

1. A confident, erect posture with eyes that convey a spiritual energy and a knowing beyond the rational, logical, simplistic knowing of everyday living. They seem to know that their role of observer is crucial to what they will see.

2. Experience with several crises, and in the process, the development of a psychic toughness, plus awareness that there is always a complementary positive side to even the most apparently hopeless situation.

3. A yearning for much more from life than mere coping, survival, success, and security. A desire to behave in ways compatible with our transcendence of the here and now. A simplicity of lifestyle free of the need to acquire goods and to possess expensive, complex things. Freedom from "stuffitis."

4. An abnormal attitude in the sense that they are creative and have avoided becoming "well adjusted" to a linear, stressful, see-and-touch world.

5. A tendency to be psychic gamblers because they are willing to take risks for the fulfillment of their dreams and to give meaning to the signals sent by the coincidences in their lives. They think in a freewheeling style that reflects the uncertainty of all of life.

6. Patience, forgiveness, generosity, truthfulness, and equanimity that manifest in loving-kindness.

Patsy helped Pearsall create the miracle of his recovery, inspired other patients with her courage in enduring the treatments she was receiving, while also helping the staff to find the determination to continue performing the painful, life-saving work they were doing.

Like the little balloon that floated away to heaven, Patsy died a few days after the parade.

The question is, how do you go on after death has come calling for one of your loved ones?

Chapter 9: Key Points

1. Creating brightness of the future is a critical component in triumphing over a life-threatening event.

2. Confront life-threatening events by speaking the language of miracles and "walking in the outcome that you want to achieve." Remember, "You are not the situation."

3. When someone is fighting a serious illness treat that person the way you did before he or she became ill.

4. To the best of your ability, make sure that the person's environment and their routines stay as close to normal as possible.

5. As Paul Pearsall observes, "Miracles are not reserved for heroic 'survivors.' Miracles are made when people live life with meaning and satisfaction, even when negative circumstances surround them."

Chapter 10:
When Death Comes Calling

Bad things do happen; how I respond to them defines my character and the quality of my life. I can choose to sit in perpetual sadness, immobilized by the gravity of my loss, or I can choose to rise from the pain and to treasure the most precious gift I have—life itself.
Walter Anderson

There is probably no greater test of your emotional resilience than losing a loved one. If your loved one has experienced terrible pain and suffering, your cortex rationalizes that their suffering is now over. The cortex's rationalizations, however, do little to alleviate the pain in the emotional and reptilian parts of your brain, even if you believe that your loved one has gone to a better place.

When someone you love dies, the death leaves a gaping hole that only your loved one can fill. Memories make your heart ache. Tears flow relentlessly or they don't come at all. You feel totally exhausted and tightness permeates your body. You try to rationalize that this is part of God's plan or you scream at God over the unfairness of it all. The pain and suffering is so intense you wonder if it will ever stop. In the meantime, the world continues on around you, laughing and loving, even though your loved one is no longer there to laugh and love. You struggle to put your life back together and, in some cases, may even question whether you have a reason to continue at all.

What does it take to weather this ordeal? When my mother was dying of cancer, I met a man who had lost his mother to cancer just six months earlier. What he shared about his experience with death has helped me to withstand the losses in my life: "You never get over it, but you do learn to live with it."

Death is All Around Us and We're Still Unprepared to Cope

Every year we see hundreds of deaths in movies and on television. The media's portrayal of death has desensitized us to death on the screen without providing us with the actual coping skills we need when we face the death of a friend or loved one. In fact, morticians shelter us from seeing the ravages of injury, illness, and death by creating the illusion that our loved one is merely sleeping peacefully in their coffin.

Elizabeth Kübler-Ross (1969), in her book *On Death and Dying*, identified the stages we experience when we face death. Even in her work, however, there is no clear path for dealing with the grief. When we receive the terrible news, our first response is often denial. Next, we may become angry or sad and then lament, "Why is this happening to me and/or to the person I love?" Often it seems unfair that people are struck down in the prime of life or that innocent children must undergo horribly painful surgeries or treatments in a futile attempt to keep them alive. Given the circumstances, it's easy to play the "woe-is-me" card.

The path through grief is unique to each individual. Also, even if you have laid out a plan and believe that you're as well prepared as you can be for whatever does come, you may respond quite differently from what you expected. Will you become angry, play the martyr, or respond with courage and determination? Or will you go deep into denial like the mother of a friend we lost to AIDS who insisted upon telling her son right to the moment he died, "You can beat this if you just put your mind to it."

Will your suffering and loss overtake you or will you view your suffering as Ralph Blum describes it in *The Book of Runes*?

> *Remember that "suffering" in its original sense, merely meant "undergoing." Thus you are required to undergo the dark side of your passage. To control your anger, to restrain your instincts, to keep your faith firm—all this is at issue here. Modesty and good temper are the essential blessings at such a time.*

Disconnecting

There's an interesting phenomenon that often takes place shortly before people die. I watched this happen with my father's death and I have observed it with others as well. In my father's case, we spent a substantial amount of time on the phone every day. It was especially hard for me when I left California to move to Texas. As I climbed into the cab at his house and waved goodbye, I had this sinking feeling that this moment would be the last time that I would see my dad alive.

For the next month, we continued to talk daily. He was planning on flying out to see me after I wrapped up my speaking gig in Florida. Two days into my Florida trip, my brother called to let me know that my dad had experienced another heart attack and was in Intensive Care. I was desperate to get back to California as quickly as possible. Unfortunately, the earliest flight I could find was my original ticket back to Austin booked for that Monday.

When I called my dad back to tell him, it seemed as if our close connection had been severed. In fact, it seemed as if he didn't want me there at all.

After I arrived home and was trying to get on the next flight to Los Angeles, my brother called from the hospital to tell me my dad had died of a second massive heart attack. My brother was shaken to the bone as he witnessed the violence of the attack. I hated that he had to face this alone, but was also grateful that I didn't personally witness my dad's death. In a strange way, I believe this was my dad's final act of protection. We were so close I'm certain he knew how devastating it would have been for me to see him die that way.

A similar event took place when Byron's stepfather died. His stepfather experienced his third heart attack a few days before Christmas. Because the prognosis was grim, most of his family had arrived in town to be with him. My mother-in-law was unable to go to the hospital that day, but most of his family was there that morning. After his family stepped out for a few minutes to get some lunch, he passed away.

In contrast, I have countless friends and relatives who were present when their loved ones died. Many of them described the experience as being one of the most meaningful and profound events in their lives.

Hospice: Nightmare and Blessing in Disguise

When someone receives a terminal diagnosis and is admitted into hospice, it can be a tremendous blessing but it can also become a total nightmare. Hospice is a facility or program designed to provide a caring environment for meeting the physical and emotional needs of the terminally ill.

Hospice care has allowed several of my family members to die peacefully in their own homes. Family and friends came to see them, their ministers were there to give them comfort, and almost everyone had a chance to say their farewells.

On the other hand, a close friend's mother chose to forego nutrition because she was very near death. She lingered for almost two months with no food. No one on the medical team could understand how she could possibly live so long. The experience was a nightmare for all involved.

While we rightfully sing the praises of hospice care, very few people are prepared for the challenges they will face in terms of coping with the hospice process itself. In her book, *From Hiccups to Hospice*, Betty Garrett (2008) catalogues her journey as her husband was diagnosed with esophageal cancer, their experience with hospice, and his subsequent death. This detailed guide can help anyone dealing with cancer or another life-threatening illness to navigate the process. There is also an excellent glossary plus other helpful resources.

Garrett's book outlines specific steps to take as your loved one faces the end of his or her life. She also provides numerous lists including how to work with the patient's medical team, handle insurance issues, and deal with financial matters. Taking care of all the medical paperwork and the complicated reimbursement requirements is extraordinarily difficult under the best of circumstances; it is infinitely harder when your loved one is in hospice. Garrett's book is a place to start.

While you are there to support your loved one, make sure that you have someone who can be there to support you. This can be a close friend, clergy, therapist, or anyone who is willing to listen and be present for you. Having a strong support group is critical to persisting, but it's never more critical than when you face the death of a loved one.

Unexpected Death

An unexpected death can be one of the most serious losses that you will ever face. Several years after my father died, one of my colleagues dropped dead. I took his death almost as hard as I had my father's and couldn't understand why I was so devastated.

As I searched for a reason for my reaction, I realized that my colleague had been an important part of my support network. When I lost him, one of the invisible supports in my community was gone. He was always there. Only after he died did I realize how important he was to my sense of connection and to my ability to do my job.

Most people are unaware that when they lose a loved one, they are not only mourning for the person; they are also mourning the loss of the relationship and the place that person held in their lives. It's almost akin to losing a tooth. Once it's gone, the original will never be back again. You might find a replacement to fill the space but it's not the original. The gap will always be there no matter how you try to fill it.

What's particularly painful about unexpected deaths is that many people mean to tell their loved ones how they feel about them, but fail to do so. They may also have unsettled issues with the deceased in terms of anger, disappointment, or unfulfilled expectations. Furthermore, disputes over money and the person's belongings can trigger lifelong feuds that prolong the grieving period by adding anger to the mix.

Prepare for the Unthinkable

Have your parents called you in for that dreaded conversation about where all their important documents are, who has medical power of attorney, and what their wishes are if they're declared brain dead, as well as how they want their funeral handled and their belongings divided? If so, you're luckier than those who are forced to deal with these decisions with no prior input from their loved ones.

In some cases, your loved one may refuse to draw a will or to take any other steps to address these issues. Their attitude may result from fear and denial. In other cases, the person believes, "I'll be dead—what does it matter?"

Addressing these issues prior to a person's death will help to minimize everyone's pain. Here are just a few of the issues you will need to address.

1. Durable power of attorney

In case you ever become mentally incapacitated, you will need a "durable" power of attorney for both your medical care and your finances. The durable power of attorney is in effect as long as you are incapacitated and unable to handle matters on your own. Be sure to spell out what your wishes are regarding a diagnosis of brain death or other debilitating condition that results in mental incapacity, such as Alzheimer's disease. It's especially important to have this in place any time you undergo anesthesia or surgery.

2. Last will and testament

Every adult needs a will, but most people procrastinate about making one. Formalizing how you want your estate handled now can minimize disputes that can rip your family apart after your death. It's important to speak to both your tax advisor and an estate attorney about the best ways to transfer your estate to your heirs.

For example, the IRS allows you to gift a certain amount each year to various people. Some people have used this as a mechanism to transfer their real property to their children. This can be done in conjunction with creating a life estate that allows you to continue to use the property as long as you live. You could also set up a living trust that can determine how assets are distributed to the beneficiaries both during your life and after your death. If you have accounts, properties, or a business that operates outside the state where you currently reside, you may need expert assistance from legal and tax professionals familiar with that state's or country's laws.

3. Important documents and assets

It's wise to create a list of important documents including where these documents are located. This can include death certificates of a family member who has pre-deceased you, your will, all your credit card and bank account numbers, any insurance policies, plus contact information for your attorney, tax professional, financial advisor, etc. Also be sure to provide any property deeds, notes that secure any debts, plus any other important documents.

4. Emotional preparation

While the documents above are important, how you prepare emotionally for your death or the death of your loved ones is even more important.

Resilience Tip #6: Avoid Looking Back in Regret
Byron had a life-changing realization that has helped him to avoid looking back in regret after losing someone he loves.

During a self-help workshop it became abundantly clear to me that I did not want to be standing over my mother's or father's grave wishing I had told them all the things I appreciated about them. Much to the initial discomfort of my family, I began telling them how much I loved and appreciated all that they had done for me. I started saying "I love you" whenever I saw them or before I hung up the phone. My father died just a few weeks after Bernice and I were married. While I miss him and his wisdom, he died knowing exactly how much love and gratitude I had for all that he'd done for me as a father.

Farewell Trips
In 2006, my closest friend from college died from a heart attack. For months I had this nagging feeling that I needed to go see her and I didn't get around to it. I still regret that choice to this day. Since then I have resolved to make those trips no matter how inconvenient they may be. I've never regretted a single one.

When the Diagnosis is Terminal
As noted in the last two chapters, you can be optimistic and you can walk in solution, but death ultimately calls on all of us. When you know death is near, what actions can you take to support the person who is dying? Moreover, what steps do you need to take to survive this tumultuous time?

While your loved one is facing death, your brain's "A" team is processing everything around that event. This means that you are less likely to be dealing from strength as you rely on the "B" team to handle work and your other responsibilities.

This shift can show up in a variety of ways. For example, you may be more distracted while you are driving, increasing your risk for getting a ticket or having an accident. You may forget important appointments or discover that you're having problems concentrating at work or at school. You may also be more prone to cry or to lash out in anger.

One of the best ways to address these issues is to engage in extreme self-care. (This concept will be discussed in detail in the section on "Self-Ish.") Steps to take include immediately freeing yourself from any non-essential commitments, eating well, exercising to work off the stress, sleeping more, and avoiding alcohol and other depressants.

Remember, there is no need to suffer alone. When people hear about what you are experiencing, many want to help—they just don't know what to do. For example, if a good friend who loves to bake offers to help, ask her to prepare one of her favorite treats to share with you and your loved one. If another friend enjoys gardening, ask your friend to make sure that your plants are watered or ask her to bring your loved one a bouquet from her garden. These are small things, but they make others feel like they are doing something to help. More importantly, it's a way for them to cope with their own sense of hopelessness about the situation.

Helping your loved one through their transition

When one of my close friends confided in me that her husband had metastatic cancer, I offered to work with her as she went through this process. During that time, I never mentioned that my mother died from metastatic lung cancer. My reasoning was that my role was to support her and avoid dampening her enthusiasm that her husband might recover.

Instead, I suggested that she share as many happy memories with her husband as possible. Based upon Paul Pearsall's research on how laughter strengthens the immune response, I also encouraged her to watch funny movies with her husband and to look for ways to make him laugh every day. When their children flew in to see him, they created even more happy memories.

I saw my friend two days before her husband died. She thanked me for helping her through this time, especially for helping her and her husband to create a whole new set of happy memories. She seemed at peace with his death and what it would take to bounce back from the loss. The special memories they created during the last months of his life eased the pain of her loss and made it easier for her to move forward after his death.

When the Dreaded Phone Call Comes

No matter how much you believe that you are prepared for losing someone you love, when that moment arrives, most people go numb. The day before my mother died, I could hear the so-called "death rattle." The doctors had started her on high doses of intravenous morphine and told us she only had a few hours left.

The call from my dad came while I was in the shower. He was crying and I told him, let me call you right back. I finished my shower, called him back, and made plans to head to his house. I was surprised that I seemed to feel nothing. We went through the process of making arrangements, letting family members know, and handling a variety of other issues. As I was driving home that night, the numbness wore off and the grief rolled over me like an avalanche.

When you receive this type of news your body releases large amounts of beta-endorphins and adrenaline as a protective mechanism. It's very common to feel completely numb because these neurotransmitters block pain. The haunting pictures of Jackie Kennedy following John F. Kennedy's assassination are one of the saddest illustrations of this phenomenon. Not only was Mrs. Kennedy mourning, the entire country was numb from the shock of what had happened. History repeated itself as our country went numb from the events on 9-11.

Consequently, even though you may feel that you can drive or handle what needs to be handled, avoid getting behind the wheel unless there is absolutely no alternative. Let others who are not as connected to the loss handle as much as possible. This is especially important when it comes to contacting family and friends. You are already experiencing so much pain that having to repeatedly tell the story of what has happened only deepens your sorrow. Let someone else handle this for you. Fortunately, posting to Facebook or on other social media is much easier than having to call people one at a time.

Four Different Farewells

During the last year, I have attended two funerals and one celebration of life—one for the man that I was engaged to in college and who died from Alzheimer's disease, Byron's stepfather's celebration of life, and just a few days before writing this chapter, a first cousin's funeral. A week later, my uncle passed away. Although I was unable to be at my uncle's funeral, like the other three farewells, there was an important theme that ran through each of the services.

Unselfish commitment
In the case of my former fiancée, the only people who attended his funeral were his gardener and his family, a first cousin and her son who hadn't seen him for 30 years, and a close friend whom I have always been able to count on for moral support. The gardener had become a surrogate son who had managed my friend's finances, medical care, and had taken time from his family and business to respond to whatever needs my friend had. This man's dedication was nothing short of astonishing. In fact, I have seldom seen this level of commitment in anyone, much less in someone who was not a family member.

The priest who conducted the service had spent 30 years of his life as a missionary serving the poorest parts of Central America. In his simple but beautiful message, the priest spoke of service. The priest had dedicated his life to service, but as he spoke, it became clear that he was also making a beautiful acknowledgement of the gardener's service to my friend.

Celebrating a life of contribution
Byron and I deeply loved his stepfather. We were aware that he was actively involved in starting at least one charity and that he also routinely gave to other charities. What we were not prepared for at his celebration of life was the magnitude of not only what he gave financially, but also how much he gave of himself. Person after person recounted his importance in mentoring them in their leadership roles, teaching them how to raise money, and going over and above in helping their respective charities achieve their goals. The stories dated back over decades. Coupled with the sadness and loss were the laughter and memories of an individual who truly made a difference in the lives of so many people.

A life of service
My perception of my cousin was always somewhat influenced by my father's attitude—he had little use for his smart-mouthed, prankster nephew. The minister's sermon totally reframed that perception for me as he talked about my cousin's life of service.

My cousin had served in the National Guard for over 30 years plus working as a sheriff and a prison guard. He also belonged to numerous organizations and was one of the people who volunteered with other law enforcement officers trying to stem the tide of illegal drugs coming into this country.

Because my cousin was in hospice, he had a chance to plan his funeral. Instead of hymns, some cousins sang several country western songs including one about "My Granddaddy's Gun" and what those memories represented. Given the motorcycle-riding retired soldiers and police officers present, the songs my cousin chose were a perfect fit for the story of his life.

The motorcyclists led the way to the cemetery. Seven soldiers and their commanding officer composed the honor guard detail. As the bugler began to play Taps, the wind picked up and the large American flags adjacent to the gravesite began to wave gently. As the wind increased, the flags unfurled fully for the 21-gun salute.

A long, joyful life
My beloved uncle Palmer died just a week after I lost my cousin. Palmer had measles as a baby and it left him totally deaf. Nevertheless, he went to deaf school, learned to dance, married, and was one of the happiest people I have ever met. His life of service was working as a janitor at the same school he had attended. The Deaf community was a place of belonging, support, and love.

I remember when he and one of his friends (both who were in their late 80s at the time) showed up in Austin to see us. His sense of adventure and that impish twinkle in his eye were there right up until the day he died.

Given that my uncle would be turning 98 in just a few weeks, I decided to tack on an extra leg to a business trip to see him. He wasn't able to write any longer but my cousin translated for us. I had a chance to hug him and to tell him how much I loved him.

The morning he died, he showered, ate a big breakfast, and then took his walker outside to sit in the sunshine. He passed away on that beautiful morning—he started to get up, sat back down, and was gone.

I wasn't able to attend the funeral, but my cousin shared how they said their final farewell. They gave everyone a balloon and at the end of the service, they all said goodbye together by releasing their balloons.

When my cousin told me, I had just finished writing about Patsy's balloons. I couldn't imagine a more appropriate send off for my uncle than his balloon, surrounded by so many others, floating away together in the sky.

Farewells and closure

As painful as attending a funeral can be, it is almost always a deep and meaningful event. If your loved one had time to plan the service as my cousin did while he was in hospice, the event is a final opportunity to connect with that person and understand how he or she wanted to be remembered. It is also a time of sharing and acknowledgement, especially when that person has made a meaningful contribution to the lives of others. Finally, there is a reason these rituals exist in every culture—they help those experiencing a loss to achieve some degree of closure and to hopefully find meaning in their time of loss.

> **Resilience Tip #7: Avoid downloading your past grief on others**
> When Byron's father died, he was both hurt and surprised at how people reacted to his loss. Although his father had died only a few hours before, when he contacted others about his father's death, almost everyone began telling him their stories about what happened when they lost a loved one. Rather than being present to support him in his grief process, they were still dealing with their own grief. If you take nothing else from this book, please take away this one thing. If at all possible, avoid dumping your unprocessed grief on top of someone who has just lost a loved one. Instead, ask how you can best support them both now and during the difficult months ahead. If you are the person who has experienced the loss and someone begins processing his or her grief with you, simply say, "I'm sorry for your loss," and walk away.

Chapter 10: When Death Comes Calling

And Life Goes On

Everyone is willing to accept that you will mourn for a few days. After that mourning period, however, you're supposed to function normally. People may ask how you are, but few want to rehash your loss—in many cases, it only serves to bring back their own unprocessed grief.

The day after my mother's funeral I was back to work. Everyone seemed surprised to see me. What I didn't realize was that I was using work to push down the pain of my mother's death. That pattern has repeated itself in my life over and over—work was always the place where I could escape to numb the pain. Other people may choose to withdraw, turn to alcohol or drugs, or take their anger at their loss out on others. Everyone's process is different. Nevertheless, there are healthy steps you can take to recover from your loss, especially if the person died and you had unresolved issues.

The most powerful technique for processing your grief

As I have worked with students and clients who have lost loved ones, there is one technique that has proven to be the most effective in helping them to process their grief. It is especially powerful where there is a lack of closure, anger toward the deceased, and even in cases where the person who died abused the individual who is seeking help now.

The technique is simple: write a letter to the person who has died. In the letter, thank the person for all the good things the person did for you. This can include providing you with food and shelter, helping you with your homework, or any other positive thing that you can recall.

The second step is to write down all the things that person did to make you angry, to disappoint you, or to hurt you. Get it all out, preferably using ink and paper rather than your computer. Allow yourself as many weeks or months as necessary to complete the process. This allows you to express the many ways that this person impacted your life. It is also a powerful way to release your grief.

Once you have finished your letter, you are ready to release the emotions you expressed and to write the conclusion of the story. Some people choose to burn the letter in a fireplace. Others may choose to write out the key points in the sand and let the waves wash the words away. A third option is to go to where your loved one is interred and to read what you have written out loud. Another approach is to read your letter to a favorite picture of your loved one. No matter which approach you choose, the process of writing down everything you wanted to say is a powerful step in healing your loss while simultaneously helping you to move on with the next chapter in your life.

Cry often
After the funeral you will find that grief comes in waves. You'll have good days where everything seems back to normal, especially when you are at work. Other days, the grief comes flooding back as intense as it was when your loved one first died. Rather than ignoring the emotion, have a good cry. It releases the pent-up energy and actually helps you to process your grief.

Tap your way away from grief
After the funeral it's especially important to pay attention to what triggers any strong grief response. Typically it is tied to the funeral or the days immediately preceding it. As mentioned in Chapter 2, emotions can be anchored in your body. As I watched people respond at my cousin's funeral, everyone was patting the family members on the back. It is quite probable that when someone pats them on the back in the future, they will experience a strong sense of grief.

If you discover that you have a strong physical anchor from your loved one's funeral, you can change it in the same way that it was anchored. Specifically, if the anchor is tied to a pat on the back, when you're with a friend or a loved one, ask that person to pat you on the back whenever you laugh or you're feeling happy. That will replace the grief anchor with a new anchor that will make you laugh and feel happy.

Resilience Tip #8: Plant a tree
Byron's family members have a great sense of humor. When Byron's dad died, his mother decided to plant a tree in his father's memory—a crabapple tree.

As one of our former coaching clients explained, planting a tree can also help you to recover from your loss.

For years, my father and I didn't get along very well. We just didn't talk much and were both kind of stubborn. About four years ago, dad died pretty quickly. Over the years, I never told him how much I appreciated all the things he did for me. I found myself experiencing lots of guilt and shame. Standing over his grave and saying all the things I wanted to say just didn't seem to be working. A good friend then made a suggestion—plant a tree in honor of my father and care for that tree like my father took care of me. Today, I've got one healthy tree and a wonderful place to sit and remember him.

Avoid falling prey to the kick-the-cat syndrome

Anger releases energy but often in an unhealthy way. A classic example is what psychologists call "displacement" or the "kick-the-cat syndrome." To illustrate how this works, a man's boss yells at him. The man goes home and yells at his wife. The wife yells at her oldest child who then yells at his younger brother. The younger brother then kicks the cat. In each case, the angry person displaces their anger on a person (animal) that has nothing to do with the reason the individual is angry.

Sadly, this dynamic occurs way too often when there has been a death in the family. People are grieving, are often angry about their loss, and can be emotionally volatile. They can't take their anger out on the person who died, so take it out on others around them.

If you find yourself feeling like you would like to hit someone or something, pound on a pillow, punching bag, or do something else physical to release the pent-up energy in a positive way.

> **Resilience Tip #9: Throw your anger away**
> My good friend Marilyn Naylor shared a technique that she has used in her fear and anger workshops. I also used the same approach at our Awesome Females in Real Estate leadership conference. The exercise is quite cathartic and allows you to release your anger in a healthy way. Here's what to do.
>
> Go to your local thrift store or any other place where you can pick up undamaged plates. Be sure to select plates that allow you to write the name(s) of those who have made you angry or who have hurt you. This will probably require a magic marker. If you are processing a lot of pain around a particular individual, you can use multiple plates to cite specific instances of their hurtful behavior.

Next, find a large trashcan and place some large rocks in the bottom. Line the trashcan with a heavy-duty plastic bag to make disposal of the broken plates safe. You will also need a set of protective goggles to avoid injury from any flying shards.

Once you have finished writing on your plates, put on your goggles, read what's on the plate, and then fling the plate into the trashcan. If it doesn't break, you haven't released the anger. Dig the unbroken plate out and throw it again.

I remember the first time I did this—several of my friends said that they had never seen me look so angry. Nevertheless, I definitely felt better afterward.

If you feel that you have a lot of anger to process, keep the plates and the lined trashcan with the rocks on hand. When you feel the need to throw away the anger, take your magic marker, write what is making you angry on your plate(s), put on your goggles, and throw those plates.

How You Can Help

The minister at my cousin's funeral made an observation that really rang true for me. While those closest to the person who died will be dealing with their grief for months or years to come, most of us attend the funeral, give our condolences, and return to our normal routines. The most difficult time for those who experience profound grief comes in the weeks and months after the funeral, when friends have stopped visiting, family members have returned to work, casseroles have stopped appearing magically at the door, and there's only a looming and lingering emptiness. Those who are still mourning find themselves terribly alone, their loss profound and real in an entirely new way.

If someone close to you is experiencing a profound loss, share your condolences and offer to help them through the following months. Meet them once a week for a funny movie or for a cup of coffee. Most people desperately need someone just to listen to what they're experiencing. Do so without commenting.

If you're an attorney, a real estate agent, or have a professional counseling background, let the grieving person know that when they are ready, you would be happy to assist them in finding whatever professionals they may need to deal with the next step in their life. This can include helping them to find a cleaning service, repair people, moving services, probate attorneys, etc. The job of navigating through this process may be more than they can handle. Provided the person is open to receiving your help, your offer to assist them can be a real godsend. Keep in mind that they may be overwhelmed, so avoid pushing. Instead, be there to lend a helping hand as they start the journey of learning to live with their loss.

Everyone Dies Alone

I would like to end this section with a quote from the television series, *Person of Interest*. In the series finale there is a final battle between two super artificial intelligences (AI) that monitor everything that people do. Finch, the creator of the compassionate AI that he calls "the machine," has infected both his machine and Samaritan (the other AI) with a virus that will destroy both AIs.

During the final battle Finch is wounded. As Finch appears to be nearing his own death, he asks the machine, "After seeing so many human deaths, what have you learned?"

The machine responds, "Everyone dies alone." Due to the virus, however, the machine struggles to recall one last important piece.

Later, the scene cuts to two cops sitting at a bar. One repeats the machine's response: "Everyone dies alone."

His buddy responds, "Everyone dies alone, but if you meant something to someone, if you helped someone, or loved someone, if even a single person remembers you, then maybe you never really die."

Like Patsy and her little balloon, your story lives on.

Chapter 10: Key Points

1. The path to coping with grief is unique to each individual. Some people fare best when surrounded by loved ones while others will choose to undertake their journey alone.

2. If you're supporting a loved one who is facing the end of his or her life, be sure to have someone there to support you as you navigate through your own personal ordeal.

3. Write a will, record your wishes regarding your medical care, catalogue important documents and assets, and prepare your loved ones emotionally for your death.

4. If you have a strong sense that you need to call or go on a trip to see a loved one—do it.

5. When someone you know loses a loved one, listen to him or her without commenting on what happened when someone you loved died.

6. When one of your loved ones dies, write a letter thanking him or her for all the wonderful things they did for you as well as all the things that made you angry. Take as much time as necessary to make the letter as complete as possible.

7. Be there for those who are mourning during those long, difficult months following the funeral.

Be Self-ish, Not Selfish

You are reminded you must first draw from the well to nourish and give to yourself. Then there will be more than enough to nourish others.
Ralph Blum

Chapter 11:
To Nourish Others,
Nourish Yourself First

*When we truly care for ourselves,
it becomes possible to care far more
profoundly about other people.*
Eda LeShan

Most people use words such as *egocentric, egotistical, self-centered,* and *self-serving* as synonyms for *selfish.* The dictionary defines *selfish* as "lacking in consideration for others; concerned chiefly with one's own personal profit or pleasure."

Consequently, you may be surprised that increasing your PQ will require you to become more selfish—but not in the sense above. Instead, being "Self-ish" is about nourishing yourself first so that you can ultimately nourish others.

Coach University founder Thomas Leonard (1995) believed that being selfish was the cornerstone of having a happy, successful life. His definition of *selfish,* however, was quite different from what most people consider the word to mean. According to Leonard,

> *Selfishness doesn't include egocentricity or insensitivity, but many people feel that these three words are synonymous. They are not. "Egocentricity" means that you only think about yourself or feel that the world revolves entirely around you. "Insensitivity" means that you have no heart and do not care about others. By being selfish, by keeping commitments to yourself, and by communicating with others in a way that keeps you responsible to you and your life while allowing others to be responsible for their outcomes, you automatically bring more balance into your daily life.*
>
> *Think about what it would mean to you and your life happiness if you learned the art of selfishness. How will your attitude change once you learn to honor your commitments to yourself? How will you feel once you start to communicate*

> *in ways that are loving and caring toward yourself and that empower others to take responsibility for their own needs?*

Echoing Deanna Scott's (2015) belief that "You are not the situation," Leonard goes on to say:

> *You are distinct from your roles. You may have roles, but there is still the YOU in YOU, independent of your roles. Men and women often defer to or are defined by traditional roles. As a result, they seek to fulfill the role, even if it means they don't get what they want personally. To become incredibly selfish may require an abandoning or restructuring of your roles. By the way, most roles come from others who help to condition us to believe in them. Selfishness disrupts that belief, so it's controversial.*
>
> *"Selfish" is about getting your needs met and reaching a point where you have enough in reserve to share with others (time, money, space, opportunities, network, love).*

Bud Harris (2002), author of *Sacred Selfishness: A Guide to Living a Life of Substance*, distinguishes between selfishness and what he terms "sacred selfishness" in the following way:

> *Sacred selfishness is the opposite of how we usually think of selfishness. It means to value our lives enough to become people of substance, to be people whose very presence gives more because our cup is overflowing. Imagine for a minute how it might change your life if you constantly asked, "Is what I am doing and how I am being treated diminishing me or adding to my life?"*

Executive Coach Krissy Jackson (2007) offers a slightly different distinction:

> *"Selfish" means being concerned excessively with oneself, for one's own advantage without regard to the well-being of others. This isn't about living your life at the expense of others. Instead, I'm talking about "Self-ish"—about being loving, kind, and caring toward yourself. It's about honoring the commitments you make to yourself; it's about taking care of you in all aspects—body,*

mind, and spirit. Without this attitude of self-care and nurturing, you are of no use to anyone—not to yourself and certainly not to others.

When *The PQ Factor* references *selfish*, it is the usual dictionary definition of the word. *Self-ish* references nourishing yourself in a healthy way so that you can nourish others.

Self-ish Tip #1: Who is actually being selfish?
Harry Browne (2004) in his book, *How I Found Freedom in an Unfree World*, says that if someone accuses you of being selfish, the reality is that person is only upset because you aren't doing what he or she selfishly wants you to do.

Symptom, Source, Solution

Thomas Leonard's (1995) "Symptom, Source, Solution" model provides a powerful framework for identifying the symptoms that are hampering your ability to persist. It also is a crucial component in your self-care and in the healthy pursuit of "Self-ishness." Many times people resist change because they are unable to get past the symptom to address the source. The result is that symptoms continue to pop up until the source is addressed. Here's a simple example that illustrates how this model works.

Assume you have just started sneezing 20-30 times per hour. Taking an antihistamine stops the sneezing for several hours. When the medication wears off, however, the sneezing (the symptom) returns. The symptom returns because you did not treat the underlying source. If the source is a cold, the sneezing will stop in a few days. If the source is an allergen, the sneezes will continue to plague you until you eliminate the source. As long as the source remains unaddressed, the problem will persist.

Once you identify the source, the final step is to select and then implement a solution. For example, you may realize that being around your cat is causing you to sneeze, but what actions will you take to eliminate the source? Would you take allergy shots? Would you continue to tolerate the sneezes because you love your pet so much? Would you reluctantly put your cat up for adoption? These are all viable solutions once you understand the nature of the source and your options for dealing with it.

Being Self-ish Begins with Self-Care

Every commercial airline flight in the United States begins with a safety warning that includes what to do in case there is a sudden loss of pressure: first, place your oxygen mask over your face and begin breathing. You can then help your child or anyone who needs assistance with their masks. You are of no use to others if you haven't secured your own mask first.

Everyone knows that self-care is essential. Nevertheless, few people eat well, exercise regularly, get enough sleep, and live stress free. Instead, obesity rates, diabetes, and other stress related diseases are at all-time highs. As a society, we suffer from sleep deprivation and never seem to have enough time to accomplish all that we "should" do.

To apply the Symptom, Source, Solution model to your self-care, begin by taking the inventory below to determine how well you care for yourself.

Self-Care Inventory
Answer each item as "True" or "False."

_____ 1. When others look at me, it's clear to them that I'm in excellent health.
_____ 2. I have had an annual physical, a full dental checkup, and my teeth cleaned in the last year.
_____ 3. I eat the right foods, exercise regularly, and get plenty of sleep.
_____ 4. If I have an unusual symptom or problem, I seek the appropriate medical care immediately—I never procrastinate when it comes to my health.
_____ 5. I seldom have pain anywhere in my body.
_____ 6. I wear clothes I love and that make me feel good.
_____ 7. I take time every day to do at least two things for myself that make me feel great.
_____ 8. I treat myself at least as well as I treat others.
_____ 9. I get enough sleep. I almost never feel tired or worn out.

Chapter 11: To Nourish Others, Nourish Yourself First

____10. I seldom feel down or depressed.
____11. I'm surrounded by people who support me in all that I do.
____12. I seldom raise my voice or become angry.
____13. I am extremely grateful for all the good things I have in my life.
____14. I have a strong sense of community and connection.
____15. I have strong relationships with both friends and family.
____16. I don't allow people in my life (friends, family, or colleagues) who drain me of my time, energy, or resources.
____17. The people I am closest to have happy and fulfilling lives.
____18. I have what I truly need.
____19. My home environment is perfect for me.
____20. I love my work and find it fulfilling.
____21. I enjoy spending time at home.
____22. The people in my work environment think highly of me.
____23. There is no one that I would hate to run into at a party or other event.
____24. My office/work area is neat and well organized.
____25. I have sufficient time to accomplish whatever goals I set.
____26. I have enough money saved to cope with an emergency.
____27. My retirement plan will allow me to retire with an income.
____28. I feel appreciated by the people in my life.

Scoring:
Each item that you marked "True" indicates a positive area in terms of your self-care. The questions that you answered "False," represent areas where better self-care will make increasing your PQ and achieving your long-term goals easier.

"Feather, Bat, Splat!"
How to Recognize Symptoms Early

Recall a moment when you had a gut feeling or an intuition that you ignored and the situation turned into a major mess. As mentioned in Chapter 1, your cerebral cortex often overrules the signals being generated by your limbic system and reptilian brain. One of the most powerful models for preventing this from happening is called the

"Feather, Bat, Splat!" model. The goal is to catch the symptom at the "feather" stage before it evolves into the "bat" or "splat!" stage.

The "feather" is typically the little voice inside that suggests something is wrong. The baseball "bat" is much more serious. Continued failure to deal with these symptoms can have devastating results like the experience one of our coaching clients shared:

> *I had a funny red lump on my ankle. It didn't hurt, but it didn't go away either. I took my annual physical but didn't mention it to my doctor. A number of months later I did mention it to a friend who is a nurse. She scared me into seeing my doctor the very next day. Unfortunately, the lump was malignant melanoma. Procrastination not only cost me a major part of my leg; it nearly cost me my life.*

In this case, the red lump was the feather. The client dealt with the issue at the "bat" level and lost part of his leg. Had he waited, his "splat" could have cost him his life. The bottom line is that when it comes to recognizing symptoms, catching them at the feather stage is crucial.

The process of recognizing a symptom as a "feather" is actually fairly simple. All you have to do is to pause long enough to check for warning signs. Warning signs can include having an uneasy feeling about a situation even though you cannot identify the source. The warning may be a fleeting thought that says, "Maybe I shouldn't do this" or "Something seems off." Other types of warning signs can come from family, friends, and the people with whom you work. If someone suggests that you are heading down the wrong path, take note of whether you are having any misgivings about your course of action. If so, avoid rushing forward and see if you can uncover the underlying source.

Be Wary about How You Label Your Symptoms

A symptom signals that you are in a situation requiring your attention. When this occurs, be extraordinarily careful about how you describe the symptoms/signals that you are experiencing. This can be exceedingly difficult, especially when it comes to your health. As the story below illustrates, even a doctor, a friend, or a well-meaning family member can sabotage your effort to stay positive and optimistic.

Chapter 11: To Nourish Others, Nourish Yourself First

Do you have arthritis?
Over dinner one night my friend Joeann Fossland shared an interesting conversation that she had with one of her coaching clients. She was having some issues with her back and she flinched as she got up from the table. Her client asked her, "Do you have arthritis?"

After careful thought Joeann responded by saying, "Having arthritis sounds like something is broken and that it can't be fixed. I prefer to think that there are some days when I have some pain and other days when I don't."

A key point to note in Fossland's response is how she separated herself from the situation. Agreeing that she had arthritis would put Fossland into the situation. By saying that some days her body hurts, she responded in a way where the days that were painful were periodic, not chronic as her client suggested. She also avoided falling into the trap of self-fulfilling prophecy. If you say have arthritis, you will be more likely to view every twitch and pain as a result of that disease.

Self-fulfilling prophecy can have both positive and negative effects. For example, if your partner comes down with a cold and you tell yourself, "Great—now I'm going to be sick," that's usually exactly what will happen.

At each of the colleges where I have taught, a number of my fellow instructors were in their 70s and 80s. Most were healthy and led active lives outside the classroom. As I look back over three decades of being on the faculty, I have no recollection of anyone focusing on their aches and pains. Part of the reason is that our students have zero interest in that conversation. Instead, most students were looking forward to starting their careers and raising a family. Regardless of your age, when you are surrounded by healthy people who have a positive, optimistic outlook, you are much more likely to be healthy.

There are two key takeaways here. First, pay special attention to how you describe any symptoms that you may be having. Second, surrounding yourself with people who are healthy and positive will also help you to persist in being more healthy and positive.

Are You a Hot or Cold Reactor?

According to Paul Pearsall's (1996) book, *The Pleasure Prescription*, there are two behavior patterns that contribute to major illness. He's termed these two patterns, "Hot Reactors" and "Cold Reactors." To

The PQ Factor

determine if either of these patterns of symptoms fit you, mark each of the following items as "True" or "False." (Scoring is at the end of Part 2.)

Part 1
1. I'm very good at multitasking.
2. People sometimes tell me I'm too quick to anger.
3. I'm extremely competitive.
4. I have absolutely no patience for long lines or for stupid people.
5. I tend to be very restless—sitting still is simply not my style.
6. I don't have as much power as I really need and deserve.
7. I don't let people get too close to me—you never know when they're going to double cross you.
8. I tend to hold my tension in my neck and shoulders.
9. When I look in the mirror, there are brown circles under my eyes.
10. I have a deep vertical crease where my earlobe joins my face.

Part 2
1. When things go wrong it's generally my fault.
2. I like to check and double check my work.
3. My life is pretty dismal—there's not much to be happy about.
4. I usually give in even when I know I'm right.
5. I have a tough time deciding what to do—it's hard for me to make up my mind.
6. I often feel inadequate—it seems like everything I do is simply not good enough.
7. I pretty much view the world as being black and white—what's right is right and what's wrong is wrong.
8. I worry constantly about being separated from those I love.
9. I keep my emotions to myself.
10. I spend a great deal of my time and effort on nurturing others.

Scoring:
Count the number of times that you responded "True" for each section. If you marked five or more items True in Section 1, you are what Pearsall calls a "Hot Reactor." This is the behavior pattern associated with heart disease, autoimmune disorders, lupus, multiple sclerosis, diabetes, arthritis, allergy, and asthma.

If you answered, "True," to the last two items in Section 1 (the brown circles under the eyes and a deep vertical crease at the base of the earlobe where it joins the face), be aware that Pearsall's research has found these two features to be physical markers for heart disease. If you haven't done so recently, please see your health care professional for a complete evaluation of your cardiac health.

If you marked five or more items True in Section 2, these symptoms are indicative of someone who is a "Cold Reactor." This behavior pattern is associated with an underactive immune system resulting in increased viral and bacteriological infections and cell disease (cancer).

If you marked four or fewer items in each section as True, you are probably leading a life that puts you at a reduced risk for serious illness.

Below are two examples of how past coaching clients shifted away from being a "hot reactor" (The Queen of multitasking) and a "cold reactor" (There's a right way to do things).

The queen of multitasking

I used to be the queen of multitasking. I had no problem conducting business while I was driving and eating. I always had tons of projects going and managed to get most done. I was running on caffeine, sugar, and adrenaline and wondering why I always seemed to be getting angry and why I had no energy. If anything got in the way to slow me down, I would blow a gasket. My coach suggested that I try an experiment for one week. She asked me to replace my regular coffee with decaf, to only eat when I was sitting at the table, and to turn off my phone when I was driving and to listen to calming music instead. I also had to agree to be home for dinner with my family no later than 7:00 PM. At the end of the week, was I surprised! My energy had increased dramatically, I actually felt happy, and I was more efficient. I decided to make this experiment permanent.

Today I'm happier, I seldom become angry, and my family is thrilled. What came as the biggest surprise, however, is that I'm also making more money in my business!

There's a right way to do things

I used to be a perfectionist. There is a right way and wrong way to do things and that's the way it is. I was constantly frustrated but never let anyone know what I was experiencing. I was so busy nurturing my family and making everything perfect that I didn't take time for me.

I was always catching colds and had lots of troubles with allergies. The wake-up call came when my husband told me that although he still loved me, he simply couldn't live with what I was doing to him and the family.

In addition to encouraging me find to a good therapist, my coach helped me to get on a self-care program. She also asked me to start being honest with my husband about what I was really feeling rather than just saying, "Everything's fine."

Today, I'm still working on the childhood issues that created my perfectionism, but being honest about my feelings has really helped. My self-care program has resulted in fewer allergies and virtually no colds. Things are a lot better for both my family and me.

The Symptom, Source, Solution model allows you to quickly identify symptoms and then dig deeper to find the underlying source. Chapter 12 focuses specifically on some of the most common sources that will block your ability to persist and to be Self-ish. In Chapter 13, you will learn proven strategies that will help you to implement solutions that will increase both your "Self-ishness" and your PQ.

Chapter 11: Key Points

1. Be Self-ish (kind, loving, and caring toward yourself), not selfish.

2. Use the "Symptom, Source, Solution" model to move beyond the symptoms of your problems and to address the source of the issue.

3. Being Self-ish begins by taking care of your needs.

4. Use the "Feather, Bat, Splat" model to spot symptoms early when it's easiest to correct the situation.

5. Be wary about how you label temporary symptoms to avoid having them become chronic, long-term issues.

6. Avoid being a "hot" or a "cold" reactor because both patterns contribute to serious illness.

Chapter 12:
Sources that Block Self-ishness

*Even when obstacles crop up, appreciate them,
because obstacles mean that you're moving
forward—that you're taking action
to make your dreams a reality.*
Anonymous

My husband's family has a long-standing love affair with carbohydrates. On my nephew's seventh birthday, his dad took him and my five-year-old niece out for doughnuts. My niece was feeling left out because her brother was receiving all the attention. When it came time to have the doughnuts, she promptly grabbed two of them and began shoving them into her mouth. When her dad suggested that it would be a good idea to share, her response was, "I share—I share with myself!"

Overcoming the Psychology of Lack

In the story above my niece was experiencing a lack of attention. *Lack*, the perception that you don't have enough, is one of the most widespread sources of unhealthy, selfish behavior. A primary reason lack is so common is that advertisers constantly bombard you with the implied message, "You must buy our product if you want to be happy and have a great life." There's no regard as to whether you need their product, can afford it, or even if it's good for you.

An excellent place to begin countering your personal feelings of lack is by identifying the areas where you are willing to share. These are the areas where you have a sense of abundance rather than lack. For example, are you willing to share your sandwich with a colleague who forgot to bring their lunch to work?

In contrast, what are some areas where you are unwilling to share? Your unwillingness to share may indicate lack, but it may have an entirely different source that has nothing to do with lack. To illustrate this point, very few people are willing to share their bed with a stranger. The question is where do you draw the line between what you are willing to share as opposed to what constitutes lack for you personally?

Standards and Boundaries

How and when you share provides an opportunity to observe the difference between a standard and a boundary. A standard is a behavior that we expect of ourselves. A boundary is the dividing point between behaviors that we are willing to accept from others and behaviors that we refuse to tolerate.

To understand how this process works, what are some of your personal standards and boundaries when it comes to sharing? For example, when you go to a restaurant are you willing to share your food with another person at the table? Are you willing to let someone who is not named on your insurance policy drive your car? What types of information are you willing to share with your family vs. the types of information that you are willing to share with the people at work? Your attitudes regarding standards and boundaries usually originate in childhood as the two stories below illustrate.

> ### Would you share your toothbrush?
> *I grew up in a small family. I had my own room and my own things. I was so surprised when I was traveling with a girlfriend and I forgot my toothbrush. When I mentioned that I had forgotten my toothbrush, she said, "Oh—use mine!" I was so stunned I was speechless. No one ever shared a toothbrush in my family. Sharing a toothbrush simply wouldn't be "sanitary."*
>
> *She looked at me strangely when I didn't respond and then she laughed and said, "I grew up in a big family—I'm used to sharing everything." I still didn't share her toothbrush, but it was a great lesson for me about how people differ in their attitudes toward sharing.*
>
> ### Who gets the last piece?
> *When I was growing up, my two brothers and I were very competitive around the issue of food. To make sure we all had equal portions, I made up a form that would allow us to equally divide a pizza, a cake, or a pie into five equal portions. While we still always wanted more, the fact that we all shared equally stopped the fighting about who was getting more. As adults, we now share equally. When it comes to the dessert when we're together, however, there's still a competition for that last piece.*

The experiences described above illustrate that where people draw the line can be quite different. How you learn to share depends upon a variety of factors. For example, only children usually have their own room and their own toys. When they become adults, they are likely to have clear-cut rules about what belongs to them and what belongs to others.

Now compare someone who comes from a large family, especially if the family members had to share bedrooms and bathrooms. In this case, no one really has a space that is designated as "mine only." Instead, everything was shared. As an adult, these individuals are accustomed to sharing and may not even think about using something that is not theirs. This difference can become a source of conflict both at home and at work. The person who clearly identifies "my things," resents it when someone who is accustomed to sharing everything decides to "share" a pen, a piece of clothing, or the food from the office refrigerator. The root cause of this conflict is simply two people with differing standards and boundaries.

What makes dealing with these differences difficult is that other people are unaware of where you draw your line. Conflicts occur when your expectations lead you to believe that someone else's boundaries and standards are identical to yours.

Boundaries tend to be stable and often apply in multiple areas of your life. It's important to identify your personal boundaries including the behaviors that you are willing to tolerate, the behaviors you find to be unacceptable, and how you plan to respond when you encounter a behavior that is unacceptable to you. Again, standards and boundaries differ tremendously from person to person.

> **Self-ish Tip #2: How to avoid being slain by an expectation**
> Byron once coined the phrase "slain by an expectation" to describe what happens when someone fails to live up to our standards or crosses a boundary. The 2016 presidential election was so heated that no matter who won, one side was bound to experience this phenomenon. The post-election despair, protests, and the cries of "not my president" are all examples of how distressing it can be when our expectations are not met.

> The next time you find yourself angry or upset because someone failed to live up to your expectations, take a moment to ask yourself where the anger originated. Did you have different expectations because your standards and boundaries differed? If you are angry because the other person crossed a boundary, note exactly where that boundary is located. If at all possible, identify how the other person's standard differs from yours. If your expectations about a situation were not met, seek to uncover any expectations that contributed to your anger. Understanding the difference will help you avoid being slain by an expectation in the future.

Are You Imposing Your Standards on Others?

Have you ever offered someone advice on how to do something without gaining their permission first? Have you ever criticized someone else because their way of doing things didn't match with yours? A primary way that people create struggle and conflict in their lives is by using their personal standards to judge others. This costly behavior can seriously damage your business and personal relationships.

The source of this behavior is the belief that, "What is good for me is good for you." Unfortunately, when you impose your standards or solutions on another person, especially when that person didn't ask for your input, anger and resentment often result.

The need to impose our opinions on others typically results from the need to be right. To illustrate this point, recall a situation where someone tried to impose his or her opinion on you. Did you feel used or manipulated? Did this interaction cause you to think less highly of the other person? Did their behavior damage your relationship?

Next, identify a situation where you attempted to control another person's choice. Was it important to you to demonstrate that you were right? Given how you felt when someone tried to impose their opinion or standards on you, wouldn't that person have the same reaction when you tried to impose your standards on them?

The first step in overcoming this potentially damaging behavior is to notice how and when you engage in this behavior. Next, when you find yourself trying to impose your personal standards or opinions on someone else, ask, "Is being right or being in control more important than the relationship that I have with this person?"

One of the biggest mistakes you can make is to rush in and offer your assistance without first asking whether it is needed or desired. This is a classic dilemma in relationships—one person will start talking about having a bad day and the other person rushes to help them by offering solutions to the problem. In general, people resent being told what to do. Furthermore, if you insert yourself into their decision-making process, you can rest assured that you will get the blame if anything goes wrong.

A better approach is to first ask whether or not the other person would like your help. Even if someone asks for your help, remember to ask what that person wants or needs from you. You may discover that what the other person wants and needs is quite different from what you expected.

Self-ish Tip #3: Let go of telling others what to do

To avoid imposing your standards on others, recognize that each person has their own unique combination of strengths, weaknesses, capabilities, and levels of development. Because of this, what works for you may not work for someone else. So before you give someone else advice about what to do, take note of whether that person asked for your advice in the first place. If not, keeping your opinion to yourself may be the best course of action.

Even if someone asks for your advice, never forget that their situation and the people involved are different from those involved in your situation. A much better approach is to describe what happened in your personal situation and then let the other person decide which choice best fits their situation. Remember, when you impose your standards on someone else, you may be perceived as being judgmental or arrogant, even though your only intention was to be helpful. Worse yet, when the other party rejects your advice, you may feel angry and hurt, which will create even more stress in your relationship.

When Someone Inadvertently Crosses a Boundary

While it's important to honor other people's standards and boundaries, what happens when someone crosses one of your boundaries? In most cases, the other person is not deliberately trying to provoke or upset you. Instead, you may have an unspoken standard or boundary that the person doesn't know about or the behavior that you find to be objectionable is not an issue for them.

The way to deal with this issue begins with a simple request. Here's how this works. Assume that someone you work with starts yelling at you. Instead of telling the person to stop yelling, ask for a different behavior: "Would you please speak more softly to me?"

The reason for asking for a different behavior is that when you say, "don't yell," or, "stop yelling," your brain must process two requests. The first is the word "yell" and the second is "stop" or "not." This is the reason when someone says, "Don't think of a red truck," the first thing your brain will visualize is a red truck. On the other hand, when you say "Would you please speak more softly to me?" your brain is only required to process a single request. The secret here is to ask for what you need rather than telling the other person to stop engaging in a specific behavior.

When someone deliberately crosses one of your boundaries and refuses to stop, you have two choices; allow the person to continue the behavior or leave the situation. If you elect to do nothing, the behavior will continue until you either leave or stop the behavior by asking for what you need.

When you inadvertently cross someone else's boundary

If you inadvertently cross someone else's boundary, the first step is to let go of any need you may have to be right or to win. The second step is to say: "It was never my intention to upset you—what can I do to fix the situation?" There is no need to apologize because apologies require an explanation. Moreover, asking what you can do to fix the situation puts the power in the hands of the other individual without any excuses or rationalizations. It also demonstrates that you are willing to take responsibility for your actions.

Boundaries help others to know what behaviors are acceptable to you and what behaviors are unacceptable. Setting, establishing, and maintaining a boundary is not always an easy task. With practice, however, this valuable skill yields results that are well worth your time and effort.

What's Bugging You?

When someone doesn't live up to your expectations or crosses a boundary, it's perfectly normal to be aggravated or upset. There are thousands of other reasons why you may experience these feelings. Using the Symptom, Source, Solution model can be a powerful way to identify and ultimately eliminate these seemingly trivial items that, when taken together, can present a substantial roadblock to increasing your PQ and having a more happy and satisfying life.

> **Self-ish Tip #4: What's bugging you?**
> Take a few minutes to identify at least 20 things that are bugging you right now. This can be anything that pulls you off focus, distracts, or irritates you. Examples include something as small as a missing button, a leaky faucet, an online subscription that needs to be cancelled, a friend who constantly wastes your time by complaining, or something as major as ending your marriage or quitting your job. Most people have at least 100 of these, but begin by noting the first 20 that come to mind for you personally.
>
> Each item on your list of what's bugging you is an example of a "toleration." According to Thomas Leonard (1995), tolerations are the little things that drain you of your time and energy. They usually fall into three major categories:
>
> 1. Work, which includes colleagues, clients, environment, equipment, compensation, etc.
>
> 2. Other people including your spouse, family, and/or friends.
>
> 3. Personal, which can include your appearance, home environment, car, negative self-talk, or harmful behaviors.

> The next step in the process is to place each item on your list into one of these three categories. This will give you a quick picture of which aspect of your life is experiencing the greatest strain due to these energy drainers. As you look at the list, also identify which areas will be the easiest to address first.

Tolerations: An expensive yet easily fixable problem
Tolerations are one of the most expensive yet easily fixable problems in life. Taken alone each toleration may be nothing more than a minor annoyance. The cumulative effect of 100 tolerations is the equivalent of having 100 paper cuts. The result is that you waste valuable time as you repeatedly notice the toleration and then remind yourself that you "should" handle it.

Tolerations are part of your 80 percent that can hamper your ability to stay focused on the 20 percent of activities that matter most. The more tolerations you have, the harder it is to move forward. The cost is the equivalent of having the money in your checking account to pay your credit card bill and letting it go past the due date. The longer you delay in paying the bill, the more costly and difficult it becomes to eliminate. In other words, the more you resist handling a toleration, the more difficult it is to persist in engaging in the behaviors that best support you.

The Primary Sources of Tolerations

Procrastination is the most common obstacle when it comes to handling tolerations. The easiest way to avoid creating tolerations is to handle them when they first occur. For example, instead of putting off sewing on that button, do it when it first falls off. When something goes wrong or irritates you, clean it up immediately—the longer you wait, the more difficult it becomes. Handling tolerations as they occur is like developing a muscle. The more you exercise it, the easier it becomes. Learning and growth are much like this as well; the more often you deal with things when they first occur, the easier it becomes.

Psychic vampires
"Psychic vampires" can be one of the most difficult types of tolerations to eliminate. A *psychic vampire* is someone who drains your time, energy,

Chapter 12: Sources that Block Self-ishness

and resources and gives virtually nothing back in return. A good way to recognize when you have been in the presence of a psychic vampire is to check your energy after spending time with him or her. If you feel drained, the person has been drawing on your energy to their benefit and your detriment.

If you have a psychic vampire in your life, chances are you haven't been strong enough about enforcing your boundaries. For example, if a psychic vampire corners you at work, tell the person that you have only one or two minutes to talk. At that point, terminate the interaction and go on to whatever else you had planned.

Another less direct but effective approach is to ask the person's help on a project: "I'm going to be cleaning my garage this weekend—why don't you come over and help me?" The reason this works is that most psychic vampires are focused exclusively on their needs, not on helping others.

For those psychic vampires who constantly complain, their goal is to feel better by downloading their problems on you. An excellent way to stop their complaints is to ask, "Tell me one thing that is going right in your life." If the person responds by saying, "Nothing is going right," then ask whether the person had a place to sleep last night, whether there was clean running water there, and if they have eaten a meal in the last 24 hours.

The psychic vampire's goal is to take energy from you without being forced to listen to what you need or to answer your questions. By the way, if the person walks off in a huff, there's a good chance they will take their complaints elsewhere. As one of our past coaching clients noted, psychic vampires are a lot like the trash—the more you let them build up, the more they stink and the harder they are to clean up!

Start with the easy ones first
When it comes to eliminating tolerations, it makes no difference where you begin. It's the cumulative effect that you're seeking to reduce. Each toleration you eliminate allows you to devote more time to your personal top 20 percent.

Here's a case in point. Several years ago I was working with a manager who was coaching a top producing husband and wife team. They were averaging 120 business related text messages per day. Even if each text only required a minute to respond, they were still spending two hours per day handling items that distracted them from their primary purpose of being face-to-face with buyers and sellers. Their manager had them switch their cell phone number so that only their assistant and immediate family members had access. All other calls flowed through the office and were screened by their assistant. The two extra hours they saved each day allowed them to spend more time doing lead generation. This resulted in a significant increase in their production and a major reduction in the stress they were experiencing.

Remember, it makes no difference where you start. Whatever you eliminate frees up both time and energy. Again, the best strategy is to avoid creating tolerations in the first place. This means rather than procrastinating, handling each toleration as quickly as possible.

Does What You Eat and Drink Drain or Energize You?

The same test that you use to tell whether someone is a psychic vampire works equally well with what you eat. If you eat a food and you end up coughing or clearing your throat every time you eat that food, chances are that food doesn't support your body. If your stomach hurts after you eat or if you notice that on certain days you feel achy and other days you do not, see if there is a pattern based upon the type of food you consume.

On the other hand, if your energy is good after you eat and you can maintain that level of energy up to three hours or more, what you are eating probably supports your body. Do be leery of caffeine and sugar that may give you a great quick hit of energy, but the crash that follows can be a serious issue. As noted earlier, caffeine kicks up your adrenaline and cortisol levels.

When you consume something sugary without appropriate amounts of protein and/or fat to balance it, your pancreas floods your body with insulin to remove the excess sugar from your bloodstream. The crash that follows will leave you feeling even less energized than if you had eaten nothing at all. This up and down cycle has often been cited as a major cause of obesity.

> **Self-ish Tip #5: Search for the source**
> For the next ten days keep a food diary of what you eat and drink. Record how you felt prior to ingesting your meal, snack, or favorite beverage. Check back 90 minutes later and note your energy. If your energy is lower, substitute a different food to see if that food improves your energy. Keep experimenting—your body will tell you which substances enhance your energy and which ones are harmful. All you have to do is track what works and eat more of those foods and less of the foods that deplete your energy. If your mid-afternoon energy crash disappears, you know that you're on the right track.

The High Cost of Lack of Sleep

Recall a night when you slept poorly, had to get up unusually early, or didn't sleep at all. If you're like most people, the next day was pretty miserable. One of the most surprising findings from my doctoral studies was that students score better on exams when they get a good night's sleep rather than pulling an all-nighter studying. The reason is that REM (dream) sleep helps your brain to consolidate what you have learned. The consolidation effect only takes place if you go to sleep immediately after studying. If you engage in any other activity, such as watching television, texting, or connecting on social media, the effect disappears.

Reminiscence

One of my favorite Gary Larson cartoons shows a student raising his hand and asking his teacher, "Mr. Osborne, may I be excused? My brain is full." When you're feeling overwhelmed by too much to do or overly tired from a lack of sleep, your brain needs time to consolidate and to prune what it deems to be unimportant.

What psychologists have termed "reminiscence" supports this contention. *Reminiscence* is the ability to perform a task better after resting than immediately after the task was learned.

Recent research has begun to unravel how the process of neural pruning in the brain works. Pathways that are used the most often are strengthened while those that are not used are eliminated. The microglial cells are largely responsible for eliminating inactive neural pathways, especially when the person is sleeping. Going back to the student in the cartoon whose brain is full, getting a full night's sleep will allow his brain to eliminate approximately 60 percent of the least used neural pathways his brain created during that day.

Companies such as Apple, Google, and Microsoft have long recognized the importance of napping during the workday. In fact, a 26-minute nap can enhance performance by up to 36 percent. Nap pods are now commonplace in high tech companies because they improve employee productivity and creativity. This new research on the role of microglial cells and neural pruning during sleep provides a partial explanation for how this process works.

Pay special attention to what you concentrate on before going to sleep
Last night before you fell asleep, what activities did you engage in and what did you think about? The thoughts and the activities that you engage in just prior to sleep appear to direct the brain to strengthen those neural connections. The remaining new or lesser connections are likely to be eliminated as you sleep.

For example, if you studied and then played a video game prior to going to sleep, your brain will strengthen the video game playing circuits while eliminating the new neural connections that you worked so hard to create while you were studying. Just to reiterate, studying and then going to sleep as soon as possible is the best way to lock in your learning.

Self-ish Tip #6: How to control what your brain prunes
Whether you realize it or not, you can take control of what your brain prunes including which circuits it strengthens. Getting plenty of sleep is critical, but what is equally important is being very selective about what you think about prior to going to sleep. Concentrate on what is positive and optimistic and banish any thoughts of what is negative, pessimistic, or unimportant to you prior to going to sleep.

If you are unable to get your self-talk to make the shift, get up out of bed, write down 5-10 positive things that you would like to focus on or remember. At that point, go back to bed and continue to review what you wrote down until you fall asleep.

A slightly different approach is to review all the positive things that happened during the day. Next, express gratitude for those events. When you wake up, take note of the difference in your alertness and your state of mind. Chances are you will be pleasantly surprised.

The fact that the brain strengthens what you think about before you fall asleep is another reason why maintaining an optimistic outlook is so important—the more you focus on the negative, the stronger those neural pathways will become. In contrast, when you focus on thinking positive and optimistic thoughts, those pathways will be strengthened while the pessimistic pathways are reduced.

We have identified the symptoms and some common reasons blocking you from being healthfully Self-ish. Chapter 13 does a deep dive into the Self-ish solutions that will help you to reduce your resistance and increase your persistence.

Chapter 12: Key Points

1. Overcome your feelings of lack by identifying those areas where you are willing to share.

2. A "standard" is a behavior that we expect of ourselves. A "boundary" is the dividing point between behaviors that we are willing to accept from others and behaviors that we refuse to tolerate.

3. Avoid being slain by an expectation by understanding how other people's standards and boundaries differ from yours.

4. Avoid telling others what to do or trying to impose your standards on them. These actions can cause serious harm to your relationships.

5. Instead of telling others what not to do, ask for what you need. For example, "Stop yelling at me" vs. "Please speak softly to me."

6. If you make a mistake or someone becomes angry with you, say, "It was never my intention to upset you—what can I do to fix the situation?"

7. Tolerations are an expensive, but fixable problem—start eliminating one a day, every day.

8. Track how your body responds to various foods. Then select those foods that best support how your body feels. Also, be sure to get enough sleep, a critical component in nourishing yourself.

Chapter 13:
Moving from Source to Solution

*It isn't that they can't see the solution.
It's that they can't see the problem.*
G.K. Chesterton

When it comes to eliminating the source of self-care challenges, the situation you find yourself in often results from hundreds of decisions made over time. For example, someone who smokes may experience relatively good health for decades before being diagnosed with lung cancer or chronic obstructive pulmonary disease (COPD). In most cases, undoing the impact of this many choices requires repeated effort over time. There's no magic bullet for undoing the effects of smoking, drinking, or overeating for thousands of days. Consequently, when people take those first steps toward moving from resistance to persistence in their self-care goals, failure to achieve instantaneous results may leave them discouraged and can cause them to give up.

The High Cost of Instant Gratification

Winning the lottery, fast food, instant messaging, and movies on demand are all testament to our society's increasing need to have what we want when we want it. People shell out millions of dollars on hoped-for instantaneous solutions to their financial challenges. Americans reportedly spend $60 billion on weight loss including diets, gym memberships, and "diet" food and drinks. In truth, instant gratification is a major stumbling block standing in the way of achieving your long-term self-care goals.

Although being overweight or having financial difficulties often result from hundreds of choices over time, the latest drop-pounds-fast-diet or get-rich-quick scheme is the siren call for people seeking instantaneous solutions. Even if you do win the lottery or drop the weight quickly, if you fail to change the underlying behaviors that created the original problem, the probability is high that the financial or the weight problems will return. A prime example is the lottery curse.

The Lottery Curse

Have you ever wished that you could wave a crystal ball that would give you the winning lottery numbers? How great would that be? The truth may surprise you.

Did you know that 70 percent of lottery winners actually end up becoming bankrupt? (Murray 2016). Dave Ramsey, radio host and author, reports on his blog that the divorce rate among lottery winners is four times higher than the rate in the general population. The suicide rate is also higher.

A primary reason lottery winners end up losing their money is that they give too much away to their family and friends. Putting it a little differently, they lack the boundaries necessary to turn down the psychic vampires who guilt them by saying, "You have plenty of money—you should share some of it with us." When the person receiving the windfall turns down the never-ending demands from family and friends for money, close relationships are often destroyed. As one lottery winner described it, "My friends and family turned into vampires trying to suck the life out of me." In one extreme case, a woman who befriended a lottery winner murdered him when he refused to share his winnings with her.

I have a friend whose husband did win multi-millions in the lottery. She went from being a happy, well-adjusted mom and businessperson to facing severe depression. The reason? The lottery changed how she viewed her value. With therapy and the advice of a wise financial advisor, she overcame these issues. One of the most important things that financial advisor did was to put her family on a charitable giving plan. In other words, the financial advisor helped them set up very specific boundaries about how and where their funds would be spent.

As predicted by the Symptom, Source, Solution model, if the source of the issue remains unaddressed, the challenge you are facing will continue to reappear. When you finally do address the source, as my friend did by working with a therapist and a financial advisor, that's when the issue can finally be resolved.

How Good Are Your Observation Skills?

For many years I opened my introductory psychology class with an observation exercise. I asked the students to pair up and to carefully note as many details about the other student's appearance as possible.

Chapter 13: Moving from Source to Solution

I also explained that I would be asking the students to turn their backs to each other and to make two changes to their own appearance. Once the students made the changes to their appearance, they would then face each other and see if they could identify what the other student had changed about his or her appearance.

We often had 100+ degree temperatures during the opening week of school. Students were dressed in shorts, t-shirts, and flip-flops. It was interesting to watch as students kicked off their sandals, took off a piece of jewelry, or removed some other item of clothing in order to change their appearance.

After the students finished identifying the changes their partners had made, I asked them to repeat the process and to change two more things about their appearance. The moans and groans were audible as many of them struggled with what else they could take off. A few students changed their hair or put an item of clothing on backwards.

After the second trial, I asked how many students correctly identified all four items that the other student changed. The numbers typically ranged between 25 and 40 percent. I explained that this is an important point to note about eyewitness testimony. Even when the students knew they would be required to note the changes the other student made, the majority failed to note all four items.

I went on to explain that when psychologists conduct experiments, their instructions almost never reveal the real purpose of the experiment. So what was this experiment really about?

Student responses included that it was an icebreaker where they could get to know each other, that it was a way to illustrate how scientific research works, and of course, to show them how accurate they were at observing others. The experiment was definitely designed to do all those things.

I then asked them to watch as I changed four things about my appearance. I put on my sunglasses, slung my purse over my shoulder, picked up my class notebook, and stuck a pen between my teeth.

The real purpose of the experiment was to illustrate how they viewed change. Very few students changed their appearance by adding something rather than taking something away. This is the crux of the issue when it comes to changing your behavior—as long as you view change as loss or giving up something, it is extremely difficult to achieve any sort of long-term, meaningful change.

Self-ish Tip #7: Learning how to "add to"
Change has elements of both adding to and taking away. This creates what psychologists call an approach-avoidance conflict. (An approach-approach conflict forces you to choose between two desirable outcomes, such as deciding between two favorite flavors of ice cream. An avoidance-avoidance conflict forces you to decide between two undesirable choices, such as moving with your company to a new city where you don't want to live or being laid off.)

To illustrate how approach-avoidance works, assume that your heart scan reveals early signs of calcification of your arteries. The doctor gives you the speech about losing weight and increasing your physical activity.

If you view the choices necessary to make these changes as taking away your freedom to eat what you want and having to replace an activity you enjoy with an activity you hate (exercise), your resistance mindset will make persisting in the activities that support your health more difficult.

On the other hand, it will be easier to persist when you seek ways that these changes may be able to add something you enjoy to your life. What are some ways that a change in your diet and your activity level might create an added benefit you? Clearly, avoiding a heart attack is at the top of the list, but what else? The more reasons you can cite (lowering your high blood pressure, being able to see your children graduate from college, better energy, etc.), the easier it will be to persist in the long-term behaviors that will limit your risk for having a heart attack.

How Many Diets Have You Been On?

The challenge with almost every diet is that if you don't make a lifestyle change in terms of your post-dieting behavior, you will probably gain the weight back. There are a number of reasons this happens.

If your weight has held steady for a year or more, you have established what biologists call a set point. No matter what you weigh, your body will "defend" this set point if you attempt to change it. The problem with dieting, especially if you're eating less than 1,300 calories per day, is that your body perceives this reduction in food as being a famine. As soon as the famine is over (i.e., you quit dieting), your body will prepare for the next famine by storing more fat. In fact, some researchers have had success putting underweight people on temporary calorie restriction as a means to help them gain weight.

Most people believe that dieting requires you to give up eating the foods that you enjoy. Giving up something you love can work for a short period of time, but it can be especially difficult to maintain over an extended period.

Another component is the language that you choose to describe your diet. When most people think of dieting, they say, "I want to lose weight." Your brain is wired to understand that when you "lose" something, you naturally want to find it again.

Because dieting and weight loss are so strongly linked in our language, a better approach is to focus on the process rather than the final outcome: "I will make healthy eating choices every day that support me to be my ideal weight." In other words, avoid making a temporary shift in favor of making a longer-term lifestyle shift.

"My 600-Pound Life"

The Learning Channel's *My 600-Pound Life* follows morbidly obese people on their weight-loss journey. Many of these patients are totally bedridden and completely reliant on others for their self-care. At the beginning of the show, the credits read, "Their chance of success is only five percent." While the show generally focuses on the patients who achieve success, their struggle highlights how difficult in can be to disconnect their eating addiction from emotional issues that are usually the root cause of both overeating and anorexia.

Dr. Younan Nowzaradan, the pioneering surgeon who developed many of the laparoscopic techniques used for bariatric surgery today, will only conduct weight-loss surgery on those patients who have shown that they can lose 30-50 pounds on their own prior to surgery. The only exception he makes is for patients so near death that immediate intervention is required for the person to survive.

Many of these patients hope that the surgery will magically make their weight issues go away. In fact, even with the surgery, they must be willing to make a change in their choices and to stick with the hard work of eating only a fraction of what they are used to consuming.

Many people are emotional eaters, but these individuals have a powerful addiction to food that is rooted in their childhood, often due to sexual molestation. In case after case, the patients struggle until they are referred into counseling to treat the source of their issue—the childhood trauma that created the situation in the first place. This comes back to the core of the Symptom, Source, Solution model. The only way to achieve a permanent solution is to eliminate the source rather than just treating the symptoms.

Easy Ways to Shift Your Eating Behavior

If you're struggling with your weight, the smart move is to make long-term, sustainable lifestyle changes rather than to engage in crash diets. To avoid feeling that you are giving up something, look for different choices that allow you to eat the same amount of food, albeit with fewer calories. Here are some strategies that can help you make this shift with a minimal amount of effort.

Be aware of the choices you are making

Changing your eating patterns can be easier than you realize. As noted earlier, it's merely a matter of substituting a better choice for the less healthy choice you may now be making. In my case, one of those choices is to avoid the potato chip aisle at the market. This is a case of controlling my environment early in the process (at the store) as opposed to trying to resist a favorite food in the pantry.

One way this choice becomes easier is to read the labels on food or on a menu if you're dining out. If the restaurant doesn't provide the calories, most major chain restaurants post their nutritional information online. For example, that healthy Cobb salad you ordered at the Cheesecake Factory has a hefty 1,130 calories and that 16-ounce non-fat Frappuccino you ordered later that afternoon at Starbucks has 390 calories. Compare this to a Wendy's full-size apple pecan chicken salad at 570 calories plus a 16-ounce Starbuck's non-fat decaf cappuccino for 80 calories. That's an 870-calorie difference (enough to cover a Big Mac plus a full order of fries).

Here's another example. Most people think of yogurt and granola as being healthy foods. The label usually tells an entirely different story. Most low-fat yogurt products are packed with sugar, as are most so-called healthy cereal bars. If the label lists sugar, high-fructose corn syrup, and fructose, you are actually eating three different types of sugar. You must add the calories from each type of sweetener listed on the label to determine the total sugar content. A healthier, longer lasting source of energy would be oatmeal and fresh fruit plus a protein such as lean meat, eggs, or almond butter.

When most people realize how much they're consuming, it becomes easier to choose a better alternative. A healthy, persistence behavior is to simply check the calorie, fat, and sugar counts on what you order when you dine out and to read the labels when you shop. Look at your favorite items and then choose the ones that you still enjoy but are the better nutritional choices.

Ditch dieting and focus on making different choices
Once I hit 35, I began gaining about a pound a year. I tried all kinds of diets, some of which worked and others that didn't. For example, I gained weight on Atkins and on Nutrisystem, even though I followed both diets religiously. Straight calorie reduction worked, but it was difficult to maintain over time, especially when I was on the road speaking or attending a special event.

What has worked for me is having two days per week where I have a 600-700 calories day. I eat normally the other five days. (The pattern is low-calorie day, normal day, low-calorie day, followed by four normal days.) When I follow this plan, I lose about 1½ pounds per month. This approach allows me to indulge in the goodies at a great dinner party, enjoy a rich dessert, or occasionally enjoy that plate of barbecue. The reason this has worked is that it doesn't seem like I'm dieting—I'm just having a low-calorie day a couple of days per week.

On low-calorie days, I do my best to eat the same amount as on normal days, just with fewer calories. Having 8 ounces of an 80-100 calorie soup, a salad with a zero-calorie dressing, and 2-4 ounces of lean meat is not only filling at meal time, but it also doesn't feel as if I'm depriving myself.

The low-calorie days have also taught me some great alternatives that I use on my normal days. For example, Bai drinks, at 10 calories per bottle and sweetened with a natural sweetener called stevia, make an excellent substitute for high calorie fruit and cola drinks. Instead of cookies, cake, or pie, I found a very high grade Belgian chocolate that has just 30 calories per serving and because of the intense flavor, satisfies my sweet tooth.

This approach has allowed me to go on a cruise, enjoy the great food, and then return to my starting weight fairly easily. Also, if I'm going through a stressful time or I'm out on the road, I can eat what I want, although the weight does come back. When I get home, low-calorie days let me gradually lose the weight again with little effort. This is a lifestyle choice that has helped me lose that 15 pounds I could never seem to get rid of and to maintain a healthier BMI.

CAVEAT: Always check with your physician before you tackle any type of weight-loss diet, especially if you're diabetic or dealing with any other illness or health condition.

Chart Your Course to True Wealth

According to a recent study by GoBankingRates.com, 69 percent of Americans have less than $1,000 in savings. (Huddleston, 2016). A 2015 Nielsen survey showed that 40 percent of the respondents were living from paycheck to paycheck, even though 24 percent of this group earned between $100,000 and $150,000 per year. Lack of savings and living from paycheck to paycheck are usually indicative of someone who spends more than they make.

Money is a terrible master but a wonderful servant

Do you have money for emergencies? Are you funding your retirement and paying cash as you go? If not, you're like most other Americans and money is your boss. As my friend Michelle Holt puts it, "Money is a terrible master but a wonderful servant."

Michelle Holt understands money. Before joining REDX as their Director of Marketing and Strategic Relations, Holt was managing billion dollar portfolios for Goldman Sachs. At my recent Awesome Females in Real Estate leadership conference in Scottsdale, Holt outlined a five-point plan that can put you on the road to true wealth.

What constitutes true wealth? According to Holt, "Wealth is measured in time, not dollars. Wealth is the number of days you can live without working." While many people are rich, the truly wealthy are those who don't have to worry about money. In order to become the boss of your money rather than having money as your boss, Holt recommends that you follow this five-point plan.

1. Know your financial obligations

The first step in this process is to identify how much you take home each month by taking your total 1040 or your 1099 annual net income and dividing it by 12 to achieve a monthly amount. If you operate a business, the next step is to list all of your regular business expenses. Use your Schedule C, your LLC, or your corporate tax return and Profit and Loss statement to make this determination.

You must also determine what it costs you to live. This includes rent/mortgage costs, utilities, food, medical, dental, insurance, etc. If you are carrying any debt, include the amount that goes to reducing the principal and the amount of interest you pay. These numbers are listed separately on both your monthly and year-end auto, credit card, and mortgage statements. Pay special attention to how much you are paying in interest. This is one of the easiest places to begin slashing your expenses by paying cash or using a debit card.

Once you have scheduled your living costs, schedule your savings and tithing.

Now look at your discretionary spending. Where are you spending your money? To become the boss of your money, write down everything that you spend beyond the expenses you've already listed. This might include such things as clothing, entertainment, travel, and gifts.

Your goal is to tell your money what to do, not to let it get away from you on an impulse. By recording what you spend, you can quickly see where the money is going while also identifying the easiest places to cut back. Dave Ramsey provides a number of free tools, strategies, and sources to help you to achieve your financial goals. (See the Appendix for more details.)

2. Budgeting is an active, not a passive activity

A major mistake most people make is failure to pay themselves first. Your budget for yourself must include funds for clothing, car, hair, entertainment, cleaning, postage, prescriptions, cosmetics, gas, gifts, fun, etc. Holt recommends that you break these into categories such as your annual beauty fund (shampoo, cosmetics, toothbrushes, etc.), a household fund (soap, detergent, toilet paper, etc.), clothing, car, and gifts. Prioritize this list so you know what must be funded first.

Now here's the secret (the solution) to making this work. Label your money for each purpose. If you don't, it disappears! When you receive extra money, allocate it based upon the priorities you have established. Remember, every penny you don't label will probably disappear.

A major money drain can be your bank, especially if they charge for checking or other services. Instead, join a credit union where you are a member and there are no fees.

Also, if you haven't done so already, take steps to automate your regularly scheduled bills. This includes house payments, electricity, internet, phones, garbage collection, water, etc. These payments should come out of your household expenses.

For any annual memberships or other expenses that you pay once a year, take the annual number and divide it by 12 to obtain the cost per month before entering it into your expense schedule. Finally, start a car fund so you pay cash rather than using financing for your next vehicle.

3. Create an emergency fund

Your emergency fund is not an investment—it's insurance against emergencies. You need a minimum of $1,000-$2,000 that you can access when you face a true emergency such as a fire, accident, or hurricane, earthquake, etc. Holt calls this your "sleep well at night fund." Set it up as quickly as possible.

4. Avoid snowball debt—pay yourself instead of paying THEM

Rather than using a credit card, get in the habit of paying cash or using a debit card. This means that you save for purchases rather than financing them. If you can't pay cash for it, do you really need it? Remember, every time you spend money it should be mindful.

5. Retirement—know your numbers

If you're saving for your kids' education, fund your retirement first. Your kids can get loans for their educations. There are no loans for retirement. This goes back to paying yourself first.

Many experts now estimate that up to one-third of the men in the United States between the ages of 22 and 34 are living at home. Holt, who is a millennial says, "Kick them out. You're doing them no favors by allowing them to live at home and it's damaging your ability to fund your own retirement."

To help you curb your spending, check out one of the so-called "latte factor expense calculators" that illustrate how small amounts can turn into big dollars. To illustrate this point, a $6.00 daily latte over five years costs $13,000. Moreover, that $6.00 expense equals $8.00-$10.00 in pre-tax dollars.

Holt's motto for her own life is drawn from Dave Ramsey and Ayn Rand. "Live like no one else now so that you can live no one else later." Remember, "Money is only a tool. It will take you wherever you wish, but it will not replace you as the driver."

How to Escape Credit Card Interest Hell

When people face serious financial problems, getting out of a credit mess may ultimately involve going bankrupt or losing their home. In many cases, credit card spending is the culprit. A key step in turning the tide is eliminating as much credit card interest as possible and paying down the principal. If you're carrying high credit balances or your credit cards are maxed out, you can turn the tide.

During the recession our home's value dipped so that it was worth less than the mortgage on the property. Our real estate consulting and speaking business also took a 70 percent hit in terms of revenue. During that time, I also had six surgeries in a 12-month period. We decided to use our personal credit cards to keep the company going.

We were managing to make the payments on our credit cards but the 15-21 percent interest rates were killing us. I had heard of people who had negotiated zero percent interest rates on their debt, or in some cases, even a debt reduction. Even though we had a perfect payment record, when I called the various credit card companies and asked for a lower rate, the answer was, "No" or, "you already have the best available rate." Sorry, but a 15-21 percent interest rate certainly doesn't seem that way. What's especially frustrating is that if we were to fall behind, our interest rates would have shot up 28 percent or more, placing us in an even more precarious position.

Break out of high interest rate jail
One of my close friends who owned several successful businesses was in the same position we were. Her house was worth 50 percent of what she paid for it and her businesses were also down by 50-60 percent. The way she climbed out of her credit mess was to give the keys to her house back to the bank and to hire a credit attorney. Because of the issues we had faced, I wanted to explore whether working with a credit attorney could be a solution for us.

When I contacted the firm she recommended, their attorney explained that there was an upfront fee. The way you could get the credit card companies to negotiate with you was to miss six months of payments. While this was going on, you would have to put up with the on-going calls from the credit card companies and collection agencies. Nevertheless, this would you give you the money you needed to pay the attorney fees.

The psychological cost of doing this seemed so high to me that it didn't feel like it was worth it. I then decided to see if the credit card companies had some other option that could work for us. It turned out that they did.

Ask for a balance liquidation program
Since our highest balances were on our business cards, I began there. The first thing I did was to explain the nature of our hardship and that we wanted to pay off our current balances. I repeatedly mentioned our intention to pay our credit balances in full—this is a key point.

I explained to the customer service representative that we could no longer sustain payments at the high interest rates. The representative repeatedly inquired what rate would work for us. I indicated to her that our goal was to pay the amount in full and asked if there was a workout program if we closed the account. After a two-hour back and forth, we settled at a six percent rate, closed out the card, and agreed to a plan that would pay the full amount over the next five years. The program we were enrolled in was known as a balance liquidation program.

Encouraged by the results, I tackled three more cards with a different company. We went through a similar process with a couple of different representatives. Again, I repeatedly told them our goal was to pay the amount owed in full. They asked us to continue to make the same payment, except that our interest rate would be zero percent. The entire amount was going to the principal and it would also be paid off in five years.

A key point to note in each case is that if you miss a payment, you agree to be bumped out of the program and your rates will be even higher than they were before. They also required automatic payments from our checking account.

I wish we could say we had a similar experience with American Express. At the time, they had a single program: one percent for three months, nine months at nine percent, and back to your original rate after that. Trying to negotiate anything else was a waste of time.

Every person's situation is different. Please also note that bank policies and programs are constantly changing depending upon the economic climate and other factors.

For us, a balance liquidation program has been a godsend, dropping our interest payments by $30,000 per year. To learn more about what your credit card provider may be able to do for you, search online for "credit card companies balance liquidation."

Unfortunately, if you have poor payment record, the balance liquidation option may not be available. Virtually all credit card companies can direct you to a credit card counseling organization. You could pursue the course my friend used. By the way, my friend's credit is back in the excellent range and she recently purchased a new home.

If you are stuck in high rates and have legitimate hardship, there are alternatives. Explore what is available and if you're still using those credit cards, do your best to transfer over to a prepaid credit card or debit card. The money you save will be substantial.

Self-ish Tip #8: Eleven fun ways to keep more of what you make

When we were struggling to stay afloat during the Great Recession, I remember having a major disagreement with Byron and heading off to the mall before saying something that I might later regret. I decided a good whodunit was what I needed to improve my mood, but the one I wanted to read was $32.95. Then it dawned on me—there's a library just a few doors down the street.

Much to my surprise the book I was about to pay for was on the shelf. The librarian also explained about being able to read books on my mobile device using Overdrive. I was thrilled because I could indulge my love of reading at zero cost. Again, persistence isn't about deprivation and pain—it's about making smarter decisions that support your long-term financial goals. Here are eleven other fun ways that I learned to cut costs while persisting in achieving my long-term financial goals.

1. **Shop in your closet**

   When your budget is tight, rather than going to the mall try shopping in your closet. Look for ways to combine different pieces and update your look with different accessories—a scarf, different jewelry, or perhaps one good jacket that pulls a number of other items together.

2. **Three-day holiday weekend discounts**

   I love shopping on three-day weekends. Search for online coupons for additional savings. One weekend I bought Byron ten name-brand golf shirts that retailed for $50.00 to $60.00 each for a total of just $78.00.

3. **Dining in rather than dining out**

   After we joined three other couples for dinner where the check came to $475 for the eight of us, the group decided to start our own dinner club. We usually meet monthly and each couple is responsible for bringing one or two dishes. We've done Thanksgiving in July, tried cooking different types of food from all over the world, and had an incredible amount of fun and terrific food for a fraction of the cost.

4. Dinner deals
If you're someone who absolutely must eat out, consider doing so during the week, preferably during happy hour if you like to drink. On weekends, have a leisurely breakfast or lunch instead of dinner. For example, one of the best restaurants in our area has a two-for-one breakfast every Saturday from 9:00-11:00. New restaurants offer great deals to have you try their food. Also, look for restaurants that serve large portions that make great leftovers the next night.

5. Moving? Consign first
When our house finally regained some equity, we decided to downsize. The challenge was that much of our furniture didn't fit, nor did a number of the decorating items. We have a very good local consignment store that has sold almost everything that we have consigned to them. For items they won't take, try eBay and Craigslist. Also, see if your area has a local online swap site where you can post your items. If you are giving to charity, the Salvation Army website posts the values that you can legitimately deduct at tax time.

6. Purchasing a new appliance?
Check your local utilities for rebates on energy efficient appliances. For example, when we had to replace our washer, we were able to reduce our water

consumption from 60 gallons to only 16 gallons of water per load. Best of all, we also got a hefty rebate.

7. **Watch for price reductions at warehouse department stores**
   If you don't belong to a warehouse club like Costco or Sam's, you are losing out on major savings. Look for items you normally buy and load up when the store offers deeper discounts. Note that seasonal items such as patio furniture and barbecues are cheaper at the end of summer than in spring. Also be sure to keep track of any items you purchase at the store or online. We saved $600 at Costco on a television for our new home. Two weeks later, the Costco newsletter showed they were offering the same TV for $200 less. I called them and they agreed to credit us the additional $200. The same thing happened on our patio furniture. By the way, both stores offer an extensive array of additional online items such as furniture, rugs, and appliances that are not available in the store.

8. **Factor upkeep into the total cost of ownership**
   The total cost of ownership is the cost of the item plus upkeep. For example, assume that you buy a $100 silk shirt on sale for $20.00. You have the shirt cleaned for $6.00 once per month. If you keep the shirt for three years, the cost of the shirt was $20.00 plus $216.00 in dry cleaning costs—the total cost of ownership was $226.00—not such a great deal after all.

9. **Reduce costs by buying top quality**
   My laser printer, my favorite carry-on bag, and my clothes dryer are literally old enough to vote and still going strong. Purchasing the best quality means you can go longer between having to replace items.

Cheap items often cost more in the long run because they must be replaced more frequently.

10. Online deals

Amazon, Overstock, Priceline—these and many other online companies offer significant savings on the items they sell. If you're traveling, bundling your airfare with hotel or a car can save you up to 50 percent over the price of booking those separately. Also note when various types of items go on sale. For example, airline prices normally drop right after the holidays and again in September after school starts. If you're a member of Amazon Prime, you also get free shipping.

Moreover, if the store where you are purchasing a product has an online store, always check the online price. Online prices are often much lower and the brick-and-mortar store will usually price match.

11. Can't afford it? Rent it

You may dream of owning a sailboat or driving a convertible with the top down—renting a sailboat or sports car for a day allows you to indulge your dream without incurring all the acquisition and maintenance costs.

When implementing any solution, try one step at a time rather than trying to change everything all at once. Especially when it comes to your finances, small steps taken over time can result in a significant improvement in your financial situation.

Self-Renewal: Become More Self-ish by Nourishing You

Self-renewal specifically refers to making a deliberate effort to restore, rebuild, or to re-energize your body, mind, and/or spirit. Again, if you don't nourish yourself first, your ability to take effective action can be severely hampered. Whether it is eating healthy foods, exercising, sleeping, meditating, or engaging in any other behavior that supports your well-being, self-renewal requires a deliberate choice. The challenge is finding time to engage in the activities that renew your energy and spirit when there are so many other things that you "should" do. Below you will find suggestions on how to strengthen your self-renewal in four important areas.

1. Physical self-renewal

You already know that getting enough sleep and engaging in moderate exercise such as walking, practicing yoga, dancing, swimming, and lifting weights are all ways to renew your physical energy. Many people have also found that eliminating alcohol, caffeine, sweets, drugs, or other types of food also increases their energy. Because everyone's body is different, experiment with various approaches until you find the two or three that work best for you.

2. Mental self-renewal

Mental self-renewal occurs when you take a break from your work, the computer, or the video games that you may be playing. Examples include listening to your favorite music, sleeping in, watching an old movie, attending a sporting event, solving puzzles, playing games such as chess, or any other activity that allows you to turn off your normal mental chatter and to sit back and unwind.

3. Spiritual self-renewal

Spiritual self-renewal can take various forms, whether it's attending your place of worship, meditating, or engaging in an activity that inspires you and fills you with a sense of awe. Many people find hiking in the woods, cross country skiing, or activities such as tai chi to be both physically and spiritually renewing.

4. Emotional self-renewal

There are thousands of ways to experience emotional self-renewal. It can be taking a long walk along the beach with a loved one or a quiet dinner at home after a hard week. A daily hug and an, "I love you" as you awaken each day are also emotionally renewing. Other emotional renewal activities include expressing gratitude to those around you, telling someone you haven't seen for some time how much he or she means to you, or spending time with a beloved pet.

Self-ish Tip #9: Four easy steps for building self-renewal in your life

1. For each of the four areas above, identify three activities that you find to be renewing (e.g., running, golf, reading a good book, gardening, etc.)

2. Add these activities to your schedule just as you would with a regular doctor or dental appointment.

3. Never miss these appointments unless it's an absolute emergency.

4. When other people make demands on your time, tell them you have another commitment. There's no need to explain is that your commitment is to take better care of yourself so that you can better care for the people who matter in your life.

What to Expect on the Road to Becoming Self-ish

When you start down this road of nourishing yourself, creating a health-focused lifestyle, and taking time for self-renewal, you may encounter resistance from both your friends and family. Here are some of the most common reactions you may face.

1. The psychic vampires in your life may call you selfish
The people who have counted on your generosity and selflessness may call you "selfish" when you no longer put their needs first. Don't be surprised if you feel angry when you recognize how they are trying to manipulate you to meet their selfish needs. Also, be wary of anyone who makes demands by telling you what you "should" do. Remember, "should" is used for manipulation. In many cases, these individuals may be the source of a number of

your challenges. When you stop yielding to their attempted manipulations, you eliminate them as a source of future problems.

2. Friends and family may try to sabotage your healthy, new behaviors

If you begin exercising and eating a better diet, your friends and family members who are not engaging in these activities may try to sabotage your new behavior. This creates a curious dynamic—do you let their resistance stop you from achieving your long-term goals or do you stay the course, even as they try to derail your efforts?

3. Long-time friends may disappear

One of my past business coaches observed that a successful client relationship could only occur when the coach was one step behind, even, or one step ahead of where the client was. If the gap is greater, the relationship will not work. The same is true as you upgrade your life. As you practice greater self-care and become more Self-ish, the people who don't change may drop out of your life. This has certainly been my experience. On the other hand, those who do remain and the new people who have shown up in my life have been nothing short of amazing. This new support system has made persisting in my self-care goals much easier.

4. You will feel happier, stronger, and more confident

As you increase your level of self-care and consistently engage in self-renewal, you will find that you feel stronger, are more confident, and will have more energy to pursue your goals while also helping others. You will also find that you are resisting less, and persisting more.

Did you eliminate the source?

When you find yourself facing a challenge, notice what happens as you take action. Did you resolve the challenge? If so, you eliminated the source. If not, you took action on a symptom. If the symptoms return, keep digging until you find where the real issue is. Sometimes this may require the help of a counselor, minister, therapist, or coach.

Also, be patient with this process. Trying to change too much at once can overwhelm you. Take it one step at a time and be consistent. That's the best way to create long-term, sustainable improvements in your life and to ultimately obtain your PERSIST goals.

Chapter 13: Key Points

1. Undoing the effect of any long-term behavior requires extended effort over time. The need for instant gratification often undermines people's efforts to persist in the long-term changes needed to make lasting improvements.

2. Symptoms will continue to occur until you eliminate the underlying source of the behavior you want to change.

3. To achieve long-term results, you don't necessarily have to eliminate a behavior. Instead, all you have to do is to make a different choice. For example, you can enjoy a favorite salad that has a lower calorie account instead of a different favorite with a much higher calorie count.

4. Be informed—read the nutrition information on products before buying them and choose items that you enjoy most that are also good choices nutritionally.

5. Make money your servant rather than your boss by knowing your numbers, tracking where your money goes, and allocating it to specific accounts.

6. If you can't pay for it in cash, do you really need it?

7. Balance liquidation programs can help qualified borrowers reduce their debt, sometimes for as little as zero percent interest.

8. Have fun keeping more of what you make by looking for creative ways to enjoy life while still keeping your costs down.

9. Schedule regular self-renewal time physically, mentally, spiritually, and emotionally.

Become More Internally Anchored

You cannot control what happens to you, but you can control your attitude toward what happens to you, and in that, you will be mastering change rather than allowing it to master you.
Brian Tracy

Chapter 14:
Take Control of Your Life

You can look for external sources of motivation and that can catalyze a change, but it won't sustain one. It has to be from an internal desire.
Jillian Michaels

Are you someone in charge of your own destiny or is fate or luck more important in terms of what happens in your life? The answer to that question has important ramifications for not only your ability to persist, but also for your long-term health. Julian Rotter coined the terms "internal locus of control" and "external locus of control" to describe these two dimensions of behavior. To determine whether your preferred style is more internal or external, answer the five questions below.

1. You're on a diet. You go to a movie with your friends who decide to get ice cream afterwards. Do you join them in ordering ice cream?

2. You are in a meeting and the leader asks for your opinion. Your opinion differs from those voiced by the rest of the group. Do you voice your opinion anyway?

3. You are given the responsibility to complete a project. Are you a self-starter who will complete the project on your own or does having your boss check your progress periodically make it easier for you to meet the deadline?

4. You share a secret about a co-worker with your closest friend at work who fails to keep the secret. The co-worker becomes very upset when he finds out. Do you blame yourself or do you blame your friend who didn't keep the secret?

5. Do you believe that people chart their own course in life or do luck and outside forces really determine what happens in most people's lives?

Scoring:
1. Sticking to your diet is internally anchored. Going along with the crowd and ordering ice cream is externally anchored.

2. Stating your opinion even when others disagree is internally anchored. Going along with the group opinion is externally anchored.

3. Self-starters tend to be internally anchored. Those who do better with deadlines and having a boss checking their progress are externally anchored.

4. If you blamed your friend for revealing the secret, you are externally anchored. If you took responsibility for not keeping the secret, you are internally anchored.

5. If you believe that you chart your own course in life, you are internally anchored. If you believe luck and outside forces determine what happens in your life, you are externally anchored.

If you have an internal locus of control, you feel that you are in charge of what happens to you. You may not be able to control events, but you can control how you respond to them. In contrast, if you have an external locus of control you believe that what happens to you is due primarily to luck or to forces beyond your control. Internal anchors make persisting in long-term, healthy goals easier. External anchors make achieving goals more difficult, especially when the person lacks a supportive environment. Nevertheless, as the story below illustrates, combining both styles often creates the best results.

Going Out on a Limb

When I first started teaching, I wanted to get to know the other faculty. The school was few years old and had a faculty of about 100. No one

Chapter 14: Take Control of Your Life

was running for Academic Senate Secretary so I volunteered for the position.

Two years later one of my good friends decided to run for Senate President. Because no one was interested in serving as Vice President, he asked me to volunteer. Several months later when the Senate didn't support him on a major issue, he decided to resign.

At age 26, I found myself President of the Academic Senate. My friend's parting words to me were, "Just remember, Ross, when these folks ask you to go out on a limb and tell you that they'll be there for you, they'll be there all right—sawing it off in back of you."

The college was about to hire a new President and the Academic Senate President would be the faculty's representative on the hiring committee. We had several great candidates, but the one from Illinois had stellar references and appeared to have done an extraordinary job at his current college.

It wasn't until after we hired him as President that we learned the truth. It was the Vice President at college in Illinois who was responsible for the college's achievements. In fact, the college in Illinois was delighted to see their past president leave.

Budgeting is one of the most critical jobs for any college administration. We were using zero-based-budgeting, which meant that you placed your budget items in priority order. The district would fund all the items above a specific cut-off mark. Anything below that line would not be funded.

The new president insisted on cutting key programs to fund his pet projects. He was unable to understand why we couldn't fund both sets of priorities. Cuts to those key programs not only would have delayed our students from earning their degrees, they could also threaten our accreditation.

I was stunned to discover that the seemingly omnipotent deans and administrators were too terrified to confront the issue. The president had the power to fire them or to bust them back to the classroom. Behind closed doors they encouraged me as faculty president to lead the charge. My friend's warning about the tree limb came to mind.

I examined my options. I had tenure and wasn't worried about being busted back to the classroom—it was where I wanted to be. I decided to pursue what I felt was in the best interest of the college. If I was out there alone, so be it.

What stopped the administrators was their belief they had no control. If they fought the president, the only possible outcome they could foresee would be loss of their jobs. This is a classic example of what happens when people are externally anchored, feel that they lack a support system, or that there are no viable options, i.e., they lack hope.

When the faculty learned the details about what was happening, they united in the effort to remove the president. The administrators cheered the effort in private.

If I had been a lone voice I would have been easy to ignore. After all, I was too young and too inexperienced to understand how things work.

As the faculty continued to clamor for action, the Chancellor contacted me to find out was happening. I explained the issues and provided him with concrete examples about how the college's programs were being jeopardized. After an investigation by the Board of Trustees, they voted to relieve the president of his duties and to assign him to a staff position elsewhere in the district.

Long-term meaningful change often means making a decision to take action even when those in your support system may disagree. These decisions are easier to make if you are internally anchored. If you are externally anchored, having a strong support system is critical. Nevertheless, the more internally anchored you can become, the easier it will be to cope with adversity and to achieve your goals. As this example illustrates, however, the best results occur when you have a strong internal motivation coupled with an external support system that backs your effort.

While it may be tempting to suggest one style should be preferred over the other, both styles have their strengths and weaknesses. Also, you may be internally anchored in some situations while being externally anchored in others. The key to success is discovering your style and then leveraging the strengths of your style while compensating for any weaknesses.

Internal vs. External Locus of Control: Key Differences

People often use the terms "spinning out of control" or "lack of self-control" to describe situations where they have little ability to influence outcomes. When the situation begins to improve, they often observe that they're "getting things under control" again.

Those who have an internal locus of control often believe:

- They are personally responsible for their choices and their actions.
- The choices they make are responsible for the outcomes they experience.
- Self-improvement is worthwhile because it helps them to be better prepared to handle life's events.

The downside of being internal is that these individuals may have a strong need to control the actions of others.

Those with an external locus of control often believe:

- They have little influence over what happens to them.
- What happens to them is due to luck and that life is unfair.
- Outside influences such as their family, social group, job, and peers have more control over them than their own choices have.
- They are not responsible for their successes and as a consequence they are more likely to be humble.
- Compliance and conformity are important. Because of that, they are often drawn to the fields of accounting, computer programming, the military, etc.

The downside of having an external locus of control can be poor health, lack of motivation, poor school performance, and possible neglect of their children due to their belief that fate is responsible for what happens to them rather than their actions.

Internal vs. External
Locus of Control: What the Research Says

Five decades of research on locus of control have proven one very important point: being internally anchored has huge benefits across the board. Fortunately, if you are externally anchored there are simple steps you can take to become more internally anchored. Combining the best of both internal and external styles can help you to achieve your goals more quickly. When you are driven by a powerful internal goal coupled with a strong, supportive external environment, you will feel more empowered to achieve your long-term PERSIST goals, no matter what those goals may be. Here is just a sampling from the many studies illustrating the power of being internally driven.

Your health
People who are internally anchored believe that their choices have a strong influence on their health. Externally anchored individuals often feel they have little control over their choices and because of that, they have little ability to change things. In other words, health just happens to them rather than being tied to their actions. The following studies illustrate this point.

- An internal locus of control coupled with self-esteem and optimism is associated with increased life expectancy, greater life satisfaction, increased alertness, and a slower rate of cognitive decline, especially in the elderly. These individuals also have lower cortisol levels, which is associated with less stress and better health. (Pruessner, et al. 2005)
- Women with an internal locus of control are less likely to experience postpartum depression. (Hayworth, et al. 1980)
- Diabetics who believe that health outcomes are controlled by chance (external locus of control) are at greater risk for health-related problems as compared with those who have an internal locus of control. (Peyrot and Rubin, 1994)
- In a seven-year study of 215 patients awaiting coronary artery bypass surgery, those with an external locus of control had poorer outcomes. (Rideout, et al. 2016)
- A study of 2,589 fifth and sixth grade students showed that those with an internal locus of control were less likely to use alcohol, marijuana, and cigarettes or to express an intention to use these substances. (Dielman, 1987)

Locus of control and cheating
- Physical punishment (an external control) retards the development of internal morality in children. Psychological forms of discipline, especially pointing out the consequences of one's actions for others, inscribe a learning pattern that results in internal control. (Eysenck, 1964)

- In terms of cheating, internals are more likely to follow an honor system while externals are more likely to cheat unless external monitoring is used to discourage deception. (Johnson and Gormly, 1971)

Locus of control at work
- Daft's (2005) research found that:
  ○ Job satisfaction is directly correlated with how well the employee's locus of control matches that of his or her boss. Internals do best with a boss who trusts their ability to complete tasks on their own and uses a participatory style.
  ○ Internals are more likely to assume or seek leadership opportunities. They handle complex information and problem solving more easily and are also more achievement-oriented than externals.
  ○ Externals do better with a boss who is directive. People with an external locus of control typically function better in structured, directed work situations. They are more able than internals to handle work that requires compliance and conformity, but they are generally not as effective in situations that require initiative, creativity, and independent action. For those with an external locus of control, directive leadership is best because it parallels their belief that outside forces control their circumstances.
- Locus of control separates good managers from bad managers. The reason is that internals are more likely to demonstrate helping behaviors, take steps to circumvent obstacles, and initiate actions to correct problems as they occur. They are also more likely to take personal responsibility for their successes and their failures. (Yukl, 2006)

Locus of control and coping with loss
- People with an external locus of control have smaller declines in life satisfaction the year they lose their spouse, as compared to those who are more internally based. Because externals typically don't take credit for their successes, they are less likely to feel responsible for any losses they experience. (Specht, et al. 2011)

Some of the most compelling research on the dangers of believing that you are at the mercy of externals comes from Martin Seligman's (1998) research on learned helplessness.

Learned Helplessness

Chapter 7 highlighted Martin Seligman's research showing that optimism has an extraordinarily powerful effect on longevity. Again, people who are optimistic are much more likely to be internally anchored and to feel that their actions influence what happens to them.

Seligman coined the term "learned helplessness" to describe what happens when an animal is exposed to an aversive stimulus it cannot escape. Eventually the animal stops trying to avoid the stimulus and will behave as if it is utterly helpless to change the situation.

A classic experiment demonstrating this concept involved cutting off the whiskers of rats in the experimental group; the rats in the control group did not have their whiskers cut. Rats rely on their whiskers to navigate.

Each rat was placed in a pool of water where they could not escape. The experiment measured how long the rats would swim before they gave up and would have drowned. The rats whose whiskers were cut (the experimental group) gave up much more quickly than the rats whose whiskers were not cut (the control group).

A second part of the experiment tested what would happen when the researcher picked up the rats in the experimental group just as they stopped swimming. When the researcher placed the rats back in the water, they swam for as long as the rats that had not had their whiskers cut. In other words, hope counteracts learned helplessness.

In humans, learned helplessness is a powerful predictor of death and serious illness. Learned helplessness occurs when people lose hope and are no longer willing to take actions in response to changes in their environment. As noted in the introduction, the death rate among people placed in a nursing home against their will is 50 percent during the first year. When people perceive that they no longer have control, the risk of experiencing a serious illness increases dramatically. Putting it a little differently, that cranky old controlling person in your life may be the best role model for living well into old age.

In fact, people who take steps to exert control in their environment, no matter how grim the situation is, fare much better than those who give up hope. Many of those who survived the Nazi concentration camps were able to exert control over their dire circumstances, however minimal that control was.

Internal Tip #1: It's your decision, not theirs

When you go to the doctor, hire a lawyer, or listen to someone who is an expert, it's easy to take what the person says at face value or to follow that person's recommendations, especially if you trust the person and are externally anchored. Below are three strategies to help you exercise more control in your life and to avoid the trap of learned helplessness.

1. When you speak to an expert, such as a doctor, pharmacist, or teacher, listen to what they have to say. At the same time, realize that you have final say about the actions you take based upon the information they give you. If something about what the expert says troubles you, seek out additional information before deciding on a specific course of action.

2. The next time someone asks you what you'd like to do, avoid saying, "I don't know," and give the person a specific answer instead.

3. No matter what happens to you, remember that while you may not be able to control the event, you can control how you respond to it.

Increase Your Control

If you are externally anchored, you will benefit from shifting your perception about your ability to control events. The two simple steps below will help you to recognize how much control you actually have in your life. These tips also work well for anyone who is experiencing a situation where they feel they lack control.

1. **Start by acknowledging where you already have control in your life**
   Every day you make hundreds of decisions over which you have control. For example, you control what time you get up in the morning, what you have for breakfast, what you wear, whether you exercise before work, how fast you drive, just to name a few. Simply becoming aware of what you do control is an important first step to becoming more internally anchored.

2. **Keep a choice journal**
   Making the shift from feeling that you lack control to feeling that you have control is a process. To strengthen your "control muscle," jot down five situations where you controlled a choice each day for the next month. For example, if you ordered food at a restaurant, write down the choice you made about the food and the beverage you ordered even if it was only water. It makes no difference if the choice you make is as trivial as deciding between wearing your sandals or tennis shoes or as serious as quitting your job.

   At the end of one month you will have a list of 150 deliberate choices that you have made. This list provides external validation of how much control you actually have. The next step is to expand your sense of control to the other areas of your life. You can do this by making a list of five opportunities where you will have to make choices tomorrow. This could include what time you will get up in the morning, what you will have for breakfast, lunch, and dinner, what you will do when you home from work, and what time you will go to bed. To get the best results from this activity, select choices that you have not used in the past. By becoming consciously aware of where opportunities to make choices exist, it becomes easier to recognize how much control you really do have.

Taking Personal Responsibility

Owning up to a mistake is never easy, yet internals are more likely to do so as compared to externals. The stumbling block for externals is accepting personal responsibility for the choices they make. If you believe what happens to you is due to luck or chance rather than due to your choices, you may see no need to be accountable for your actions. While the degree of control you can exert varies from situation to situation, you always have a choice—you just may not like the options that are available.

Become accountable for your choices
To better understand how being accountable for your choices works, picture two end points on a horizontal graph, with zero percent accountability on the far left side where you assume no responsibility for your actions and 100 percent accountability for your actions on the far right side where you assume complete accountability.

The next step is to recall a significant choice you made—it could be deciding to get married, to have children, or to change jobs. Now rank yourself on the graph as to how much control you believe that you had over the important choice you named above.

For example, if a couple uses birth control and still becomes pregnant, they still made the decision to engage in sex even if it wasn't their intention to create a pregnancy. On the other hand, a couple that is trying to become pregnant using in vitro fertilization may feel they have no control over the outcome. They do have control about continuing with the procedure, stopping the procedure and taking time off, deciding to accept that they may not be able to have a child, or pursuing adoption.

As you considered where to rank your level of responsibility on this scale for your choice, did your energy level go up or down based upon the number you selected? If your energy level dropped, you may be associating personal responsibility with fault or blame.

Marilyn Naylor (Naylor, Ross 1997) described this situation in the following way:

> *Many people frequently fight to avoid responsibility because they equate responsibility with fault or blame. When you accept responsibility, you have no need to point a finger and refuse blame for that which you are accountable. Blame and fault are twins that deny the choice you made. When you accept your accountability you have a clear mind and have no need to make excuses. Your choice is clear and you know why you made the choice. Once someone begins to justify or explain their choice, they begin to question whether or not they made the right choice. If it is the truth, it requires no explanation; if it is a lie, there is*

no explanation. Accept accountability and make your choices with thought and care.

Internal Tip #2: When you make a mistake, own it
No one is perfect. We all make mistakes, say things that we regret later, and create pain for our loved ones. An important lesson I learned from selling real estate was how to handle the situation where you were at fault for a problem in the transaction.

According to Clotaire Rapaille's (2006) research into American culture codes, Americans actually rank a company that makes a mistake more highly if the company corrects the mistake as opposed to getting everything right in the first place. Part of Costco and Nordstrom's success has been their willingness to correct any issues customers have with their products or their customer service. (Please note that based upon Clotaire Rapaille's work on culture codes, this is not the case for people from Germany, Japan, or Switzerland where "perfection" is part their culture code.)

Consequently, if you make a mistake, the following statement often works to move the situation forward: "It was never my intention to make you angry. What can I do to fix it?" According to Rapaille, Americans value "fixing it" above perfection.

This simple statement allows you to take responsibility without assigning blame or fault. You can't go back and undo your previous actions, but you can ask the person what you can do to fix the situation. Sometimes you will need to listen while the other party vents, but in virtually every case that I have experienced, this statement shifts the conversation from blame and excuses to searching for actions that can improve the outcome.

Creating a Supportive Environment

Actions always have an environmental context. For example, if you have set a production goal at work and your boss keeps piling on other tasks, it's not a lack of persistence or self-discipline that is blocking your success—it's your environment. Even if you are internally anchored, a supportive environment greatly enhances your ability to resist the easy choices and to maintain your momentum toward achieving your long-term PERSIST goals.

The cost of being in an unhealthy environment is profound. According to Robert Sapolsky (2007) of the Stanford School of Medicine, listening to someone who whines or gossips raises your cortisol levels. This makes your nervous system less efficient by slowing down communication at the synaptic level. It also increases the rate of cell death while simultaneously shrinking the hippocampus, the primary seat of learning. The result is that thinking, decision-making, and the ability to adapt are reduced dramatically.

The previous section on "Self-ish" identified how to nourish yourself including how to walk away from psychic vampires who fail to support your goals or who drain you of your time, energy, and optimism.

Turning now to the environment, a supportive environment has three key components—you, the people in your life, and the physical aspects of the environment itself. It is the interaction between these three components that will ultimately determine how easy or difficult it will be to achieve your goals.

To illustrate how this works, assume that you are training to run a marathon. If you have a strong internal locus of control, you will prepare to run the race regardless of whether the people and the environment are supportive or not. On the other hand, if you don't want to run the race, your peers can pressure you all they want—you won't be persuaded.

If you have a strong external locus of control, you will be much less likely to complete the race if the people around you fail to support you. On the other hand, if your peer group places strong pressure on you and creates an environment where everyone is training together, the likelihood of you running and finishing the race is high.

Again, optimal results occur when all three components—you, the people in your life, and the environment, are in total alignment.

Environment Is Stronger than Will

In most cases, making changes in your environment is easier than exercising your will power. For example, if you're dieting and your friends decide it's time to visit the colossal calorie hot doughnut food truck, it's easiest to avoid temptation by not going. Staying away from the doughnuts is an obvious choice. What's more insidious, however, are the words people use to describe everyday events.

Daniel Ariely (2009), the author of *Predictably Irrational*, has shown how simple negative comments can have a negative impact on behavior. To illustrate this point, Ariely conducted an experiment where he first measured how quickly students walked through a hall leading to the lab where the experiment was to be conducted. Once the subjects arrived in the lab, the control group saw a cartoon while the experimental group listened to several elderly people describing the difficulties they had walking. Ariely then measured how quickly the subjects walked through the hall as they left the lab. As compared to the control group that watched a cartoon, the students who heard the negative descriptions took longer to walk through the hall.

Masaru Emoto's (1994, 2004) work provides a vivid illustration of how human thoughts and intentions can alter physical reality. In one study, Emoto (1994) filled two jars with water. Elementary school students were then instructed that whenever they walked by one jar they were to tell the jar that it was bad. When they walked by the second jar, they were to tell the water it was beautiful. When the water from each jar was examined under an electron microscope, the water molecules in the "bad" water were ragged and ill formed. The molecules in the "good" water formed beautiful, well defined patterns.

In a second experiment, Emoto (2004) placed portions of cooked rice into two containers. On one container he wrote, "thank you," and on the other he wrote, "you fool." He then instructed school children to say the labels on the jars out loud every day when they passed by them. After 30 days, the rice in the container with positive thoughts had barely changed while the rice in the other jar was rotten and moldy.

Most people give little thought to how powerful their words can be. These three experiments illustrate how mistaken that belief actually is. They also highlight how important creating an optimal environment can be.

How to Build a Supportive Environment

Regardless of your locus of control, maintaining an optimistic view and a positive mindset can be challenging when you are immersed in an overwhelmingly negative environment. Unless you are completely off the grid, it's impossible to avoid the talk of war, terrorist attacks, and the endless stream of natural disasters. Here are some simple steps to follow to improve your environment both at work and at home.

1. **Surround yourself with like-minded people**
   Choose friends that fully support your goals as evidenced by their thoughts, comments, and actions. For example, if you are interested in losing weight and one friend keeps encouraging you to eat dessert, avoid eating meals with this person. This is one of the reasons that groups such as Weight Watchers and Alcoholics Anonymous (AA) are so successful—members find support from others who are going through the same experience.

2. **Clean and upgrade your existing environment**
   Start small, whether it's your bedroom, office, or even your car. If cleaning your office or your desk is too overwhelming, then clean at least one area where you can work. Next, commit to keeping this area clean. To experience the effect this has on your productivity, work in the clean area for an hour and then work in one of the chaotic areas for an hour. Normally there will be a substantial difference in your productivity.

3. **Eliminate the background noise**
   Many people believe that they are more effective in a busy, noisy environment. The research shows otherwise. Eliminating as many distractions as possible allows you to complete your tasks quickly and more accurately. As noted earlier, it may take "Mother" up to 20 minutes to regain total concentration after an interruption.

   This is especially true if you are working on the computer, studying, or doing some other mental task while listening to music that has lyrics. Your brain will focus on spoken words over written words. If you must listen to music while you work on mentally challenging tasks, choose songs without lyrics. This prevents the competition between your occipital lobes that process visual information and your temporal lobes that process auditory information. In this scenario, hearing always trumps reading. Remember, "Mother" can only process one bit of information at a time.

4. Turn off the negativity

Listening to negative comments from others can quickly destroy your positive attitude. Turn off the news, stop reading the paper, and run from those who always complain about how bad things are. If you can't escape a negative rant, you can ask, "Please tell me one thing that went right today." If the person says, "Nothing is going right," you can point out that they have their health, a roof over their head, clean water, good food, etc. If you catch yourself falling into being negative, stop immediately and identify at least three things that are right about your life.

5. Join a mastermind or a support group

An excellent way to upgrade your environment is to join a mastermind group or some other group of highly successful people that meet regularly to help grow their business. *Chicken Soup for the Soul* author Jack Canfield explains how he didn't start making lots of money until he changed his peer group. According to Canfield, if you take the average income of your ten closest friends and/or colleagues, you can accurately predict what your earnings will be. Upgrade your peer group and you will upgrade your income.

Internal Tip #3: Create an "energy efficient" home

Chances are that you own at least one energy efficient appliance. Have you ever given any thought to the energy that exists in your home? Like electricity, this energy is taken for granted until something goes wrong. Nevertheless, this energy influences how productive you are, how good you feel, and even how you interact with others. To make your home environment more supportive by being "energy efficient," follow these tips:

1. **Begin with awareness**

   The first step in increasing your home's "energy" efficiency is to discover how each primary area of your home makes you feel. Take at least 15 minutes to experience the energy in each area. Next, write down what you experienced, whether it's light, happy, relaxed, drowsy, depressed, etc. Use as many words or descriptions as needed to get a complete sense of the energy in each area.

2. Does the energy you noted match the room's purpose?

Does your primary living area energize you? Does your bedroom feel calm and relaxing? If you have an office, is it easy for you to work in or is it filled with distractions? To maximize the efficiency of your actions, match the energy in each area with the activity best suited to it.

For example, your bedroom is a place to feel calm and relaxed. Consequently, if you work on your laptop computer, pay bills, or do other types of work in your bedroom, you are now bringing in work energy that would be more appropriate in a different part of your home. This is especially important for students. If they must study in their bedroom, have them sit at a desk or any place other than their bed, even if it is on the floor. The reason is that each of us has been strongly conditioned to go to sleep when we go to bed. This conditioning is so strong that when a student reads a book in bed and starts to doze off, the book itself becomes a stimulus for sleeping.

3. Insulate

Everyone needs a place to escape. To whatever extent possible, establish your own private area in your home that is insulated from distractions, kids, or visitors. Even if you live in a tiny apartment with other people, you can still take a relaxing soak in the tub or stretch out on your bed, close your eyes, and listen to your favorite music or audio book. If you are an early bird, that time may be in the morning rather than at night. Having personal time to relax and unwind will help you to replenish your physical energy and to be better prepared to meet whatever challenges you face.

4. Stop cleaning up their messes

If you've been asking someone in your household to do something for over 30 days and it hasn't been done, it's an energy drain for you both. You have three options: you can continue to drain your energy by making a request that yields no result, you can clean up the problem yourself, or you can delegate the problem.

For example, some parents have found the following approach to be very useful when their teenager refuses to clean up their room. Instead of nagging the teenager to clean up or doing it themselves, the parents allow the mess to accumulate. When the room finally gets too bad, they tell their teenager that a cleaning crew will be coming in one week. The cleaning crew will be instructed to discard anything that is on the floor or not put away. The goal here is to shift the energy drain away from yourself while still holding your teenager accountable for the energy he or she creates. While this may sound harsh, you are actually giving your teenager a clear-cut choice that has very real consequences and that will help him or her to be more responsible in the long run.

5. Avoid conflicts in areas devoted to sleep and relaxation

If you have ever walked in on two people having an argument and it stopped when you entered the room, you know what it's like to feel tension in the air. While arguments can't always be avoided, avoid having them in your bedroom or kitchen where relaxing and nourishing energy is more appropriate.

6. Replace what is no longer energy efficient
Like an old electricity-guzzling refrigerator, there are certain aspects of your environment that will waste your valuable energy. If your garage, closets, or attic are packed with things you no longer use, these items drain your energy every time you think, "I need to clean the garage" or, "I wish I had more room in my closet." The reason people become overwhelmed by this task is that they believe they have to change the situation all at once. If you allocate just 30 minutes each week to cleanup, you'll be surprised by how quickly the task goes.

Self-Control vs. Controlling Others

Think of control as a continuum. On one end is chaos and total lack of control; on the other end is a total need to exert control over oneself and others. The balance point is where you have control over yourself without needing to control others. Many people are unable to distinguish between controlling their reactions to life's events (healthy) and attempting to control others (unhealthy).

When someone is strongly attached to the outcome of a situation, he or she may try to influence the outcome by controlling the action of others. The need to control others can set up a vicious cycle where the individual expects to be in control. When these expectations are not fulfilled, the individual experiences an even greater loss of control, which leads to escalating attempts to regain control. This only causes the situation to deteriorate faster, with anger and frustration as the result.

If you have a strong need to control others and would like to break this detrimental pattern, the best place to begin is by letting go of your attachment to results. This can be extremely challenging when you're accustomed to trying to control others as the following example illustrates.

"It was my fault"
Assume that your friend's husband is physically abusing her. You could step in and report the abuse to the authorities, but if she denies there is a problem, you have only made the situation worse.

My friend Marilyn Naylor (Ross, 2007) made an important observation based upon her years of work with women who had been abused. A large percentage of these women will say, "It's my fault—I made him do it." In my own work with women who have been abused, I was extremely surprised to observe the same phenomenon. Furthermore, when I asked, "If this is your fault, then who was in control?" The response? "I was." If these women truly believe that their actions are responsible for the outcome, are they the perpetrator rather than the victim? As disturbing as this notion is, it provides at least one explanation as to why breaking the pattern of abuse can be so difficult.

As much as we would like to end such horrific situations, please remember you are only responsible for your choices—not those of any one else. You can offer your assistance and advice, but I have found it's best to end by saying, "It's your choice. If and when you're ready to take action to change the situation, I'm happy to support your choice."

Letting go of how things should be allows you to focus on doing the best you can under the given circumstances. Again, while you cannot control the outcome, you can control how you react as you experience the situation. If you can honestly say that you did the best that you could at that moment in time, there is nothing to regret. Each event in your life offers the opportunity for you to learn something to help you meet future challenges. Take advantage of it.

Coping with What Can't Be Controlled

When discussing locus of control, there are some aspects of life that are beyond human control including the weather, natural disasters, your genetic makeup, etc. Nevertheless, you do control how you respond. For example, if you live in a flood-prone area, would you really want to buy a lake house that flooded in the past? If you live in an area where there are hurricanes, earthquakes, or brushfires, have you taken steps to be prepared for a major disaster by carrying the appropriate insurance, having a contingency plan if a disaster strikes, plus having sufficient food and water on hand if there is a serious disruption of services? Although these events are outside your control, you can choose to be as prepared as possible. Better yet, it's smart to avoid putting yourself in harm's way in the first place.

Using past successes to cope with current challenges
Self-development begins with observation or the nagging feeling that something just isn't right. To regain control in your life, begin by paying attention to that uneasy feeling that suggests there may be an issue that you need to address. This book has already provided you with a number of tools and strategies to work through challenges. The issue is spotting these situations earlier rather than later. A good analogy is weeds growing in a garden: the longer the weeds are allowed to grow, the harder it is to remove them. If you wait too long, the weeds go to seed. Instead of having to deal with a few weeds, you could end up contending with hundreds.

Internal Tip #4: How to strengthen your coping mechanisms
Foreseeing challenges and minimizing their effects will be easier if you leverage your strengths to cope with them. The best place to begin is by identifying what is and is not working for out.

1. **Where do you draw the line on control?**
   In order to identify your personal coping strengths, list three decisions where you successfully coped with a difficult situation. For each situation write down at least one coping skill you utilized that influenced the final outcome of that situation. For example, you may have been assigned a difficult problem at work and you coped with it by doing extensive research on your own and seeking help from a professor friend who is an expert in the area.

   Next, list three additional situations where you were unable to control the outcome. Record any unrealistic expectations that you had about the situation including what made those expectations unrealistic.

   For the three situations where you exercised control, what elements did they have in common? By the same token, what did those three situations where you lacked control have in common?

>   Finally, record the outcome including what you experienced before, during, and after each of the six events. Your goal is to identify a framework of what works and what does not work. It's also important to recognize the warning signals about what you really cannot control so that you can focus your efforts on what you can control.
>
>   Consequently, the next time you encounter a problem, review the strategies that have worked in the past and determine if any of these strategies would be useful in coping with your present challenge. Employing approaches that have been successful in the past can be an excellent starting place for overcoming any new challenges that you may face.
>
> **2. Baby steps increase your sense of control**
>   It's common for a major life challenge to overwhelm you so completely that you are unable to take any type of action. When this happens, identify one simple step that you could take, no matter how small it may be. This simple first step boosts your self-confidence while also restoring your sense of being in control. If possible, handle a small aspect of something important rather than handling something easy but unimportant.

Ultimately, how you exercise control is your choice. Exercising control over your responses promotes your health and well-being. Giving up hope, being paralyzed by overwhelm, or trying to exercise control of others undermines your health, happiness, and your ability to function effectively.

Chapter 14: Key Points

1. Those with an internal locus of control feel that they are in charge of what happens to them. Even if they cannot control an event, they believe they can control how they respond to it.

2. Those with an external locus of control believe that what happens to them is primarily due to luck or to forces beyond their control.

3. Five decades of locus of control research has consistently shown that having an internal locus of control is correlated with increased self-esteem, better health, less cheating, and increased effectiveness in leadership positions. Those with an external locus of control are more likely to have poor health, lower self-esteem, and to work best in positions that require compliance and conformity.

4. Learned helplessness is a powerful predictor of death and serious illness, but hope counteracts it.

5. To become more internally anchored:
   - Recognize what you can and cannot control by keeping a choice journal.
   - When you speak to a doctor, pharmacist, or teacher, listen to what they say and remind yourself that you are in charge of the actions you take.
   - The next time someone asks you what you'd like to do, avoid saying, "I don't know." Give the person a specific answer instead.
   - When you make a mistake, own it.
   - Be aware of the power of negative comments. Thrive by surrounding yourself with happy, optimistic, successful people.
   - Create an energy-efficient home by matching the energy in each area with the activity best suited for it.
   - When you are feeling overwhelmed, baby steps work best. That baby step requires a choice and an action, which helps you to restore your sense of control.

Serve

*The highest destiny of the individual is
to serve rather than to rule.*
Albert Einstein

Chapter 15:
Give the Gift that Gives Back

*Help others achieve their dreams
and you will achieve yours.*
Les Brown

Several years ago I interviewed Frank McKinney, one of the world's most successful custom homebuilders. McKinney's homes are fully furnished masterpieces with unique features such as a James Bond room, shark aquarium, and even 18-karat gold toothbrushes. At a $1,000 per square foot, no detail is overlooked. He is also the builder of the "greenest mansion" in America.

McKinney's website describes his marketing events as, "legendary, professionally choreographed symphonies of the senses." For his "Pirates of the Caribbean" event, he arrived in a hot-air balloon dressed as a pirate, accompanied by a massive fireworks display. Given his flair for building and the dramatic, his business model may surprise you.

The mantra that McKinney lives by comes from Luke 12:48: "To whom much is entrusted, much is expected." This biblical passage is the foundation for both McKinney's business and personal life:

> *I build houses for the world's most wealthy to fund houses for the world's most desperately poor. The homes I build at $1,000 dollars per square foot contain the finest quality, artistry, and unique features in the world. In Haiti, the most desperately poor, distressed property market in the world, I build concrete and steel houses for $10.00 per foot to house 8 people who are currently living in a mud hut or a cardboard box.*

To date, McKinney has built over 10,000 houses in 23 self-sufficient villages. One of his most recent projects is the Doug Doebler Village that will contain 40 concrete and steel homes to house a total of 400-500 children and their families, plus a large school/church/community center, 20 concrete and steel latrines, water well, water filters, solar light, and hundreds of goats and chickens. According to McKinney, "That legacy will outlive any oceanfront home that I build."

Service Tip #1: Create your own opportunity
McKinney believes that "you create your own opportunity." Here are the steps he recommends that you follow to create your own opportunity by being of service.

1. **Develop your personal "Three T's: time, talent, and treasure"**
   McKinney argues that each person has a unique combination of the "Three T's: time, talent, and treasure." When you first start out on this path, you may not have talent or treasure, but you can volunteer your time to help others as you grow your talent. The development of your talent leads to your treasure.

2. **Mindset matters**
   McKinney explains that if you want to make money in your business, your mindset must be right. Creating the right mindset requires you to address three different issues: motivation, inspiration, and aspiration. Aspiration is a goal or objective that is strongly desired. As McKinney observes, "Motivation washes off in the shower, inspiration fades like the effects of a sunburn, but aspiration can alter your DNA and forever change your life and the lives of those you love."

   Have you ever attended a seminar where you bought books and products, or signed up for a multi-level marketing product and then did nothing with what you purchased? You probably felt motivated or inspired, but these factors are external. As noted in the previous chapter, you need the internal self-starting energy that McKinney calls "aspiration."

   He goes on to say, "Snake oil salesmen sell on the intoxication of motivation and inspiration. When the intoxication stage wears off, motivation and inspiration fade away quickly. The result is nothing happens."

3. Become an "executioner"
What does it take to become someone who actually takes action and achieves results? McKinney calls this being an "executioner." Action arises from aspiration, which is internally driven. It allows you to push through the drudgery stage and to keep moving to complete your goals, even as you encounter fear and risk along the way. Being an executioner means that you are able to take focused action to relentlessly pursue to completion every important endeavor you undertake.

4. Overcoming what stops you: fear, risk, change, and challenge
Aspiration keeps you going when you encounter the fear that is normally associated with risk taking. McKinney says that he is "afraid everyday—my fear runs rampant." Nevertheless, his commitment to his work allows him to create the amazing properties he builds, which, in turn allow him to invest in his legacy of creating sustainable villages for the world's most impoverished people.

As McKinney urges, if you haven't found your aspiration, begin by considering how you can serve others. It's devotion to serving others that leads to long-term success and to a meaningful life. It also increases your ability to resist selfishness while supporting you to consistently engage in long-term, persistent service to others.

Self-Serving vs. Service vs. Selfless

If you had no knowledge of Frank McKinney's charitable work, it would be easy to assume that his motivation for building $50-$100 million houses was to grow rich and to derive the benefits associated with an ultra-luxury lifestyle. It's abundantly clear that McKinney uses his talent to serve others rather than for his self-aggrandizement. This raises the issue of what it means to serve or to be of service to others.

To gain a better understanding about how this process works, imagine a continuum with "self-serving" at the far left, "being of service" as the middle point, and "selfless" at the right end of the continuum. Here's how the dictionary defines these three terms:

1. *Self-serving:* being preoccupied with one's own selfish interests, often disregarding the truth, the interests, and the well-being of others.

2. *Being of service:* to be useful or helpful to others.

3. *Selfless:* having little or no concern for oneself, especially with regard to fame, position, or money—unselfish.

Millions of people contribute to charities every year. For those who are self-serving, their motivation may be more about the power, status, or lining their own pockets. In fact, there are some charities where less than ten percent of donated funds reach the people who were to benefit from donor contributions.

At the opposite end of the continuum are those who are "selfless." For example, a real estate agent we know was spending half of her time helping other agents in her office while her company searched for a new manager. Her business was down, she was missing precious time with her family, and she wasn't even being paid.

Being "of service" exists somewhere between being self-serving and selfless. The question is where do you draw the line between nourishing yourself as opposed to being selfish and disregarding others?

Service Tip #2: Money better spent
Several years ago another business coach shared an interesting story about one of his clients. The real estate agent was paying over $500 per month to an online lead generation company but the program wasn't working. The agent decided to terminate the service and to donate the money to a local food bank. He and his daughter also decided to volunteer there on Saturdays. Their special Saturday time together deepened their relationship. What the agent didn't anticipate was a 15 percent increase in his business. As noted in the discussion regarding attraction, when you give to others it comes back in ways you may never have anticipated.

Eliminate "Help"

When most people think of service, they think of someone helping others by volunteering, raising money, or working in the service professions such as psychology, law enforcement, nursing, etc. Few people, however, pay attention to the other side of the equation—receiving service from someone else.

For over two decades I have asked those who want to become psychologists, business/personal coaches, or real estate agents about their motivation for choosing this type of work. Common "helping" responses include:

- "I want to help people who suffer from depression."
- "I want to help people to have a better business and a better life."
- "I love looking at houses and I enjoy helping people."

Whenever someone begins to explain their choice using the words "I want to help," I flinch. I never gave much thought to this reaction until I began writing this chapter. While helping others is laudable, there's an interesting distinction between helping behavior that is focused on others and helping behavior that is self-serving.

Healthy vs. unhealthy helping

To better understand this distinction, consider these two statements:

"I work with women who have been sexually abused."

"I want to help women who have been sexually abused."

This is subtle, but in the second sentence the words, "I want," indicate that the person is self-focused rather than other-focused. Sadly, this situation is extremely common. When someone is focused on fulfilling their need to help others rather than focusing on what the other person needs first, a dysfunctional relationship often results. This is especially true when the person providing the help has a strong need to control others.

Service Tip #3: When to use "I" vs. "you" language
When you begin a sentence with "I want," the focus is on you rather than on the person who needs help. For those who work in the helping and sales professions, keeping your focus on the other party is critical. To do this, remove the word "I" from your conversations and substitute the word "you" instead. Using an example from real estate:

- *I think your house should be listed at $200,000.*
- *Where would you like to position your house in the marketplace?*

The first sentence sets up the agent as the expert who tells the seller what to do. The second sentence turns the power over to the sellers. After all, it's their house, it's their mortgage, and it's their decision.

In personal situations, it's important to use "I" language if you are having a disagreement with a friend, colleague, or loved one. Using "you" may come across as an accusation and can cause matters to escalate. For example,

You're always late and you never even bothered to text or call. You have absolutely no consideration for my feelings!

> *I'm no longer willing to wait in a restaurant by myself. In the future, I will wait no more than 15 minutes and then leave.*
>
> The first sentence casts the speaker as a victim. The second approach allows the speaker to take control of the situation. It also gives the other person a clear-cut choice about the consequences if he or she is late in the future.

Ask "How" and "What" Questions

As you set out to help others, ask what is wanted and needed. As good as your solution may be to a challenge the other person is facing, it's still your solution. A better approach is to ask "how" and "what" questions to uncover the solution best suited for the person who is receiving your help. In fact, it's smart to ask whether the other person is interested in hearing any additional input or if your input would only make their decision-making process more difficult.

For example, assume that a friend's company is moving out of state. Your friend is in charge of caring for her elderly mother and she also has two children in high school. Moving would be highly disruptive for the entire family. On the other hand, she loves her job, will probably be promoted to a senior position with the move, and the homes are less expensive in the new area, so she could put more money toward her kids' college education and her retirement.

As you listen to her describing this scenario, you may feel tempted to jump in and tell her what you would do. A better approach is to ask questions. For example:

- *You have quite a few important points to consider as you make this decision. What are the three factors that you would rate as being most important in terms of what you decide?*
- *When you have faced a conflict between your work and your personal life in the past, how did you go about making the decision to resolve the situation?*

If you want to share your solution without forcing it on the other person, here's what to say:

- *When I have faced a tough decision like the one you're facing, I've found it helpful to write down all my options, rank each option, and then make the decision.*
- *My brother faced a similar situation a couple of years ago. He listed the advantages and disadvantages of each choice and then asked his family about how they felt about each choice. His family agreed to stay put. There's no way to know what your family will decide until you sort through the various options.*

Recognizing When Helping Behavior Isn't Helping

Sometimes the very people we turn to for help are not in a place to help us. Byron has a simple test that he recommends for anyone interviewing a personal or a business coach. To determine whether the coach is a good fit, ask yourself, "Do you feel more energized at the end of the interview than you did at the beginning?" If so, you have probably found the right coach for you. If not, keep searching.

This same test applies to a wide variety of situations in your life, whether it's choosing a doctor, therapist, or which friends to rely upon when you face a crisis. If you feel better after working with that person, chances are that you two are a good fit. On the other hand, if you feel drained, you may be in the presence of a psychic vampire. Furthermore, if your gut tells you something is off, listen to it. It's better to spend more time searching for someone who is a good fit than to select someone who may make matters worse.

Red flags

It's one thing when someone is not a good fit for you. It's a much more serious issue when the person helping you is using you to cope with their own issues. Understanding Sigmund Freud's theory of psychological defense mechanisms can help you to circumvent those individuals who may be using you to work out their issues rather than yours.

Freud believed that anxiety could produce emotional defense mechanisms, most of which operate on an unconscious level. These result due to a conflict between the id (instinctual needs and drives) and the superego (the conscience, which adheres to social standards imposed by others). This conflict plays out in the ego, which mediates between these two forces. According to Freud, defense mechanisms are the ego's attempt to resolve these conflicts. Two of Freud's defense mechanisms are particularly useful when it comes to explaining helping behavior that really isn't helping.

1. Projection

Projection refers to attributing one's own unacceptable feelings to someone else. A classic example is the obese physician who harshly criticizes a diabetic patient for failing to lose weight. In other words, the doctor is attacking the patient for the very behaviors in which he is engaging. Another example is the husband who is cheating and who accuses his wife of cheating on him. If you find yourself working with a doctor, therapist, or other professional whom you believe is projecting their feelings and issues on you, seek assistance elsewhere.

In contrast, working with someone who has successfully coped with the challenges you are facing provides you with hope for success as well as a role model to follow. This is one of the reasons why organizations like Alcoholics Anonymous are so successful. Active members are coping with their addiction while also helping others to manage the same challenges they face daily. This means that even when a group member suffers a setback, other group members are still there to support that individual. A personal support network can play a major role in helping you to face a devastating crisis or to overcome a difficult life challenge.

2. Reaction formation

According to Freud, *reaction formation* occurs when the person's id has a strong desire to engage in a behavior that the superego finds to be abhorrent. In many cases, this shows up as an obsessive opposite behavior to which Freud claims their id is drawn. Examples include a drug addict who campaigns for strict punishment of all substance abusers or a person who has strong homosexual desires who rails against homosexuality.

Again, if the person you have turned to for support tries to force their solution on you, go elsewhere. The goal is for you to find the solution that will work best for you. The only person who can make that choice is you. There is one caveat however: denial.

3. Denial

Denial is the refusal to accept reality or fact. It is also acting as if a painful event, thought, or feeling did not exist. For example, if someone's family, friends, and the people they work with are voicing concerns about the person's drinking, that person is probably in denial about how serious their drinking behavior has become. Even in the face of being arrested for drunken driving or being hospitalized for alcohol poisoning, it's common for alcoholics to deny that they have a problem. In many cases, the individual is using alcohol to self-medicate for an underlying medical problem such as bipolar depression. Until the source of the issue is discovered and treated, changing the behavior is extremely difficult.

The same is true with using drugs or any other self-destructive behavior. If a number of people in your life are voicing concerns about your behaviors, it may be time to visit a health care professional for an objective assessment. Also, please give the person you see the straight facts about your behavior—not the edited version that may be supporting your denial.

Build Your Karmic Bank Account

If you believe in karma (what goes around comes around) or the law of attraction, the concept of building a karmic bank account will come easily to you. If you are skeptical about these beliefs, a different way to approach building a karmic bank account is to focus on the benefits that come from laughing with another person, sharing a fun memory, or delighting a child with a story. The more you add to your karmic bank account, the more emotionally resilient you will be. This in turn supports your persistence, good health, and well-being.

When most people think of service, they think of volunteering or giving money to a charity. There are thousands of other ways to be of service that sometimes go unnoticed, especially by the person who is being of service. For example, are you the person who always cleans up after a meeting? Did you volunteer to take a sick friend to the doctor? Are you the neighbor who happily helps the elderly woman down the street with the smoke detectors and other little repairs at her house?

Chapter 15: Give the Gift that Gives Back

You probably didn't even give these acts much thought because they're just simply part of who you are.

On the other hand, anger, adrenaline, and toxic people can drain this account. Your goal is to add as many positive experiences to this account as possible and to minimize what empties it. Here are some proven ways to be of service that you may have never considered before.

1. Smile

When you smile, your body releases beta-endorphins, dopamine, and serotonin—the brain's feel good neurotransmitters. Smiling also activates the release of neuropeptides that fight stress, lower blood pressure, and make you feel more relaxed. People who smile are considered to be more personable, trustworthy, and attractive to others, which also makes them more approachable. Smiling boosts your mood, makes you feel better, and contributes to better health.

In a Swedish study (Sonnby-Borgström, 2002) subjects were shown pictures of someone who was smiling. The researchers then asked the subjects to frown. It took a conscious effort for them to do so. In other words, smiling is so contagious that it's hard for people not to return your smile.

To increase your smiling behavior, smile back at anyone who makes eye contact with you. If appropriate, you can also say, "Good morning" or, "beautiful day today." Tell the parents of a new baby how beautiful their baby is. Whether you're standing in line at the grocery store, being served food in a restaurant, or riding up an elevator with your co-workers, instead of looking down at your phone, look up and smile at people around you.

When you smile at someone and they smile back, you have just given them all the benefits that you obtain from smiling. Flashing a smile is one of the easiest and most beneficial ways to be of service.

2. Laugh

While smiling has tremendous benefits, laughter has even more. Laughter can reduce stress, anxiety, and depression, strengthen your immune system, and diminish pain. A good, hearty laugh also relieves physical tension and stress. Dr. Paul Pearsall's (1999) work has shown that 100 deep belly laughs per day can ward off both cancer and heart disease. This results partially because laughter increases blood flow, T-cells, and infection-fighting antibodies, all of which help to strengthen your cardiovascular health and immune system. As an additional benefit, laughing 10-15 minutes per day burns about 40 calories—that's good for a 4.17-pound weight loss over a one-year period.

Laughter strengthens relationships, enhances teamwork, promotes group cohesiveness, and can defuse conflict. Furthermore, humor is a powerful way to heal resentments, disagreements, and hurts while also increasing your emotional resilience. All these benefits add up to increased longevity.

Service Tip #4: Seek opportunities to laugh

Both smiling and laughter are contagious. If you want to laugh more, here are some suggestions:

- Spend time with family and friends—more laughter comes from reminiscing with loved ones than from listening to jokes.
- Keep track of funny events or pictures that you come across and share them by text, email, or on your favorite social media sites.
- Surround yourself with people who like to laugh.
- If you're in a group setting, gravitate to where the laughter is.
- Go to a comedy club or spend time with those who like to make others laugh—every comedian appreciates an audience.
- Watch funny YouTube videos.
- Learn to laugh at yourself. Some of our most embarrassing moments make for a laughter-filled story at a later date. When you laugh at yourself, others laugh with you rather than at you.
- Subscribe to any of the joke sites that deliver daily jokes directly to your email.
- Read a comic strip.

- Share a funny story.
- Spend time being silly with your kids, grandkids, or fun-loving friends.
- Sing your heart out on karaoke night.
- Go bowling or play miniature golf.

Like smiling, laughter is a seldom-recognized gift of service that each of us can engage in daily. Give generously.

3. Express gratitude
Whenever you have an opportunity to do so, smile and express gratitude to another person. It can be thanking the person who packs your groceries or who clears your table at a restaurant, acknowledging a co-worker for how hard they work, or any one of a thousand other opportunities. Every one of these actions builds your karmic bank account and it costs you nothing more than a smile and a few kind words. You never know the impact that your smile and gratitude can have on someone who is having a difficult day.

I experienced one of those moments at my father's funeral when my cousin Winston, who had been a minister for 50 years, shared a story I had never heard about my father. When Winston was six years old he almost died from pneumonia. He was so weak that he couldn't walk to school. For six months, my dad carried Winston on his back three miles each way to school, through the ice, rain, and mud. Winston then went on to explain that whenever he had too big of a load to carry he remembered my dad carrying him on his back and then dipped down into his heart to find the strength to carry on.

The gift of that story helped me navigate through one of the most difficult days of my life. More importantly, it reminded me of the importance of being there for others when they face difficult times. Winston paid forward my father's gift at the exact moment I needed it most.

4. Listen to and hear what others have to say
For two decades I have incorporated the Native American Talking Circle into many of my classes, seminars, and conferences.

Various versions of the circle exist in native cultures across the world. These circles allow everyone to voice their opinion and to walk away knowing that their voice has been heard. When people feel they are not heard, anger and harmful behavior often result.

The way the circle works is that you can only speak when you are holding the "talking stick." (This can be a feather or just about any item that you select.) When you have the talking stick you can share your perspective, but you are not to comment on or reference anything that others have said.

I ask those who are listening to look at the person who is speaking without commenting or moving their head to agree or disagree. Also, what is shared in the circle stays in the circle. Each individual can share what he or she said, but not what anyone else said. The talking stick is always passed clockwise, honoring the forward progression of the sun through the day and the seasons.

The level of trust and intimacy created within these circles is profound. When I conducted these with my Psychology 1 classes, almost every one of the students said it was the first time that they felt that someone had really listened to and heard their concerns. Many said they felt closer to the people in their circle than they did to their closest friends. More importantly, I've seen people share some of their most challenging situations for the first time because of the safety they felt within the circle.

Talking circles work equally well in a corporate setting. One company hired me to address an outright revolt against their new CEO. I came in armed with power points and my feathers (talking sticks). The looks in the room told me that quite a few people in the room thought what I was asking them to do was beyond stupid. At the end of the day, however, the circle had worked its magic and the revolt was averted. Again, when people feel they are heard, even if the group decides to go in a different direction from what a specific person wants, it's much easier for everyone to accept. It also strengthens the bonds within the group because people who have participated in a circle consistently report having greater feelings of trust with those in the group.

5. Give the gift of your undivided attention

Children don't need fancy toys and expensive games to keep them happily occupied. I watched a friend play make-believe with a couple of four-year-old girls. The imaginary game began with each girl selecting an animal they wanted to buy as a pet. They then went to the library to check out a book about the animal. After they read their book, they had to return the book to the library on time. Next, they went to the pet store to "buy" the animal and to get all the supplies their pet would need. Once they had picked out their pet, they had to name it. When the animal got sick, they had to take it to veterinarian. The game went on for quite some time with each girl happily giggling as she shared her imaginary experience. I wouldn't be surprised that they will play the same game when they have children.

Service Tip #5: The attention game
Interested in learning how your undivided attention can positively impact someone else's life? If so, try this game as an experiment for the next week.

Each day when you get up, identify at least one person who could benefit from having your undivided attention. It could be one of your children, a colleague at work, or perhaps an elderly friend or relative who is lonely. Spend at least 20 minutes with that person with absolutely no outside interruptions.

At the end of the week, check two things: First, how did you feel about yourself at the end of doing this for five days? Second, were you surprised when someone did something unexpected and nice for you? Play the game for a week and see what comes up for you!

Giving and Receiving

The Law of Attraction says that giving to others results in others giving back to you. Again, the person that you help is generally not the person who will help you. *The Go-Giver* by Bob Burg and John David Mann (2015) illustrates how this process works. In a beautifully told parable, the authors not only illustrate how attraction works, but they also show how to remove the blocks that are holding you back. The jacket of *The Go-Giver* begins with a quotation:

> *Most people just laugh when they hear that the secret to success is giving. Then again, most people are nowhere near as successful as they wish they were…Giving is the secret to success.*

The authors have generously granted me permission to share their "Five Laws of Stratospheric Success," which are really a primer on how to serve others.

1. **The Law of Value:** *Your true worth is determined by how much more you give in value than you take in payment.*
   Many people confuse value with price. Price refers to the cost of purchase. In contrast, value includes the cost plus a wide variety of other factors. For example, if your accountant charges you $500 for preparing your tax return and saves you $2,000, your accountant made a profit and still gave you more in value than what you paid. He or she saved you the time required to prepare the return, the tedium of checking the tax laws, plus knowing that you have an advocate should you face an audit. A key point to recognize is that, "All things being equal, people will do business with and refer business to those people they know, like, and trust."

2. **The Law of Compensation:** *Your income is determined by how many people you serve and how well you serve them.*
   People often ask why teachers are not compensated as well as actors, athletes, and CEOs. The Law of Compensation says that your compensation is directly proportional to how many lives you touch. It's not just your value; it's a question of impact. There are no limitations on what you can earn because there are always more people that you can find to serve. The value you provide is your potential for earning. The number of people you serve determines how well you will be compensated. Look for ways to serve others, whether it's your family, your friends, your clients, or people you don't even know.

3. **The Law of Influence:** *Your influence is determined by how abundantly you place other people's interests first.*
   Whether it's business or personal, the most important type of network to have is a group of people who know you, like you, and trust you and who are also invested in seeing you succeed. The way to create this type of network is to focus on creating "win-win" situations. In other words, look out for the other guy and keep your focus on the other person's win. When you place the interests of others first, your needs will always be taken care of. If you have ever wondered what makes people truly attractive, what makes them magnetic, it's because they love to give. Givers attract.

4. **The Law of Authenticity:** *The most valuable gift you have to offer is yourself.*
   Both personally and in business, when you take the time to help another person or to spend time with a lonely friend or loved one face-to-face, that action is often one of the meaningful things that you can do for that individual.

5. **The Law of Receptivity:** *The key to effective giving is to stay open to receiving.*
   One of Mann's clients once said that Laws 1-4 were like smooth, polished wood. Law #5, however, gave him splinters. The point of the Law of Receptivity is that you must give without emotional attachment. When you eliminate attachment you are more open to receiving with abundance.

When I interviewed Bob Burg, he told me he had once commented about how nice his bookkeeper's pen was. She offered to give it to him. When he told her he would be happy to go out and buy one, she offered again. He declined again. She then looked at him and said, "Take the pen and say thank you."

The key to giving is being open to receiving. All the giving in the world won't bring success or create the results you want, unless you also make yourself willing and able to receive in like measure. If you don't let yourself receive, you're refusing the gifts of others and you shut down the flow.

For me, this last Law was a huge "aha." Giving works in tandem with receiving. If you want to achieve a level of personal satisfaction and success unlike anything that you have experienced ever before, you must be willing to give (serve) and receive.

No matter how hard you persist, no matter how dedicated you are to a meaningful cause, there are times when certain paths are simply not open to you. The final step in the PERSIST model is "Timing." The next chapter addresses how to make best choices in terms of how you use your time, how to recognize when the timing isn't right, and how to recognize when it is time to stop persisting and to change directions.

Chapter 15: Key Points

1. To create your own opportunity, develop your personal "Three T's: time, talent, and treasure" and focus on your aspiration rather than on motivation or inspiration.

2. Eliminate "help" and seek to be of service rather than being self-serving or selfless.

3. Use "you" language rather than "I" language to describe helping others. Use "I" language if you have a disagreement with a friend or loved one.

4. Ask "how" and "what" questions and avoid asking, "Why?" which puts the other person on the defensive.

5. Avoid recommending what someone else should do—instead share what worked for you in the past.

6. When it comes to choosing service professionals, red flags to look for include that you feel drained after working with them or the person is actually working out their issues through you.

7. Build your karmic bank account with smiles, laughter, gratitude, and the willingness to listen to others and to really hear them.

8. The key to giving is to be open to receiving.

Time It Right

Life is all about timing...the unreachable becomes reachable, the unavailable becomes availablethe unattainable...attainable. Have patience, wait it out. It's all about timing.
Stacey Charter

Chapter 16:
Timing Is Everything

*I learned that we can do anything, but we
can't do everything...at least not at the same time.
So think of your priorities not in terms of what
activities you do, but when you do them.
Timing is everything.*
Dan Millman

The final part of the PERSIST model is timing. Timing encompasses the choices you make about how you use your time, whether the timing is right for a particular opportunity, and how long to persist before a course correction is needed.

Chapter 5 outlined a number of ways to maximize how you spend your time, including avoiding multitasking, focusing on your strengths, and applying the Pareto principle (the 80-20 rule). What is more difficult is deciding which opportunities are the best choices and, if you are not succeeding, how long do you persist before you change direction or stop persisting entirely?

When Missing the Opportunity IS the Opportunity

Two days after my seventeenth birthday my dad was hospitalized for a gall bladder attack. The doctors failed to diagnose it quickly enough and gangrene had set in. The day after his surgery he contracted pneumonia, which led to congestive heart failure. He also tore open his incision from the coughing. Because his kidneys were failing, they could only stitch him up externally rather than repairing the internal damage. For six weeks we were told that he wouldn't make it through the night. When my father was released, the doctors told me that he was the sickest man they had ever seen walk out of a hospital.

After my dad came home, I told him about my plans to major in psychology. He and my mother were adamant: "We don't want you to become one of those people!"

Instead, my father was convinced that I should major in English and learn how to write. English had little appeal to me and my writing was mediocre at best. Given the circumstances regarding his health, I reluctantly agreed.

While fulfilling the requirements for my B.A. and M.A. in English, I found a work-around—I filled every one of my electives with psychology courses. My ultimate goal was to teach. If I was lucky enough to find a job, it looked as if I would be teaching English composition rather than psychology.

As part of the master's program I took a course on learning disabilities. The eight-week lab involved working one day a week at UCLA's Fernald School. I was fascinated by their work with children and was eager to apply it in a community college setting. I then heard about at internship at El Camino College where I could work with adults with learning and reading problems. I signed up and was accepted into the program.

I spent the summer working with Gene Kerstiens in the college's new learning lab. Gene had agreed to supervise my student teaching in the fall. The problem was that UCLA required students to do their supervised teaching at one of the campuses in the Los Angeles Community College District and El Camino was outside the district.

I was unwilling to give up without a battle. I petitioned, wrote letters, and even met with one of the deans at UCLA. Nothing worked. Gene then introduced me to Loretta Newman who was doing similar work at Los Angeles Harbor College.

Loretta turned out to be one of the most important mentors in my life. She had worked with Grace Fernald who had pioneered the techniques being used at UCLA's Fernald School. Loretta expanded on Fernald's work and devoted her life to teaching adults to read. On weekends, she also held reading classes for disadvantaged elementary school kids. She combined individualized instruction with eye and brain training exercises to produce stunning results in both children and adults. Gains of three to five grade levels were common and some highly motivated students jumped from third or fourth grade reading level to college level in a single semester. What I didn't fully appreciate until much later in life was how profoundly Loretta's service impacted the thousands of students she touched during her 30-year teaching career.

Loretta's program was growing and I was hired to teach part time for L.A. Harbor. Eight months later a full-time position came open at

West Los Angeles College. At age 23, I was hired as a full-time instructor in their developmental reading program.

Two years later I began my doctoral studies in educational psychology at the University of Southern California. When I was transferred to Pierce College 13 years later, I did achieve my dream of teaching psychology full time. What surprised me most, however, was that my first love was working with my developmental reading students at West L.A. College.

It's easy to become upset when things don't go your way. In retrospect, you may have had similar experience—being stopped was the best thing that could have happened. I missed the opportunity to student-teach with Gene, but the better opportunity turned out to be working with Loretta.

To this day I still marvel that my father had some sort of sixth sense regarding how important writing would become in my life. I am saddened that he didn't live to see that, especially because it was so important to him. He died in 1998, two years before I began writing a real estate column for *Inman News* and eight years before my first book, *Waging War on Real Estate's Discounters*, became a best seller.

The most important lesson I have learned about timing is this: if the doors swing open easily, then this is the right path for me. Little perspiration and no butting your head against the door required. On the other hand, when I keep encountering obstacle after obstacle, it's usually time to step back and try something else. If something doesn't work out, learn from it, and then persist in searching for what will work.

Opportunity vs. Opportunity Cost

In order to choose which opportunities are best for you, the first step is to identify the nature of the opportunity including the opportunity costs associated with that choice. The term opportunity suggests that there is a good chance for advancement or progress. This is where most people place their focus. What most people ignore is the opportunity cost, a measure of how much they have to give up in order to take advantage of an opportunity.

Timing Tip #1: Is this the right opportunity for me?
Use the following steps to determine whether an opportunity is the right one for you.

1. **List the opportunity costs**
   Begin by evaluating the opportunity cost first rather than the benefits associated with the opportunity. Items to consider include the time needed to fully capitalize on the opportunity, the level of financial commitment required, and what you will have to give up to pursue this opportunity. Record each of these items in writing.

2. **List the benefits this opportunity could provide**
   Make a list of the benefits that you will gain from this opportunity and place them in a second column.

3. **Is there another option you haven't considered?**
   Sometimes when you focus on one choice, you may be ignoring other options that could work for you. Is there a different choice that provides many of the benefits of your first choice and perhaps additional benefits that your first choice doesn't provide?

4. **Weigh your options including both the benefits and the opportunity costs**
   The final step is to determine which option offers the greatest benefits to you. Are the gains you will experience worth the cost? Is the alternative choice actually the best choice? Examine the cost of the opportunity in light of how the same resources could be applied to a different choice you may have.

To illustrate how to weigh the opportunity costs against the benefits, assume that you are considering going back to school to finish your bachelor's degree in nursing. The opportunity costs include having to quit your current job because the nursing courses are only offered during the day. Without your additional income, you and your spouse will also have to delay starting your family and buying a house. In fact, the new student loans that you will incur will require a minimum of five years to pay off once you finish your degree.

On the benefit side, your income will double once you graduate and you will be able to fulfill your lifelong dream of working in the emergency room. Depending upon where you decide to work, you may also have the option of choosing your own hours so that you can spend more time with your family once you have children.

When you consider the situation, you discover there is an entirely different option. Your employer has indicated that she would like to groom you for a leadership position in your current company. In order to evaluate this choice, compare the positive and negatives of pursuing a career in leadership with pursuing a career in nursing.

If you only considered the benefits of pursuing a nursing degree, you would miss what you would have to give up in order to achieve your dream. You may have also passed on a career in leadership that could be as fulfilling as a career in nursing. Using this process provides you with a more complete picture prior to making your choice.

Yellow Light Moments: Stop or Go?

The PQ Factor began with the premise, "stop resisting and start persisting." In other words, avoid giving in to that piece of chocolate, buying those shoes you really don't need, or skipping your exercise (the short-term temptations) that fail to support your long-term goals. As we discussed in the section on "Perspire," most people give up just short of reaching the point where they would achieve success.

A "yellow light" moment occurs when you reach a crossroad—do you keep persisting or do you give up? Learning to recognize these moments can save you considerable pain and agony if you make the right decision. The question is how can you tell which decision is the best decision? Perhaps your intuition is already whispering that you need to slow down or to take a different approach.

Here's one case where I was very happy to have stopped on "yellow."

It was President's Day weekend and I was flying home to Austin from LAX. When I checked in at the airport kiosk, my ticket didn't have a seat assignment. I went to the counter and they told me to see the gate agent for my seat assignment. I had first tier status so wasn't worried about getting a seat.

When I reached the gate the agent apologized profusely—there wasn't a single seat available. The agent agreed that the system should have assigned me a seat. If I insisted, she was willing to offer a voucher to another passenger who would agree to travel the next day.

My gut told me not to press the issue. Instead, I asked if there were any seats available in first class on the flight out the next morning. The agent said that there were. I then asked if she would be willing to give me a meal voucher and upgrade me to first on that flight the next morning. She happily agreed.

I had a nice meal, headed back to where I was staying, and enjoyed my first class flight home the next morning.

Because of the school holiday, I didn't see my normal Sunday night commuting friends until two weeks later. They asked where I had been for the last couple of weeks. When I explained what happened they told me, "You have no idea how lucky you were. The turbulence was so bad that even the frequent flyers were throwing up. The smell was still lingering in the aircraft when we flew back on Sunday night."

If I had insisted on being on that flight, the gate agent would have asked for a volunteer. Instead, by heeding my gut's "yellow light," I missed what would have most certainly been a dreadful experience.

When does yellow mean stop?

When you come to a yellow traffic signal, the decision to stop or go often happens automatically. If your right brain recognizes a traffic camera or police car ahead, "Mother" may bounce the decision up to your cerebral cortex to evaluate. If you are too aggressive you may be ticketed. On the other hand, if you stop too soon, you could be rear-ended.

This brings us to what may be the most difficult aspect of persistence—determining when to continue to persist and when it's time to stop. Yellow light moments are easy to recognize—making the right decision during these moments is the challenge. What makes these decisions so difficult is interpreting conflicting data that may be clouded by emotion, past experience, or a host of other factors.

Chapter 16: Timing Is Everything

Stop, Go, or Change Direction?

Where do you draw the line between persisting and stopping? What are the signposts to look for to distinguish between a yellow warning light and an actual red light that means it's time to stop now? How can you recognize that the cherished goal you desire is simply not within your reach? The first part of this process is to determine whether tweaking what you are already doing will help you break through whatever is blocking your forward progress. If that doesn't work, the next decision is determining whether it's time to stop persisting. Here are some important questions to ask in making that determination.

1. **Is your goal in alignment with your values and your strengths?**
   If your goal is not aligned with your values, it may be time to reset your mindset or to try a different tactic. In my case, I have never been very successful selling our real estate training products from the stage. I've been coached on it, have top-rated products, and know all the right things to say. Nevertheless, it always felt uncomfortable because I place being of service first, not making money. When I finally let go of trying to sell from the stage my reviews improved and I felt infinitely better. I also realized that the bulk of my business was coming from creating content for Realtor associations and large real estate companies. My business picked up when I focused on leveraging these strengths rather than trying to sell products to agents at events.

2. **Are you using a hammer when you really need a wrench?**
   Sometimes your forward movement is blocked because you lack the right tools. For example, assume that you want to maximize how much you save toward your children's college education or your retirement. In order to do this, you must first be able to identify where you can eliminate unnecessary expenses. While you could attempt to figure this out manually, using a tool specifically designed for this task, such as Dave Ramsey's EveryDollar app, will make your goal much easier to reach. (See the Appendix for additional information.)

3. Did you make the wrong choice?
If you are encountering one obstacle after another and everything you do only seems to make matters worse, it's time to pause and regroup. Ask yourself whether you made the right choice in terms of the path that you decided to pursue. For example, even though I religiously followed a low carb diet, I gained weight. When I returned to my normal eating patterns my weight stabilized. I still wanted to drop the extra pounds but a low carb approach was obviously the wrong choice. This is an important point—what may be the perfect choice for someone else may be a poor choice for you. If something that you're doing is only making matters worse, take time out to determine if you need to merely change tactics or to drop the effort completely.

4. Stop staring at the corner
Here's a simple exercise to illustrate how people can get stuck and what they can do to get unstuck. Find a corner and then step as close to it as you can get without touching it. As long as you continue to stare at the corner, you are looking at a dead end. Now turn around and walk away—you have a wealth of new directions that you can take. My friend Marilyn Naylor (Naylor, Ross, 1997) summed up this scenario like this: "If you made the wrong choice, choose again." In other words, there are plenty of better choices once you are willing to let go of the choice that wasn't a good fit for you.

5. Change your perspective
Here's a problem that requires you to change perspective in order to solve it. Assume that you have six matches, all of which are the same length. From those six matches, please make four triangles whose sides are all of equal length. When I presented this problem to my psychology classes, my students rarely came up with the right solution. Solving the problem required them to shift from using a two-dimensional solution to using a three-dimensional solution. (Place three matches on the surface to form the base. Next, use the other three matches to construct a pyramid.) If you're stuck, look for out-of-the box thinking strategies that may provide an unexpected route to success.

6. Seek fresh input

I remember when we were finally ready to move into our new house. I had carefully measured the living room during the construction process and my large three-piece sectional would definitely fit. Consequently, I decided to replace cushions and ordered custom pillows to match the new décor prior to moving. When the movers brought the sofa in, it did fit but there was no way to center it on the fireplace. Every placement I tried looked horrible. I was practically in tears when one of my friends dropped by to see how the move was progressing. She looked at the situation and suggested getting rid of the center portion of the sectional. Her idea worked perfectly. Sometimes a set of fresh eyes is exactly what you need to find the right solution.

7. Are "shiny objects" pulling you off your goal?

Many entrepreneurs are pulled off focus by what is known as "shiny object syndrome." *Shiny object syndrome* is a new idea that captures your attention and causes you to go off on a tangent rather than staying focused on your primary goal. A simple way to overcome this issue is to work on no more than three goals at any time. If you are going to add one more goal or task to the list, you must decide which of your existing goals you are willing to put on hold or to stop pursuing. This strategy will help you to stay focused and to avoid going off on a tangent.

8. Are you willing to persist through the dip?

Seth Godin (2007) in his book *The Dip* says that every new project, job, hobby, or company starts out fun and then becomes difficult. The "dip" is the long, hard period between beginning something new and achieving what you set out to do. Godin says that "the dip" is the time when you should stick things out, even when it seems reasonable to quit. He goes on to say that the secret to dealing with the dip is to figure out beforehand if you're willing to see the project all the way through. If the payoff isn't big enough, he recommends that you quit before you reach the dip. If you begin the dip, be willing to persist because "quitting in the middle is the worst waste of both your time and effort."

9. When you hit a cul-de-sac it's time to quit

When searching for other strategies or tweaks fails to produce results, Godin says it's time to quit. Godin calls these dead ends, "cul-de-sacs." He further argues that, "Winners are the best quitters—quit fast, quit often, and quit without guilt until you are willing to commit to beating the right Dip." Furthermore, it's important that you know when you're going to quit and that you have an exit strategy. Otherwise, you end up stuck in a cul-de-sac with no way out.

10. Is the halt in your progress really a red light or is it a yellow light moment?

Sometimes you will find that you are making solid progress toward your goal and then something goes sideways that totally stops your progress. While Godin argues it's time to quit, the issue may really be that the delay is simply a step backwards that will allow you to take two steps forward at a later date. Sometimes the best course of action prior to quitting is to put the project or goal aside for a period of time. When you revisit it weeks or months later, you may find that new opportunities have arisen that will allow you to pick up where you left off, albeit in a different direction. If this is not the case, then it may very well be time to stop persisting and move on to a different project or goal.

Determining when to persist and when to quit is challenging. Past experience is an important teacher. If you make the wrong decision, learn from it, and then make a different choice. Learning a lesson once is useful, but having to relearn it is both expensive and painful. To make the best possible decision, you must listen with both your heart and your head. Moreover, if that little voice in your head is whispering that it is time to cut your losses and move on to the next opportunity, pay attention.

You now have all the tools you will need to stop resisting and to start persisting. Chapter 17 provides you with a roadmap for creating your unique path to happiness and success in your life.

Chapter 16: Key Points

1. To determine which opportunities are right for you, begin by identifying the opportunity costs prior to listing the benefits associated with the opportunity. Also consider if there are any other options that could possibly yield a better result.

2. When you hit a "yellow light moment," when do you proceed and when do you stop persisting? Issues to consider include whether the goal aligns with your values or if changing tools or technology could remove part of the blockage. Other issues include whether the timing is off and a delay could actually be beneficial. Additional strategies to consider include taking a time out, changing your perspective, or seeking fresh input.

3. When you start a project, are the rewards great enough to keep you working at it when you hit what Seth Godin calls "the dip"—the point when the fun is gone and moving forward becomes very difficult. If not, cut your losses early.

4. If you hit a dead end (what Godin calls a "cul-de-sac"), you can make a new choice. Listen to the little voice inside and if it is truly time to cut your losses, pay attention to it.

Chapter 17:
What PERSIST Choices Will You Make?

*A journey of 10,000 miles
begins with a single step.*
Lao Tzu

Writing *The PQ Factor* has been an extraordinary personal journey for me. There's a saying that you teach what you have to learn. I was surprised how almost every chapter turned into an exercise in persistence. The topics I was writing on were familiar, covered concepts and ideas I had taught, but weaving them together proved to be the most challenging writing task of my career.

On the other hand, there was an element in this book's creation that was almost magical. Just prior to the time I began writing on a specific topic, the events in my personal life seemed to perfectly mirror what I was about to cover. For example, just before I began the chapter on adversity, I ran into Lennox Scott, the CEO of Seattle based John L. Scott Real Estate, at a conference. I was very surprised when he gave me a copy of his wife Deanna's book, *Speaking the Language of Miracles*. The book provided an important reframe in terms of how to cope with adversity. Several weeks later as I began the chapter on *When Death Comes Calling*, my uncle and my cousin died just eight days apart. A few months earlier, Byron's stepfather had also died.

As I am writing the final chapter of this book, I'm sitting on a lanai in Hawaii on a cool, rainy day with the waves crashing in the background and the birds noisily chirping in the trees. Byron and I are here with his family at the end of a transitional year that has seen challenge and loss coupled with laughter and joy. It strikes me that this last year has been a study in contrasts much like Hawaii, with its fiery lava flows, black-scorched volcanic landscapes, and glorious rain forests and foliage. We all have our bright sunny days, fiery times of tribulation, and face the black hole of despair when life doles out its most trying times. It's how we choose to PERSIST, the action steps that we choose to take, that determine whether the landscape stays shrouded in black or ultimately turns into a beautiful, lush garden.

The ONLY Thing that Matters about this Book

There is only one thing that truly matters about *The PQ Factor*—the action steps you choose to take each day. Byron and I have repeatedly observed that when our coaching clients tackle too much, they become overwhelmed and nothing happens.

To avoid having this happen to you, the first step is to set a goal. This could be losing weight, exercising regularly, or putting money aside in an education or retirement fund.

Once you have identified your goal, take a few minutes to review the key points at the end of each chapter. Then, for each letter in the PERSIST model (*Perspire, Embrace* Your Strengths, Increase Your *Resilience,* Be *Self-ish* not Selfish, Become More *Internally Anchored, Serve, Time* It Right), select one action step that you could implement. If you find that there is more than one step in a section that you would like to implement, jot down both steps.

Next, reduce your list to only three action steps. Now here's the most important question—which action step will you take first? No matter how small that step may be, go take it now.

For example, if you want to lose weight, check the calorie count on two meals that you could have for lunch. Select the meal with the lowest calorie count. Another alternative would be to cut back your serving size by 20 percent.

If you want to start exercising more, walk somewhere right now for 10 minutes. Repeat the process again later today. To start saving for college or retirement, search for websites that provide on-line coupons for the major brands and stores where you shop. You could also pack a lunch for work tomorrow rather than eating out. Bank what you save.

The key point here is to choose ONE action step and to take it now. Repeat this process daily in at least one of the three areas you have identified as your priorities. As Michal Stawicki suggests, committing to taking one small step each day, (i.e., doing that single pushup), is the most direct path to reaching your goals and fulfilling your dreams.

Create Your Personal 90-Day PERSIST Plan

The three-step plan that follows is a simple way to begin the first 90 days of your PERSIST journey.

Chapter 17: What PERSIST Choices Will You Make?

1. Write down three goals you would like to achieve in the next three months.
2. Each night before you go to bed, write down at least one action step you will take tomorrow to reach one of the three goals on your list.
3. If you decide that you would like to add a new goal to your list, you must first decide which of your current goals you will delete. In other words, your list will never consist of more than three goals at a time.

As you embark on your journey, here are some additional thoughts to keep in mind:

1. You cannot change the past. What you can do is choose to take a single action step right now that will move you closer to your goals and your dreams.
2. It's easier to resist the easy choices in the beginning than it is to use self-discipline to persist later in the process.
3. Your fear and worries about the problems you may face are almost always worse than what you actually experience.
4. You ALWAYS have a choice, even if you don't like it.

At the beginning of this book, I encouraged you to think of *The PQ Factor* as a toolbox. As you encounter challenges in your life, re-read the chapters that apply to the issue you are facing. You may be surprised to find there is a piece of wisdom, a strategy, or an action you can take that you missed when you first read the book.

Finally, I would like to leave you with two things—first, my deepest gratitude and thanks to you for being one of my readers. Second, this beautiful piece of wisdom from Mother Teresa that sums up the essence of what it means to stop resisting and start persisting:

People are often unreasonable, illogical, and self-centered.
Forgive them anyway.

If you are kind, people may accuse you of selfish, ulterior motives.
Be kind anyway.

The PQ Factor

If you are successful, you will win some false friends and some true enemies.
Succeed anyway.

If you are honest and frank, people may cheat you.
Be honest and frank anyway.

What you spend years building, someone could destroy overnight.
Build it anyway.

If you find serenity and happiness, others may be jealous.
Be happy anyway.

The good you do today, people will often forget tomorrow.
Do good anyway.

Give the world the best you have and it may never be enough.
Give the world the best you have anyway.

You see, in the final analysis, it is between you and God.
It was never between you and them anyway.

Mother Teresa

About the Author
Bernice L. Ross, Ph.D.

The journey that led Bernice L. Ross to write *The PQ Factor* began when she was 17. She dreamed of majoring in psychology, but her father, who had hovered near death for six weeks and had just been released from the hospital, insisted that she major in English so she could "learn to write." She reluctantly agreed even though she found writing to be difficult and had little interest in it. That detour set her on the path to earn her B.A. and M.A. in English and to later receive her doctorate in Educational Psychology. During that journey, she met the many mentors and teachers whose wisdom is the foundation of this book.

When Bernice purchased her first condo, the college where she was teaching cancelled summer session leaving her without the ability to make her payments. Rather than going back to checking groceries that had allowed her to pay her way through college, she decided if she could sell one or two houses that summer, she could make ends meet. Her first month she sold two properties and the second month she sold eight. For the next 25 years, she balanced the demands of being a full-time Professor of Psychology with a career in real estate.

After sustaining over $100,000 damage to her home from the 1994 Northridge earthquake, Bernice decided to move to Texas. She founded her company, RealEstateCoach.com which specializes in real estate training, coaching, and consulting, in 1996. She met her husband Byron Van Arsdale in 1997 who also later became her business partner.

Bernice began writing an online weekly newsletter to build her business in 1998. When she heard of an opportunity to have her articles published on *Inman News* (Inman.com), she submitted several of her columns for consideration. Since that time, she has published over 1,000 articles and five books including *Going Where—Ancient Wisdom for People Today, No More Lame Conference Calls, Real Estate Dough® Your Recipe for Real Estate Success, Waging War on Real Estate's Discounters,* and *Who's the Best Person to Sell My House?* In fact, the overwhelmingly positive response to her July 2015 column on *Inman News* "Why the 'PQ Factor' Is the Secret to Real Estate Sales Success" prompted Bernice to draw on her psychology and coaching background to expand that content into a comprehensive self-help book.

Bernice's life has been a study of choosing to persist rather than to resist, looking inward while also constantly seeking the wisdom of others. The result of that journey is this book, something she could never have envisioned when she was 17 and her father insisted that she learned to write. We hope that *The PQ Factor* will support you to persist in pursuing your dreams of having a happy and fulfilling life.

Acknowledgements

First, I would like to acknowledge you for picking up a copy of *The PQ Factor*. I am extremely grateful to you for your business and your support. We are also deeply appreciative of our wonderful clients and readers for their support of our products and services over the last two decades.

I would also like to express my sincere appreciation to each of the following individuals who contributed to the creation of this book:

Shane Bowlin, virtual assistant extraordinaire, has guided this entire effort from start to finish including laying out the final manuscript, proofing, locating our graphics artist, overseeing the work with our publisher, coordinating the website design, marketing, and a host of other tasks to numerous to list. Without her wisdom and expertise, this project would never have come into being.

Brad Inman, Publisher of *Inman News* (Inman.com), who has been publishing my weekly real estate advice columns since 2001. I am honored to be one of Brad's weekly columnists and am also grateful to the entire Inman news team including managing editor Amber Taufen, COO Morgan Brown, and copyeditor Dani Vanderboegh. I am especially indebted to the Inman community of readers whose response to my July 2015 column, "Why the 'PQ Factor' Is the Secret to Real Estate Sales Success," prompted me to expand the column into this book.

Judy Kleinberg, my incredibly talented book editor, who is also a poet, copywriter, and the co-author of *Fat, Stupid, Ugly: One Woman's Courage to Survive*. Judy creates "exceptionally tasty writing that promotes, describes, instructs, and inspires in plain English." One of Judy's one-line comments about the tone in my first book, *Waging War on Real Estate's Discounters*, resulted in a complete rewrite of that book. *Waging War's* success was due in large part to her wisdom about how to best speak to my readers.

Whether it's a book cover or website design, Cheryl Klinginsmith of Klinginsmith & Company has created outstanding covers and designs for our print publications, audio CDs, and websites since 2005. Her work always far exceeds my expectations and captures perfectly what I often struggle to convey in words.

The late Thomas Leonard, the founder of Coach University, and Sandy Vilas, the current CEO of Coach U, Inc. Thomas and Sandy helped me write my original business plan for RealEstateCoach.com in 1997. We are still operating on the plan two decades later. A pivotal part of that plan was to write a weekly newsletter as a way to attract clients. I began doing that and it evolved four years later into my weekly column at *Inman News*. Thomas was also an innovator in virtual learning—almost all of Coach U's training was done by phone, which, by the way, is how I met Byron—on a Coach U training teleclass.

I am especially indebted to my long-time friend and mentor Marilyn Naylor, whose wisdom appears throughout this book. Her work on the Native American Medicine Wheel was the basis for my book *Going Where*. The wheel is an agrarian model based upon the seasons of the year. The model is simple—if you "move forward" through winter, spring, summer, and fall, your life flows smoothly. Problems arise when you "back up." What was especially surprising were the hundreds of articles linking season of birth to types of illnesses, addictions, learning disabilities, and a host of other factors. We started using the wheel in our coaching practices 20 years ago and found it to be one of the most powerful tools for helping people overcome life's greatest challenges and to create positive, forward movement in their lives. It can be especially helpful to those who are experiencing any type of physical or emotional abuse.

I would also like to acknowledge three colleagues who are no longer with us and who made a major impact on my teaching career—Wayne Hren, Gene Kerstiens, and Loretta Newman. It was Wayne's office I stepped into the night the disturbed student showed up at my office. He also was the one who gently persuaded me of the wisdom of teaching statistics and critical thinking. His willingness to share his work was the foundation that enabled me to tackle teaching these tough courses. As I shared in the book, Gene and Loretta's influence was profound as was their service. May they rest in peace.

I'm grateful to my family and especially to my parents for how they modeled persistence every day of their lives. As I mentioned earlier, I still marvel that my dad foresaw how important writing would be in my life—my one regret is that he didn't live to see it. I also suspect my mom would have been astounded that someone would actually buy a book that I wrote.

Last, and certainly not least, my husband and business partner Byron Van Arsdale, who has been my sounding board and de facto editor for every chapter in this book. For a number of years, Byron and I wrote a weekly coaching newsletter called *Teleclues*. Many of the practical applications and the coaching strategies in *The PQ Factor* came from those newsletters.

Byron is also a Master Certified Coach and an international speaker whose client list includes the senior executive team at companies such as IBM, Chubb Insurance, State of Texas, as well as numerous real estate companies and associations. During his tenure at Coach U, he trained over 1,000 professional business and personal coaches. He currently heads up our coaching team at RealEstateCoach.com as well as keeping me laughing and well fed when he's not busy playing golf.

Appendix

The list below contains links to online resources arranged by chapter. Please check our website at *www.ThePQFactor.com* to easily access these and other related assessment links online.

Many of these assessments will provide you with additional insight into what makes you unique. Any assessment that suggests that you may have a more serious problem, such as a mood disorder or other physical issue, should be followed up with the appropriate medical professional. Please be aware that even the most accurate assessments are accurate for groups of people, but may not be accurate for you. Each individual is unique. Again, if you are concerned about an issue, seek the appropriate type of professional help.

Chapter 2: Amp Up Your Brain Power

Neurotransmitter Evaluations:
To determine if you may be deficient in any key neurotransmitters, take any of the assessments below. If any of these inventories reveal a major issue, it is best to be evaluated by a doctor to determine whether or not you need treatment.

Brain Deficiency Quiz
http://www.pathmed.com/uploads/6/4/1/3/64134895/brain_quiz.pdf

The Mood Type Questionnaire
https://www.moodcure.com/take_the_mood_type_questionnaire.html

The UltraMind Quizzes
http://drhyman.com/downloads/UltraMindCompanionGuide.pdf

Chapter 5: Embrace Strengths, Work Around Weaknesses

Self-Esteem Inventory
http://www.mhhe.com/socscience/hhp/fahey7e/wellness_worksheets/wellness_worksheet_024.html

Chapter 7: Optimism

If you would like a more detailed account of the research on optimism, visit:
http://www.pursuit-of-happiness.org/science-of-happiness/positive-thinking/

If you would like to determine how optimistic you are, take Martin Seligman's inventory at
https://web.stanford.edu/class/msande271/onlinetools/LearnedOpt.html

There's another assessment that evaluates your optimism at:
http://www.seemypersonality.com/personality.asp?p=Optimism-Test#q1

Chapter 8: Bouncing Back from Adversity

For Paul Pearsall's complete post on "Patsy's Parade," visit http://www.soulfulliving.com/miracle_maker.htm

Chapters 13: Moving from Source to Solution
Chapter 16: Timing Is Everything

Dave Ramsey has a number of tools that can help you with your finances. His main website http://www.daveramsey.com.

Also be sure to visit his "every dollar app" (https://www.daveramsey.com/everydollar) as well as the other free tools that he offers at
https://www.daveramsey.com/category/tools/?snid=tools

To better understand how buying a latte or any other small item on a daily basis can add up to major amounts of money, visit:
https://financialmentor.com/calculator/latte-factor-calculator

Bibliography

Amen, D. (2005). *Making a good brain great,* New York, NY: Harmony Books.

Ariely, D. (2009). *Predictably irrational, the hidden forces that shape our decisions,* New York, NY: HarperCollins Publishers.

Blum, R. (1982). *The book of runes,* New York, NY: St. Martin's Press.

Burg, B., & Mann, J. (2015). *The Go-Giver,* New York, NY: Portfolio, Penguin.

Browne, H. (1973, 1997, 2004). *How I found freedom in an unfree world,* New York, NY: Avon Books.

Cialdini, R. (2009). *Influence,* New York, NY: William Morrow and Company.

Carver, C., et al. (2010). Optimism. *Clinical Psychology Review,* 30 (7), pp. 879-889.

Daft, R. (2005). *The leadership experience,* Vancouver, B.C.: Thomson-Southwestern.

Dielman, T. (1987). Susceptibility to peer pressure, self-esteem, and health locus of control as correlates of adolescent substance abuse. *Health Education Quarterly,* 14(2), pp. 207-221.

Dreeke, R. (2011). *It's not all about "me:" the top ten techniques for building quick rapport with anyone.* Retrieved from https://www.amazon.com/Its-Not-All-About-Techniques-ebook/dp/B0060YIBLK.

Dunbar, R., et al. (2012). Social laughter is correlated with an elevated pain threshold. *Proceedings of the Royal Society B: Biological Sciences,* (279) pp. 1161-1167.

Emoto, M. (1994). What is the photograph of frozen water crystals? Retrieved from http://www.masaru-emoto.net/english/water-crystal.html.

Emoto, M. (2004). Masaru Emoto's Rice Experiment. Retrieved from http://thirdmonk.net/knowledge/masaru-emoto-rice-emotions-experiment-video.html.

Eysenck, H. (1964) *Crime and personality,* London, England: Methuen.

Fowler, J. (2008). Dynamic spread of happiness in a large social network: longitudinal analysis over 20 years in the Framingham heart study. BMJ 2008, 337(a2338).

Fox Cabane, O., & Pollack, J. (2016). Your brain has a "delete" button—how to use it. Retrieved from https://www.fastcompany.com/3059634/your-most-productive-self/your-brain-has-a-delete-button-heres-how-to-use-it.

Frank, R. (2007). *Richistan,* New York, NY: Three Rivers Press.

Friedman, H. (1987). The "disease prone personality": a meta-analytic view of the construct. *American Psychologist* 42, pp. 539-555.

Friedman, H. (1991). *The self-healing personality: why some people achieve health and others succumb to illness,* New York: Henry Holt.

Garrett, B. (2008). *From hiccups to hospice.* Publisher: Caregivers4Cancer.

Godin, S. (2007). *The dip, a little book that teaches you when to quit (and when to stick),* New York, NY: Penguin Group.

Goodman, L. (May 27, 2015). Millennial college graduates: young, educated, jobless. Retrieved from http://www.newsweek.com/2015/06/05/millennial-college-graduates-young-educated-jobless-335821.html.

Haney, M., et al. (2014). Age and psychological influences on immune responses to trivalent inactivated influenza vaccine in the meditation or exercise for preventing acute respiratory infection (MEPARI) trial. *Immunotherapy*, 2014 Jan 1; 10(1) pp. 83–91.

Harris, B. (2002). *Sacred Selfishness*, Makawao, Maui, HI: Inner Ocean Publishing, Inc.

Hayworth, J., et al. (1980). A predictive study of post-partum depression: some predisposing characteristics, *Psychology and Psychotherapy*, 52, (2), pp. 161-167.

Huddleston, C. September 19, 2016. Retrived from https://www.gobankingrates.com/personal-finance/data-americans-savings/

Jackson, K. (2007). The art of selfishness: it's not what you think. Retrieved from http://www.articlesbase.com/coaching-articles/the-art-of-selfishness-its-not-what-you-think-167966.html.

Jiang, J. (2015). *Rejection proof*, New York, NY: Harmony Books.

Johnson, C., & Gormly, J. (1971). Achievement, sociability, and task importance in relation to academic cheating. *Psychological Reports*, 28 (302).

Keller, G. & Papasan, J. (2013). *The one thing*, Austin, TX: Bard Press.

Kübler-Ross, E. (1997). *On death and dying*, New York, NY: Scribner.

Leonard, T. (1995). Coach University Coach Training Program. Publisher: Coach University.

MacLean, P.D. (1990). *The triune brain in evolution: role in paleocerebral functions*, New York, NY: Springer Publishing.

Maruta, T., et al. (2000). Optimists vs. pessimists: survival rate among medical patients over a 30-year period. *Mayo Clinic Proceedings,* 2000 Feb; 75(2) pp. 140-143.

Marshall, P. (October 28, 2014). *80/20 sales and marketing,* Troy, MI: Business News Publishing.

Matthews, K., et al. (2004). Optimistic attitudes protect against progression of carotid atherosclerosis in healthy middle-aged women. *Psychosomatic Medicine,* September/October 66(5) pp. 640-644.

McCarthy, N. (September 23, 2016). Survey: 69% of Americans of Americans have less than $1,000 in Savings. Retrieved from http://www.forbes.com/sites/niallmccarthy/2016/09/23/survey-69-of-americans-have-less-than-1000-in-savings-infographic/#271a135591ee.

McRaney, D. (June 23, 2010). Confirmation bias. Retrieved from https://youarenotsosmart.com/2010/06/23/confirmation-bias/.

Medina, J. (2014) *Brain rules: 12 principles for surviving and thriving at work, home, and school,* Seattle, WA: Pear Press.

Merton, R. (1948) The self-fulfilling prophecy. *The Antioch Review,* 8(2), pp.193-210.

Milam, J. E., et al. (2004). The roles of dispositional optimism and pessimism in HIV disease progression. *Psychology and Health,* 19(2), pp. 167-181.

Murray, T. (2016). Why do 70 percent of lottery winners end up bankrupt? *The Plain Dealer.* Retrieved from http://www.cleveland.com/business/index.ssf/2016/01/why_do_70_percent_of_lottery_w.html.

Nass, C., Ophir, E., & Wagner, A. (2009). *Multitaskers pay mental price, Stanford study shows.* Retrieved from http://news.stanford.edu/2009/08/24/multitask-research-study-082409/.

Naylor, M. & Ross, B., (1998). *Simple, joyful challenges* newsletter.

Nielson Consumer (July 28, 2015). Saving, spending, and living paycheck-to-paycheck in America. Retrieved from: http://www.nielsen.com/us/en/insights/news/2015/saving-spending-and-living-paycheck-to-paycheck-in-america.html.

Nielsen Newswire. July 28, 2015. Retrieved from: http://www.nielsen.com/us/en/insights/news/2015/saving-spending-and-living-paycheck-to-paycheck-in-america.html

Ohannessian, C.M. (1994). Hassles and uplifts and generalized outcome expectancies as moderators between a family history of alcoholism and drinking behaviors. *Journal of Studies on Alcohol and Drugs*, 55(6) pp. 754-763.

Pearsall, P. (1996). *The pleasure prescription: to love, to work, to play—life in balance,* Alameda, CA: Hunter House, Inc., Publishers.

Pearsall, P. (1999). *The heart's code.* New York, NY: Broadway Books.

Pearsall, P., (2001). *Miracle in Maui: let miracles happen in your life.* Makawao, Maui, HI: Inner Ocean Publishing, Inc.

Peyrot, M., and Rubin, R. (1994). Structure and correlates of diabetes-specific locus of control. *Diabetes Care*, Sep; 17(9): 994-1001.

Pruessner J., et al. (2005). Self-esteem, locus of control, hippocampal volume, and cortisol regulation in young and old adulthood. *NeuroImage,* 28, (2005), pp. 815-826.

Ramsey, D. (no date). How the lottery can ruin your life. Retrieved from, http://www.daveramsey.com/blog/how-the-lottery-can-ruin-your-life/.

Ramsey, D. (no date) EveryDollar app, retrieved from https://www.daveramsey.com/everydollar.

Rapaille, C. (2006). *The Culture Code,* New York, NY: Broadway Books.

Rideout, A., et al. (2016). Health locus of control in patients undergoing coronary artery surgery—changes and associated outcomes: a seven-year cohort study. *European Journal Cardiovascular Nursing*, retrieved from http://cnu.sagepub.com/content/early/2016/03/07/1474515116636501.

Robinson, P., (2003). *How Ronald Reagan changed my life:* New York, NY: HarperCollins Publishers, Inc.

Ross, B., (2007.) *Going where: ancient wisdom for people today:* Austin, TX: Rossdale Press.

Rotter, J.B. (1954). *Social learning and clinical psychology.* New York, NY: Prentice-Hall.

Rotter, J.B. (1966). Generalized expectancies of internal vs. external control of reinforcements. *Psychological Monographs.* 80, (609).

Rubinstein, J., Meyer, D., & Evans, J. (March 20, 2006). Multitasking: switching costs, American Psychological Association. Retrieved from http://www.apa.org/research/action/multitask.aspx.

Sapolsky, R. (2007). Lecture for the American Association for the Advancement of Science. Retrieved from http://news.stanford.edu/news/2007/march7/sapolskysr-030707.html.

Schou, I., et al. (2005). The mediating roles of appraisal and coping in the relationship between optimism-pessimism and quality of life. *Psychooncology,* 14(9), pp. 718-727.

Scott, D. (2015). *Speaking the language of miracles.* Publisher: Deanna Scott and the John L. Scott Foundation.

Seligman, M. E. P. (1995). *What you can change and what you can't: The complete guide to successful self-improvement.* New York: Ballantine Books.

Seligman, M. E. P. (1995). *The optimistic child.* New York: Houghton Mifflin.

Seligman, M. E. P. (1998). *Learned optimism: How to change your mind and your life.* New York: Free Press.

Seligman, M. E. P. (2004). *Authentic happiness: Using the new positive psychology to realize your potential for lasting fulfillment.* New York: Free Press.

Sonnby–Borgström, M., (2002). Automatic mimicry reactions as related to differences in emotional empathy. *Scandinavian Journal of Psychology,* 43: pp. 433–443.

Specht, J., et al. (2011). The benefits of believing in chance or fate: external locus of control as a protective factor for coping with death of a spouse. *Social Psychological and Personality Science,* 2 (2) pp. 132-137.

Stawicki, M. (2015). *The art of persistence: stop quitting, ignore shiny objects, and climb your way to success.* Publisher: Michal Stawicki.

Tracy, B. (2007). *Eat that frog!* San Francisco, CA: Berrett-Koehler Publishers, Inc.

Yukl, G. (2006). *Leadership in organizations* (6th ed.). Upper Saddle River, NJ: Pearson/Prentice Hall.

Index

9-11 (September 11, 2001), 8, 129
80-20 Rule, 66, 73, 78, 237
600-Pound Life, 171

A

AA (Alcoholics Anonymous), 80, 205, 225
abundance, 41–43, 108, 153, 233
abuse, 209–10
   adolescent substance, 261
   emotional, 256
accountability, 201–2
acetylcholine, 21
actions, taking, 9, 52, 75–76, 82–83, 106, 153
action steps, 28, 78, 82, 84, 98, 249–51
adrenaline, 20–21, 129, 149, 162, 227
adrenaline (epinephrine), 21
adversity, 42, 59, 90, 101–2, 106, 115, 194, 249, 260
advice, 19, 52, 104, 156-157, 168, 201, 255
AIDS, 122
Alcoholics Anonymous (AA), 80, 205, 225
Alzheimer's disease, 72, 126, 129
Amen, Daniel, 19
American culture codes, 202
American mindset, 61
anchor, 27, 29, 134
   new, 134
   powerful, 27
   powerful positive, 27
   strong, 27
   strong physical, 134
anchor happiness, 27

Anderson, Walter, 121
anger, 46, 95, 99, 108, 122, 125, 128, 133, 135–36, 148, 156, 209, 227, 230
   triggering, 15
anger workshops, 135
anxiety, 24, 115, 224, 227
Ariely, Daniel, 204
aspiration, 218–19, 234
attachment, 209, 233
   emotional, 233
attention game, 231
attract, 33–34, 36–40, 42, 44
attract clients, 256
attraction, 33, 37–39, 41, 221
   law of, 34, 226, 231
attraction level, 37, 55
attraction mindset, 33
Attraction Step, 34, 37, 39, 41
auditory sequencing problem, 62–63
Autism, 23
avoidance, 60, 73, 76–77, 170
Awesome Females in Real Estate Conference, 33, 135, 174

B

baby steps, 71, 84–85, 212–13
baby steps work, 213
balance, 9, 141, 162, 178, 265
Balance liquidation programs, 178–79, 187
behaviors, 34, 36–37, 44, 75–76, 83–84, 154–56, 158–60, 165, 167, 169, 184, 187, 191, 225–26, 230
   costly, 156
   healthful, 115
   hurtful, 135

long-term, 170, 187
new, 83, 186
post-dieting, 170
smiling, 227
beliefs, 36, 47, 50–52, 54, 142, 156, 194–95, 197, 204, 226
  cherished, 54
  political, 50
  preexisting, 50
belief system, 79
believing, 198, 267
Bennett, United States Senator Robert F., 7
beta-endorphins, 22, 42, 129, 227
better choices, 8, 21, 48, 172, 244
  long-term, 15
Block Self-ishness, 5, 153, 155, 157, 159, 161, 163, 165
Blum, Ralph, 122, 139
boundaries, 44, 154–56, 158–59, 161, 165, 168
  personal, 155
brain, reptilian, 15, 17, 109, 145
brain synchronization, 26, 48
brightness, 101, 111, 113–14, 116, 120
Browne, Harry, 143
Buddha, 113
budget, 176, 180
Burg, Bob, 231, 233

C

caffeine, 20, 22–23, 29, 149, 162, 184
caffeine intake, 21
caffeine kicks, 162
caffeine stresses, 21
cancer, 21-22, 61, 91, 95, 98
Canfield, Jack, 206

Caregivers4Cancer, 262
Carver, C., 91, 261
celebration of life, 129–30
challenges
  facing, 36
  financial, 43, 167
  greatest, 256
  life's, 100
  new, 212
change direction, 72, 237, 243
change perspective, 244
changes
  meaningful, 169
  positive, 84
Charter, Stacey, 235
Chesterton, G.K., 167
choice journal, 200, 213
choices
  conscious, 75–76, 84
  deliberate, 184, 200
  healthy, 172
  lifestyle, 174
  negative, 60
  positive, 60
  right, 201, 244
Churchill, Winston, 89
Cialdini, Robert, 96
Clotaire Rapaille, 202
Cold Reactor, 147, 149, 151
compensation, 61, 73, 159, 232
compliance, 195, 197, 213
confirmation bias, 50–51, 264
conflicts, 47, 155–56, 208, 223–25
  approach-avoidance, 170
  defuse, 228
conformity, 195, 197, 213

control, 7, 15–16, 20, 98–99, 102, 104–5, 114, 156–57, 164, 189, 192, 194–201, 203, 209–13, 222–23
  exercised, 211
  exercising, 212
  external, 196, 266
  external locus of, 191–92, 194–97, 213, 267
  extreme, 34
  getting things under, 194
  human, 210
  internal, 196
  internal locus of, 191–92, 195–96, 212–13
  lack, 199–200
  left brain, 14
  little, 196
  locus of, 195, 197, 204, 210, 265
  regain, 209, 211
  right brain, 14
  sense of, 61, 200, 212–13
  spinning out of, 194
  taking, 7
control events, 192, 199
control group, 198, 204
control matches, 197
control muscle, 200
control research, 213
cope, 36, 61, 92, 95-96, 122, 128, 145, 151, 194, 211, 224-225, 249
coping, 101, 119, 122, 124, 137, 197, 210-212, 225, 266-267
corpus callosum, 14
cortex, 15, 17, 97
  cerebral, 109, 145, 242
cortex rationalizes, 121
cortical areas, 15
cortisol levels, 162, 203
  lower, 196
cortisol regulation, 265
credit balances, 178
  high, 177
credit card companies balance liquidation, 179
credit cards, 75, 126, 175–77, 179
credit mess, 177–78
cul-de-sac, 246–47
culture codes, 202, 265

D

Daft, Richard, 197, 261
Daniel Amen's research, 92
Dave Ramsey's EveryDollar, 243
death, 5, 7, 25, 91, 114–16, 119, 121–29, 131, 133, 135, 137–38, 249, 253, 263, 267
  cell, 203
  powerful predictor of, 198, 213
decision-making, 50, 63, 157, 203, 223
debt reduction, 177
debts, 43, 46, 126, 175, 177, 187
  eliminating, 67
  snowball, 176
defense mechanisms, 225
  emotional, 224
  psychological, 224
delegate, 60, 79, 208
delegate or dump it, 79
delegation, 60, 73
denial, 51, 61, 73, 122, 125, 226
depression, 7, 20–21, 24, 115, 168, 221, 227
Di Lemme, John, 31
Dielman, T. 196, 261
dieting, 171, 173, 203

diets, 29, 77, 167, 170–73, 191–92
  better, 186
  healthy, 115
  low carb, 244
  weight-loss, 174
Dip (Seth Godin), 245
  the, 245
disease-prone, 115
dominant hemisphere, 15
dopamine, 22–23, 92, 227
dopamine levels, 20, 22–23
  high, 23
  increased, 22
  low, 22–23
Doug Doebler Village, 217
Douglas, Jon, 65
Dreeke, Robin, 51
Dunbar, Robin, 95
Durable power of attorney, 125

E

Eating Behavior, 172
eating choices, healthy, 171
Edison, Thomas, 19
effort, 8, 20, 49, 63, 65–70, 76, 79, 82, 99, 146, 148, 186, 194, 244–45, 255
  conscious, 227
  deliberate, 183
  extended, 187
  little, 65, 174
  people's, 187
  repeated, 167
  wasted, 67
effort required, amount of, 65–66, 69
ego, 225
Einstein, Albert, 13–14, 215
El Camino College, 238

Embrace Strengths, 5, 59, 61, 63, 65, 67, 69, 71, 73, 259
Emoto, Masuru, 204, 262
energy
  internal self-starting, 218
  low, 20, 77
  nourishing, 208
Energy and persistence conquer, 19
energy drain, 208
energy efficient home, 206
environment, 36, 80, 97–98, 116, 159, 172, 198, 203, 205–6, 209
  optimal, 204
  positive, 98, 100
  supportive, 192, 202–4
environment support, 36
epinephrine (adrenaline), 21
Escape Credit Card Interest Hell, 177
everyone dies alone, 137
exercise, 23, 26, 29, 34, 45, 48, 71, 75, 81, 84, 144, 199–200, 241, 244, 249
  following, 27, 38
  moderate, 184
  tap-three-times-on-the-shoulder, 29
exercise control, 212
exercise programs, 48, 115
expectations, 47, 85, 103, 105, 155–56, 159, 165, 209, 211, 255
  personal, 104
  slain by an, 155
  unfulfilled, 125
  unrealistic, 45, 211
expecting change, 83
Eysenck, Hans, 196, 262

F

Facing Adversity, 5, 43, 101, 103, 105, 107, 109, 111
farewell, final, 131
farewells, 124, 129–30, 132
Farewell Trips, 127
FBI's Behavioral Analysis Program, 51
fear, 47, 59, 62, 76-77, 84, 99, 103-104, 106, 108, 125, 135, 219, 251
Feather, Bat, Splat model, 145–46, 150
Feeling Stuck, 81
Fernald, Grace, 238
Fernald School, 238
fight or flight response, 21
financial difficulties, 167
Fossland, Joeann, 59, 147
Fowler, J., 98, 262
Fox Cabane, O., 262
Frank, Robert, 42
Franklin, Benjamin, 19
Freud, Sigmund, 61, 224–25, 262
Friedman, Howard, 115, 262

G

GABA (Gamma-aminobutyic acid), 23
Garrett, Betty, 124
Godin, Seth, 245, 247
gratification, instant, 83, 167, 187
gratitude, 41–44, 46, 71, 127, 165, 229, 234
  deepest, 251
  expressed, 113
  expressing, 42, 184
  practice, 42
gratitude journal, 43–44
grief, 22, 27, 122, 129, 132–34, 136–37
  unprocessed, 132–33
grief anchor, 134
grief process, 132
grief response, strong, 134
grieving period, 125
grieving person, 136
gut, unconscious, 16
gut feeling, 145
gut memories, 15

H

Haney, M., 92, 263
happiness, 5, 9–10, 42–43, 45–46, 53, 59, 89–91, 93, 95, 97–99, 212, 246, 252, 262
happiness and success, 10, 59, 246
happiness neurotransmitter, 23
happiness/positive-thinking, 260
happy brain, 8, 26
Harris, Bud, 142
Hayworth, J., 196, 263
Healing Power of Aloha, 16
help, 15-16, 20-21, 25, 28, 29, 35, 39, 42-43, 48-49, 52-53, 55, 62-63, 66, 70-71, 81-83, 90, 92, 95-96, 99, 100-101, 107, 110-111,115-116, 124-125, 128, 132-137, 142. 144. 147. 150, 156-158, 161, 163, 165, 171-172, 175, 177, 186-187, 195, 199, 206, 208, 210-211, 213, 217-218, 221-229, 231, 233-234, 243, 245, 259-260
helping, 8, 42, 62–63, 99–100, 119, 128, 130, 133–34, 137, 161, 186, 220–22, 224–25, 234, 256
helping behavior, 197, 221, 224–25
helping responses, 221
helpless, 7, 198

helplessness, learned, 198–99, 213
Hill, Napoleon, 20, 75
HIV (AIDS), 92
Holt, Michelle, 174
Homo Perfectus, 64–65, 76
hope, 53, 62, 92, 101-102, 104, 113, 115, 118, 172, 194, 198-199, 212-213, 225, 254
hospice, 123-124, 131-132, 262
Hot Reactors, 147–49
how to attract your ideal, 40
how to give your best (11 steps), 70
Hren, Wayne, 256
Hubbard, L. Ron, 20

I

I have/I choose model for overcoming obstacles, 109
I vs. You language, 222, 234
id, 224–25
illness, 77, 91, 98, 104, 115-116, 120, 122, 124, 147, 149, 151, 174, 198, 213, 256, 262
illusions, 5, 45–47, 49, 51–55, 60, 63–64, 72, 122
   eliminating, 53
   resisting, 45
   shattering, 52
illusions hurt, 45
immune response, 92, 113, 128, 263
   strengthened, 100
immune system, 92, 149, 227–28
increase your resilience, 5, 9, 250
inspiration, 13, 19, 218, 234
instant gratification (high cost of), 167
instinctual, 17, 224
   basic, 15

intention, 157–58, 166, 178, 196, 201–2, 204
intuition, 14, 145, 241
Intuition Trump Thinking, 14
intuitive information system, 16

J

Jackson, Krissy, 142, 263
Jiang, J., 94–97, 263
Johnson, C., 197, 263

K

karma, 226
karmic bank account, 226, 229, 234
Keller, Gary, 66
Kennedy,
   Jackie, 129
   John F., 129
Kerstiens, Gene, 238, 256
Key to Happiness and Resilience, 5, 89, 91, 93, 95, 97, 99
kick-the-cat syndrome, 135
Kübler-Ross, 263
   Elizabeth, 122

L

lack focus, 77
lag time, 83, 85
Lamott, Anne, 45
Lao Tzu, 78, 249
Larson, Gary, 163
last will and testament, 126
latte, 260
   daily, 177
latte factor expense calculators, 177

laugh, 3, 27, 59, 103, 121, 128, 134, 227–28, 232
  hearty, 227
laughter, 22, 27, 96, 100, 113, 128, 130, 227–29, 234, 249
laughter defuses, 95
Law of Attraction, 34, 226, 231
Law of Authenticity, 233
Law of Compensation, 232
Law of Influence, 233
Law of Receptivity, 233
Law of Value, 232
learned helplessness, 198-199, 213
learned optimism, 267
left brain, 14-17
Leonard, Thomas, 141, 143, 159
LeShan, Eda, 141
Leverage Attraction, 5, 33, 35, 37, 39, 41, 43
lifestyle, 43, 119
  health-focused, 185
lifestyle change, 170
lifestyle decisions, 77
lifestyle shift, longer-term, 171
limbic system, 16–17, 145
locus, 213
  employee's, 197
  strong external, 203
  strong internal, 203
Locus of control and cheating, 196
Locus of control and coping, 197
Lombardi, Vince, 65
Los Angeles Harbor College, 238
lottery curse, 167–68
low calorie day lifestyle change to lose weight, 173-174
luck, 93, 191–92, 195, 200, 213
lucky, 109, 238, 242

M

MacLean, Paul D., 15, 263
Mandino, Og, 101
Mann, John David, 231, 233, 261
Mann's clients, 233
Marshall, Perry, 66, 264
Maruta, T., 91, 264
Masaru Emoto's Rice Experiment, 262
Matthews, Karen, 91, 264
McCarthy, N., 264
McKinney, Frank, 217-220
McRaney, David, 50
Medina, John, 24–25, 264
Merton, Robert, 90, 264
Michaels, Jillian, 191
Milam, Joel, 92, 264
Millman, Dan, 237
mindset, 38, 218, 243
  positive, 204
  right, 218
mindset matters, 218
miracle prone (six characteristics for becoming), 118
miracle worker, 116
miracles, 115–20, 265
  language of, 115, 120, 249, 266
mistakes, 25, 35, 62–63, 72, 76, 80, 106, 108, 111, 157, 166, 176, 200, 202, 213
mistakes and failures, 72
money, 35, 39, 42, 46, 52, 54, 61, 103, 105, 107, 114, 125, 130, 142, 145, 149, 160, 168, 174-179, 187, 206, 218, 220, 221, 223, 226, 243, 250, 260
Money as Your Boss Five-Point Plan, 175
Mother Teresa, 251–52

motivation, 22, 75, 191, 195, 218, 220–21, 234
  strong internal, 194
multitask, 24
multitaskers, 25, 264
multitasking, 24, 29, 70, 148, 266
  avoiding, 237
multitasking behavior, eliminating, 66
Murray, 168, 264
My 600-Pound Life, 171

N

nap pods, 164
Nass, 25, 264
Native American Medicine Wheel, 256
Native American Talking Circle, 229
Naylor, 201, 244, 265
  Marilyn, 201
neurotransmitter, 21
  relaxation, 23
Neurotransmitter Evaluations, 259
neurotransmitter imbalances, 20
neurotransmitters
  feel-good, 29
  good, 227
  important, 20
neurotransmitters block pain, 129
Newman, Loretta, 238, 256
nicotine, 20, 23
Nielson Consumer, 265
non-dominant hemisphere, 15
Nowsaradan, Younan, 171
nucleus accumbens, 20, 22

O

observation exercise, 168

obstacles, 10, 25, 54, 83, 104, 109–12, 153, 197, 239, 244
  common, 160
  encountering, 239
  numerous, 7
Obstacles Blocking, 109
obstacles crop, 153
Ohannessian, Christine McCauley, 92, 265
one pushup approach (to procrastination), 84
opportunities, 34, 36, 43, 89, 99, 103, 108, 210, 218, 228–29, 234, 237, 239–40, 246–47, 253
  five, 200
  new, 246
opportunity costs, 239–40, 247
optimism, 5, 89–95, 97–100, 113, 118, 196, 198, 203, 260–61
  choosing, 101
  dispositional, 264
  level of, 90, 92, 98
Optimism by Avoiding Vicarious Trauma, 97
optimism-pessimism, 266
Optimism-Test, 260
optimistic, 89, 91–94, 97–99, 104, 113, 116, 127, 146, 164, 198, 204, 213, 260
optimistic attitudes, 264
optimistic child, 267
optimistic outlook, 147, 165
optimistic responses, 100
optimistic solution, 94
optimistic statement, 93
optimistic thinking, 92
optimistic thoughts, 165
optimistic viewpoint, 94
optimistic ways, 92

optimistic women, 91
optimists, 89, 91, 94, 99, 264
  total, 89
optimists experience, 91, 94
overcompensation, 61, 73
overwhelm, 77–78, 84, 187, 212

P

Papasan, Jay, 66, 263
Parents Without Partners, 80
Pareto, Vilfredo, 66
Pareto principle (80-20 rule), 66, 73, 237
Parker, Christopher, 75
Patsy's balloons, 132
Pearsall, 16, 117–19, 148, 265
  Paul, 22, 95, 116, 120, 147, 227, 260
Pearsall reminds, 117
Pearsall's contention, 16
Pearsall's research, 149
Pearsall's research documents, 16
perfection, 64–65, 202
  chase, 65
perfectionism, 84, 150
perfectionist, 65, 73, 150
PERSIST model, 9-10, 16, 37, 55, 59, 63, 99, 234, 237, 250
PERSIST plan (90 day), 250
persistence, 7–9, 11, 20, 31, 63, 81, 84, 90, 94, 97, 99, 165, 167, 242, 249
  increased, 15
  little, 20
  modeled, 256
persistence behavior, 173
persistence conquer, 19
persistence muscle, 71, 73
Persistence Quotient. See PQ

persisting, 64, 76, 81, 124, 170, 180, 186, 192, 241, 243
Person of Interest, 137
Personal Standards Inventory, 34–35
Perspire, 5, 9, 31, 241, 250
Perspire Less, 5, 33, 35, 37, 39, 41, 43
perspire time, 26
Perspire Tip, 35–36, 38, 40, 43, 45, 48, 50, 52, 54
pessimism, 91–93, 99, 101, 116, 264
pessimistic, 92–94, 164
pessimistic mindset, 93
pessimistic thinking, 92
pessimistic thought, 94
Peyrot, Mark, 196, 265
Pierce College, 239
possibilities, 46, 50, 103, 107–8
  new, 53, 108
  positive, 101
possible choice, best, 109
possible decision, best, 246
possible outcome, best, 10, 53, 101
possibility, 46, 107–108, 114
PQ (Persistence Quotient), 8–9, 14, 20, 28, 33, 49, 59, 67, 90, 101, 141, 145, 150, 159
PQ Factor, 1–2, 8–10, 14, 16, 19–20, 22, 24, 26, 28, 34, 36, 38, 40, 240–42, 249–57
procrastinating, 76, 162
procrastination, 75–76, 79, 82–84, 146, 160
  quicksand of, 5, 75, 77–78, 81–85
professionals, choosing service, 234
Projection, 225
Pruessner, Jens, 196, 265
prune, 68, 73, 163
pruning, 67

neural, 163–64
psychic vampires, 160–61, 168, 185, 203, 224
psychology of lack (how to overcome), 153

Q

Questions, 96, 223, 234
quicksand of procrastination and focus, 79

R

Ramsey, Dave, 168, 175, 177, 260, 265
Rand, Ayn, 177
Rapaille, Clotaire, 202, 265
reaction formation, 225
Reagan, Ronald, 89, 99, 266
RealEstateCoach.com, 253, 256–57
Reardon, Daniel, 99
regret, 127, 180, 202, 210, 256
rejection, 93–97, 100
  social, 95
rejection proof, 95, 263
rejection toolbox, 97
reminiscence, 163
reminiscing, 102, 228
reptilian brain, 15, 97–98
resignation, 108
Resilience, 5, 9, 87, 89, 91, 93, 95, 97, 99, 101–2, 115, 250
  emotional, 121, 228
  increased, 90
Resilience Tip, 90, 105–6, 109, 116, 127, 132, 134–35
resilient, 7, 101, 226

responsibility, 35, 127, 142, 158, 191–92, 201–2
  personal, 197, 200–201
  taking, 51
retirement, 174, 177, 223, 243, 250
retirement fund, 250
retirement plan, 145
Richistan, 262
Rideout, Andrew, 196, 266
right brain, 14-16, 70, 242
risk taking, 219
Robinson, 266
  Peter, 89
Rocky Mountain Vet, 114
Rohn, Jim, 33
Ronald Reagan Changed My Life, 89
Ross, Bernice L., 2, 193, 201, 210, 244, 253, 265–66
Rossdale Press, 266
RossdalePress.com, 2
Rotter, Julian, 191, 266
Rubin, R., 196, 265
Rubinstein, Joshua, 25, 266
Rule-Shifting, 25

S

Sapolsky, Robert, 203, 266
schizophrenia, 23, 92
Schou, Inger, 91, 266
Scott, 115–16, 266
  Deanna, 115, 266

  Brandon, 115
  Lennox, 249
self-care, 143–45, 171, 186
  better, 145
  extreme, 128

self-care challenges (source of), 167
self-care goals, 167, 186
  long-term, 167
Self-Care Inventory, 144
self-care program, 150
self-confidence, 212
Self-Control, 209
Self-Esteem Inventory, 259
self-fulfilling prophecy, 90, 93, 100, 115, 147, 264
self-healing personalities, 115, 262
selfish, 5, 9, 77, 139, 141–43, 150, 185, 220, 250–51
Self-ish, 5, 9, 128, 139, 141–42, 144, 150, 165, 183, 186, 203, 250
Self-ishness, 143, 150
Self-ish solutions, 165
Self-ish Tip, 143, 155, 157, 159, 163–64, 170, 180, 185
selfless, 220, 234
self-renewal, 183–86
  emotional, 184
self-renewal time, regular, 187
self-serving, 141, 220-221
Seligman, Martin, 91, 94, 198, 260, 266–67
serotonin, 23–24, 227
service, 45, 59, 130–32, 176, 210, 218, 220–21, 226–27, 229, 234, 243, 255–56
service, being of, 220
Service Tip, 218, 221–22, 228, 231
sharing, 39, 113, 116, 132, 154-155, 226
shiny object syndrome, 245
should (used for manipulation), 47, 49, 185-186
Sigmund Freud, 61
Slain by an expectation, 155-156, 165

sleep, 22–24, 29, 77, 114, 144, 161, 163–64, 166, 184, 207–8
  plenty of, 144, 164
sleep deprivation, 144
smile, 227, 229, 234
snowball debt (how to avoid), 176
Sonnby, 267
Sonnby-Borgström, Marianne, 227
speaker, international, 257
Specht, Jules, 197, 267
spending, 63, 67, 161, 175, 177, 220, 265
Stan, Sebastian, 57`
standards, 34, 36–37, 47, 154–57, 165
  people's, 158, 165
  personal, 44, 154, 156
  social, 224
standards and boundaries, 154–56
Stawicki, 267
  Michal, 81, 84, 250, 267
stories, 14, 20, 33, 89, 95, 101–11, 113–14, 116, 129–33, 137, 146, 153–54, 221, 226, 229
  funny, 229
  laughter-filled, 228
  negative, 111
  news, 101, 105
  old, 102, 105–6
  positive, 113
  powerful, 28
  right, 101, 109
  tragic, 102
  wrong, 101
Stories Attract, 102
Stories People, 103
Stratospheric Success, 232

strengths, 5, 9, 11, 36–37, 55, 57, 59–61, 63, 72–73, 109–10, 194, 229, 237, 243, 250
success (The Five Laws of Stratospheric Success), 232
sugar, 23, 149, 162, 173
superego, 224–25
support system, 70, 84, 194
symptoms, 24, 143–44, 146–47, 149–50, 159, 165, 168, 172, 186–87
  spot, 150
  temporary, 151
symptoms fit, 148
symptoms return, 186
Symptom, Source, Solution model, 143-144, 150, 159, 168, 172
symptoms/signals, 146

T

Take Control, 5, 191, 193, 195, 197, 199, 201, 203, 205, 207, 209, 211, 213
Taking Personal Responsibility, 200
talking circle (Native American), 229-230
texting, 25, 29, 163
Three T's: time, talent, treasure, 218, 234
three-brain theory, 15
time blocking, 80
time it right, 235, 250
to-do list, 66–68, 78, 84, 99
tolerations, 159–62, 166
  eliminating, 161
Tracy, Brian, 68, 189, 267

U

UCLA (Fernald School), 238
UltraMind Quizzes, 259
up-down spiral, 106–8

V

Van Arsdale, Byron, 3, 13, 14, 27, 50, 111, 123, 127, 129-130, 132, 134, 155, 180, 224, 249-250, 253, 257
vicarious trauma, 97-98, 100

W

Waging War on Real Estate's Discounters, 239, 253, 255
walk in solution (the outcome you want to achieve), 115-226, 127
wealth, 101, 174, 244
weight, 83, 167, 170–74, 225, 244, 250
  ideal, 171
  I want to lose, 171
  losing, 170, 205, 250
weight issues, 172
weight loss, 167, 171
  4.17-pound, 228
weight problems, 167
Weight Watchers, 80, 205
West Los Angeles College, 239
What's bugging you exercise, 159
Win-lose game, 106-107, 111
workaround, 61, 63–64, 73
www.The PQFactor.com, 259
www.The PQFactor.com/assessments, 9

Y

Yellow Light Moments, 241–42, 247
you are not the situation, 120, 142
you create your own opportunity, 218
you get what you give, 41
Young, Jeff, 114, 116
Yukl, Gary, 197, 267

Z

Zander, Benjamin, 106–8
Zander's answer, 107
Zander's approach, 107

www.ingramcontent.com/pod-product-compliance
Lightning Source LLC
Chambersburg PA
CBHW070556300426
44113CB00010B/1271